NATURAL RESOURCE POLICY
AND INCOME DISTRIBUTION

Natural Resource Policy and Income Distribution

ADAM ROSE, BRANDT STEVENS,
and GREGG DAVIS

The Johns Hopkins University Press

BALTIMORE AND LONDON

The Johns Hopkins University Press
701 West 40th Street
Baltimore, Maryland 21211
The Johns Hopkins Press Ltd., London

∞ The paper used in this publication meets
the minimum requirements of American National
Standard for Information Sciences—
Permanence of Paper for Printed Library
Materials, ANSI Z39.48 1984.

Library of Congress Cataloging-in-Publication Data

Rose, Adam Zachary.
  Natural resource policy and income distribution.

  Bibliography: p.
  Includes index.
  1. Natural resources—United States. 2. United States—Economic policy—1981–
3. Income distribution—United States. I. Stevens, Brandt. II. Davis, Gregg. III. Title.
HC103.7.R67   1988   333.7′0973   87-2788
ISBN 0-8018-3523-2 (alk. paper)

For Annie, Elizabeth, and Debbi

Contents

Figures and Tables

Figures

Tables

Foreword

In a highly developed but nonhomogeneous society like that of the United States with its stark differences between the very poor and the very rich, the inequality of income distribution represents a major, possibly the major, social problem.

Modern economic theory analyzes the distribution of national income primarily in terms of its principal functional components such as wages, returns on capital, and rents. The study of the personal, as contrasted with functional income distribution, traditionally has fallen in the domain of descriptive statistics. Theoretical thinking on that subject was in the past and is still centered on numerical description of the degree of equality or inequality. The most widely used measure of this kind is the so-called Gini coefficient. As with any other index number, it provides a more or less convenient albeit arbitrary numerical description, not an explanation of income inequality.

These two different approaches, the functional and the personal, will eventually have to come together, and the focus of their meeting will obviously be the description and explanation of the behavior of individual households in their double role of ultimate receiver and spender of various kinds of incomes.

The diversity of the demographic structure of an individual household is compounded by the variety of the combinations of functional characteristics of income received by its members. The proverbial representative consumer with his "utility function" cannot possibly provide a solid base for realistic description of the internal structure of different types of households and the relationship of each of them to all other parts of a complex modern economy. Sooner or later, economists will have to take advantage of the much more concrete understanding of these structures and those relationships possessed by anthropologists, social psychologists, market analysts, advertisers, and even teachers of practical household economics.

In the meantime, the first order of business is a systematic description of the role played by households in transforming streams of functional incomes generated in different industries into personal expenditure streams, taking the form of purchases of various kinds of goods and services produced by them.

This monograph represents an important forward step in this direction. By mobilizing a great variety of sources of quantitative information, its authors succeed in describing in great detail the position of different groups of households within the intersectoral relationships that govern the flows of goods and services between the many different parts of the

U.S. economy. The loose ends that, up to now, characterized modeling of the personal and functional income flows have finally been tied together.

The new, enlarged national input-output table of the U.S. economy thus provides a data base for tracing not only the direct but also the less obvious indirect repercussions of such primary impulses as establishment of new industries or introduction of new taxes or subsidies.

Wassily Leontief

Preface

Whether intended or not, most natural resource policies have important distributive effects. The fact that much of the natural resource base of the United States is located in areas with relatively high proportions of low-income residents raises important vertical equity issues. Even without regard to relative income positions, differential impacts are reason for concern because they heighten tensions among interest groups and between these groups and policy-makers.

Unfortunately, policy-makers and analysts are hampered by a lack of operational models that can determine who gains and who loses from alternative resource allocation decisions. This book offers a way to overcome this major obstacle. It establishes a methodology for constructing models to determine the economic impacts of alternative natural resource policies on income distribution. Our research endeavors to advance the state of the art at the conceptual, methodological, and empirical levels. Examples of these advances include development of a formal set of measures that make use of distributional information for predictive purposes, construction of the first multisector account of dividend income distribution based on primary data, and development of methods for estimating the distribution of income in cases where data are limited.

This book is timely for two reasons. First, recent federal legislation has mandated increased public participation in natural resource policy-making. Conventional methods of evaluating policies, such as aggregate cost-benefit analyses do not, however, provide sufficient data for informed participation by those affected by these policies. To help remedy this problem we have developed three "positive" distributional measures:

1. to provide individuals with a probability distribution of how they will be affected,
2. to translate this probability matrix into a prediction of public reaction to a given policy, and
3. to facilitate a comparison between predicted reactions and predicted impacts.

Thus, in addition to offering policy-makers an important new research tool, we have also provided them with an improved means of communicating with their constituencies.

Second, our methodology is based on the disaggregation of the payments sector of an input-output (I-O) table according to income bracket, and thus represents a specialized version of a comprehensive approach to economic analysis, referred to as a Social Accounting Matrix (SAM). The social accounting framework calls for the inclusion of an extended set of economic interactions, beyond the standard interindustry relations, in an I-O table. While the SAM concept has received a growing amount of attention in the professional literature, few such models have been constructed. If our experience is any indication, a major reason for this deficiency is a lack of data. However, the award of the 1984 Nobel Prize in Economics to Richard A. Stone, who developed the SAM concept, should provide a major impetus to the interest in SAM's and to the eventual establishment of comprehensive data bases. It is therefore gratifying to have contributed a method that, in the interim, shows how to utilize existing data to overcome obstacles to the construction of income distribution versions of SAM's for the United States or its subregions. In addition, we seek to show how valuable these models can be by applying them to the analysis of important issues, and hope thereby to accelerate the pace of future empirical work.

The authors take pride in the fact that methodologies and models presented in this book have been computerized and transferred to the U.S. Forest Service for practical application. As such they represent an extension of the Forest Service's "Impact Analysis System for Planning," or IMPLAN, which is a major socioeconomic data base and set of procedures for constructing regional input-output tables and social accounting matrices. Beyond this, it is hoped that this book will assist researchers in several fields in building income distribution models for their own analyses and for use by policy-makers in general.

Acknowledgments

We are indebted to several individuals, institutions, and government agencies for their assistance in our study. Foremost is Dr. Gregory Alward of the U.S. Forest Service, for conceiving of the need to extend his agency's Impact Analysis System for Planning in several directions, including distributional analysis. We are grateful to Greg for making IMPLAN data and program descriptions available to us so that we could perform policy analyses of our own, and we are most appreciative of his patience in working with academics, who often chose the pursuit of an intellectual challenge over the attainment of a project deadline. Thanks also go to Jay Sullivan of the Rocky Mountain Forest and Range Experiment Station for supplying us with several IMPLAN input-output tables. Dr. Everard Lofting of Engineering-Economics Associates, who along with Dr. Gregory Alward was instrumental in developing the original IMPLAN modeling capability, answered several important questions about its operation over the course of our research.

We would like to acknowledge the support of the U.S. Department of Energy's Pittsburgh Energy Technology Center for its support of a project that overlapped slightly with the one contained in this volume. Specifically, the construction of a West Virginia income distribution matrix, which proved helpful in formulating the "regionalization" methodologies presented in chapter 8, was one output of a DOE grant.

Were it not for the foresight of the New York Stock Exchange in commissioning a survey of shareholders and the efforts of Chilton Research Services, Inc., in carrying out the survey, we would not have been able to construct the first multisector model of dividend income. We especially wish to thank Jean Lyons of the NYSE for helping us acquire and interpret the data. We also benefited from special data tabulations by federal government agencies such as the Bureau of Economic Analysis and the Internal Revenue Service.

We wish to express our gratitude for travel support from West Virginia University's Regional Research Institute, College of Mineral and Energy Resources, and President's Grant Fund, which enabled us to obtain valuable feedback on preliminary results presented at four professional meetings. Thanks are also extended to Professor Luc Anselin of the University of California, Santa Barbara, and Professor Breandan O'hUallachain of Northwestern University, who served as discussants for two of these papers.

Other helpful comments and encouragement have come from Dr. Marion Clawson of Resources for the Future, Professor Faye Duchin of the Institute for Economic Analysis at New York University, Professor Alan Randall of Ohio State University, Professor Mark Henry of Clemson University, and Professors Paul Beaumont and Gary Zinn of West

Virginia University. Professor Irwin Friend of the University of Pennsylvania provided useful advice as well as a summary of his earlier unpublished work on dividend income. Professor Paul Culhane of Northwestern University shared with us some valuable insights from his several studies on the management of public lands. Professor Paul Speaker of West Virginia University provided a useful background piece on measures of income concentration as a member of our original research team. We also wish to express our gratitude to Professor John Boland of the Johns Hopkins University, who served as principal reviewer of our manuscript and offered several important suggestions for improving our work.

Our greatest debt is owed to Professor C. Y. Chen, formerly a member of the Department of Mineral Resource Economics at West Virginia University and now at National Cheng-Kung University of Taiwan, for helping to design the computerized algorithms, writing most of the computer programs, and performing some of the computer runs to construct early versions of our empirical model. Dr. Chen is the principal author of the *User's Guide* for the U.S. Forest Service's operation of the model.

Additional computer assistance was provided by Ahmad Afrasiabi and Mostafa Aleseyed of West Virginia University, and James Murdoch of Northeast Louisiana University. Angela Durham did an excellent job of typing the final version of the manuscript. Donna Weston, Nancy Ireland, Bonita Helmick, MaryLou Myer, and Dianna Martin assisted in typing various earlier drafts.

Finally, this book might not have been completed were it not for the encouragement of the economics editor of the Johns Hopkins University Press, Anders Richter. We are also grateful to Peter Dreyer and to Nancy West of the Press for their excellent job of transforming our manuscript into a finished product.

I / CONCEPTUAL FRAMEWORK

1 / Important Dimensions of Natural Resource Policy

The public sector has had a major influence on the way natural resources have been maintained or utilized since the founding of the United States. As population moved west in the nineteenth century, natural resource policy decisions by federal and state governments became increasingly more prominent and complex. The Homestead Act, the Railroad Act, the National Park Service Act, and the Rivers and Harbors Act are examples of legislation with important consequences for the nation's resources then and now. The legislators and administrators who dealt with natural resource issues were primarily interested in stimulating economic growth or adhering to conservation. Nonetheless, their actions resulted in important distributive effects among income groups, among industries, and among regions. Some of these effects were deliberate, as in setting the homestead size at a level that would promote the most efficient scale of farm operation and discourage concentration of ownership. Others were indirect, as in the granting of rights-of-way to railroads, which has made them some of the biggest landowners in the western United States.

Federal and state involvement in natural resource management has increased in the twentieth century. Numerous examples could be cited, but a short list might include:

1. Forest Service land-use policy governing private sector activities
2. Mineral rights leasing policies on public lands
3. Soil conservation programs
4. Agricultural commodity programs
5. Irrigation water supplies in the West
6. Bureau of Land Management grazing policy
7. Wildlife preservation
8. Air and water quality regulations

Most modern-day analyses of natural resource policies have focused on economic efficiency and aggregate economic impacts. The associated distributional effects have typically received less attention than other policy issues, even though many economists view these impacts as very important. For example, Clawson (1975) has stated: "Good social policy includes identification of gainers and losers with as close an estimate as possible of the magnitude of gains and losses, and with a final decision which at least contains all major interests." Unfortunately, a lack of data, disagreement over objectives,

3

inadequate methodologies, and unresolved conceptual issues have resulted in few studies of distributional impacts.[1]

The purpose of this study is to develop an operational methodology for determining the distributional impacts of alternative natural resource policies for both positive and normative analysis. Distributional impacts refer to the absolute and relative gains and losses among individuals or interest groups. Personal income is typically the object of analysis, and we use it in the broadest sense as a common denominator for the value of environmental amenities and other nonmarket goods as well. In many instances, it may be interesting to extend the analysis of distributional impacts in the spatial sense, but the case of inter-regional transfers is beyond the scope of this study.

The methodology is based on input-output (I-O) techniques, which have a long tradition in impact analysis and have been used increasingly in resource economics in recent years. I-O's unique advantages in this context include its disaggregated structure—the ability to capture the important distinction between diverse resource-based industries (mining, logging, recreation, etc.)—and its general equilibrium character—the ability to link these industries with the broader regional economy in which they operate. This means that an I-O model facilitates the determination of income distribution impacts not only for resource-based industries but also for all sectors that are directly and indirectly related to them. However, even though I-O models have been used to address income distribution impacts for several years, they have not been adequately linked to a theory of income distribution. We remedy this omission as well.

The major hurdle in performing income distribution analysis with I-O models is the lack of data on the income class of recipients on a sector-by-sector basis. Previous studies have been able to establish a primary data base only for wage and salary income. Through the refinement of data from such diverse sources as the New York Stock Exchange, the U.S. Department of Commerce, and the Internal Revenue Service, we have been able to advance the state of the art to encompass several forms of property income. Our model is the most comprehensive multisector model of income distribution of the U.S. economy to date based on primary data. Moreover, we provide a methodology for adapting it to specific regions. Our goal is to make the distributional impacts of natural resource policy no more difficult to estimate than conventional aggregate impacts relating to net benefits or employment changes.

Income distribution impacts can be a sensitive subject because of their frequent association with judgments about "social equity," or "fairness." Social justice in the abstract is itself not the issue. The difficulty is in translating it into an objective, defensible, or popularly supported policy goal. Subjective judgments of what "ought to be" make many economists uneasy, and are therefore often avoided. Usually overlooked, however, are the positive economic aspects of income distribution. It is valuable to know "what is" or "what will be," irrespective of normative judgments, for the purpose of information dissemination or prediction. Knowledge of the number of people who will gain and lose as a result of a policy may help a public official make decisions more in line with the preferences of his constituency. Knowledge of how he will be affected by a policy may help an individual citizen make a more informed judgment in the increasing number of cases where he has an explicit input into the final decision. In these instances knowledge of aggregate net benefits is not sufficient. Our methodology is extended to yield the requisite information on the distribution of individual impacts.

Public Participation in Natural Resource Policy Decisions

Citizen involvement in natural resource policy-making has long been important. The enactment of legislation such as farm commodity programs, water storage projects, and air quality maintenance has been significantly influenced by private individuals and interest groups. However, since the early 1970s, the scope of public involvement has been broadened to allow citizen groups to affect the interpretation and administration of natural resource policy by executive branch agencies directly, i. e., through "public participation."

Some of the most prominent areas of public participation affecting natural resources are those formally required of the Forest Service by the Forest and Rangelands Renewable Resources Planning Act of 1974 (RPA) and the Natural Forest Management Act of 1976 (NFMA),[2] and of the Bureau of Land Management by the Federal Land Policy and Management Act (FLPMA) of 1976. Both agencies have exceeded the legislative requirements in encouraging citizen involvement in their decision-making processes and are considered leaders among federal agencies in this area (Friesema 1979). District level managers now treat communication with the public with the same importance accorded other professional skills (Culhane 1981). These new activities are taken seriously at all levels of management.[3]

Elaborate procedures have evolved to promote public participation, the most prominent of which is the public hearing. Though formal in nature and having some of the characteristics of a legal proceeding, the public hearing involves a statement of (proposed) policy by agency personnel with some technical explanation of why it has been selected over other alternatives. A question-and-answer period follows that allows for exchange between the agency personnel and interested groups. Prepared statements are permitted and, in some cases, written comments on the policy are solicited by policy-makers. In addition, the Forest Service and the Bureau of Land Management have agency-initiated meetings with members of the public, such as grazing advisory boards. Various interpersonal contacts, such as information and education tours, are also an important, but informal, vehicle for public participation.

Citizen groups and affected industries have sued to challenge policy decisions at the local and national level. This type of participation has occurred in place of, or in addition to, formal participation on numerous occasions (Dana and Fairfax 1979). For example, in a celebrated case the Izaak Walton League sued the Forest Service over its timber sale practices in an attempt to halt clear-cutting in the Monongahela National Forest in the early 1970s. The U.S. Fourth District Court found in favor of the plaintiffs, effectively halting timber sales in national forests in its jurisdiction and leaving the Forest Service open to similar legal challenges in all other national forests. The court's final ruling in the case suggested that new legislation could solve the Forest Service's dilemma. The ultimate result was the passage of the NFMA in 1976, which revised the agency's management practices and decision criteria not only for timber sales but also for most private activities undertaken on national forest lands.

Whether this trend in litigation as one form of participation will continue is unclear, but several factors suggest that it may: (1) the courts now recognize more parties as legitimate plaintiffs, (2) the number of successful suits encourages additional legal forays, and (3) industry learned quickly from environmental groups and now pursues legal action if beneficial to its interests. Policy-makers cannot ignore the potential of adverse legal action, especially given the relative costs of seeking public input at each stage of the policy making process compared to the costs, including the opportunity costs of delayed action, of a lawsuit. As a result, various decision-makers want to know public preferences.

Our analysis takes Downing's (1981) model of the participation process as a starting point. The model is a simplified version of interaction among three participating groups: the regulating agency, a citizen interest group, and a firm, where the interests of the citizen interest group and the firm generally contradict each other. Each group's spokesperson is assumed to be motivated by constrained rational self-interest; there is a common goal each seeks to maximize, but also a goal unique to the group.[4]

This model provides us with insight into the motivation of different types of participants and the interaction among them. It also provides us with insight into the relevant information flows in a public-participation setting. First, the lead agency is obligated to disseminate information to the parties affected. This same information is useful in interpreting the public response. The majority of the population may receive positive net gains, but owing to opportunity costs of attendance, the small size of these gains, or perceived lack of influence, they may be poorly represented at a public hearing. Our "distributional impact matrices" could help provide the requisite information on impacts and could help prevent any erroneous assessment of public reaction.

The Rural Setting

Natural resource policy decisions generally have their most immediate impact on the economies and citizens of predominantly rural areas.[5] A brief assessment of the characteristics of rural areas is therefore warranted to appreciate the socioeconomic context in which natural resource policy decisions are made.

Resource-based industries are a significant economic activity in many rural areas. Using 20 percent or more employment in any or some combination of four primary industries (agriculture and food processing; fishing; mining; and forestry, logging, wood products, and pulp/paper mills) as a meaningful threshold, 44 percent of nonmetropolitan counties (a total of 1,051) are dominated by resource-extraction activities (Elo and Beale 1984). These counties contain 27 percent of the nonmetropolitan population, or nearly 15.3 million persons. The economic base of rural areas has, however, gradually diversified (Deavers and Brown 1983). Manufacturing now engages approximately one-quarter of the nonmetropolitan labor force, trade and government about one-sixth each, and the service sector about one-tenth. Of course, there is considerable variation in sectoral composition across individual regions, and considerable regional variation in the location of resource-based, and non-resource-based, economic activity throughout the United States.

Rural population growth had been declining steadily until the 1970s, when rural population suddenly began to grow, and to grow much faster than the metropolitan population. Although this phenomenon is not fully understood, analysts have offered several explanations: (1) the large absolute reduction in the farm labor force in the first two decades of the postwar era represented a major "shake-out" that stabilized farm out-migration, (2) diversification of the rural economy provided employment opportunities and reduced out-migration, (3) lower costs of living and greater amenity values in rural areas attracted in-migrants from urban areas, particularly retirees, and (4) improved transportation and communications systems reduced the isolation of rural areas. The factors cited above suggest that this trend will continue, though not universally and perhaps at a less rapid pace.

Rural poverty levels have declined since the 1960s, but poverty is still disproportionately high in rural areas. Data from the 1980 Census indicate that 34 percent of those with incomes below the poverty level live in nonmetropolitan counties even though such counties have only 28 percent of the total population. The total percentage of persons in poverty in nonmetropolitan counties in 1979 was 15.4 percent, whereas the average in natural-resource areas is 17 percent (Elo and Beale 1984). With the exception of counties in which forestry is of prime importance, all the types of natural-resource counties have poverty rates ranging from 17 to 17.7 percent.

According to Elo and Beale, if a 9–10 percent rate of poverty represents some irreducible minimum level of poverty because of personal catastrophe (death of a spouse, disability, business failure), then a rate of poverty substantially higher may be owing to "systemic" problems (prominence of seasonal work, lack of education, discrimination, etc.). These overlap with what we refer to as "structural" and "institutional determinants" of income distribution in chapter 2. A prominent example of a structural factor is the low skill requirement, and hence low associated pay, of workers in primary industries. A prominent example of an institutional factor is the existence of labor unions, which in return for higher pay for their members may have caused significant labor displacement. In addition to their impact on poverty levels, many of these factors have contributed to the skewness of income distribution in natural-resource settings.

Does resource development hold the prospect of reducing poverty levels and/or reducing overall income inequalities? If development proceeds as it has in the past, it is likely that improvements will be limited. Clawson (1983) has noted that those with property, influence, and special skills are in a better position to capture the economic rewards of resource development. The increased economic activity generated directly and indirectly by an increase in mining, logging, or recreation may raise the overall per capita income of a region, but there is no guarantee that it will filter down to where it is needed most. For example Elo and Beale (1983) found that in 1980, Kentucky, Virginia, and West Virginia had the lowest percentage of high school graduates, the highest rate of unemployment, the lowest household median income, and the highest percentage of persons in poverty, when contrasted to other regions of mining employment dominance. Although the median household incomes of counties with at least 20 percent of the labor force employed in mining exceed the median incomes of non-resource-based counties, the distribution of income in mining-based counties is relatively more skewed. The authors conclude: "The region seemed to be a clear case of the exploitation of a rich natural resource failing to produce prosperous communities or equitable distribution of wealth."[6]

It would appear that such strategies as diversification of rural economies and retention of more of the value-added emanating from resources through further processing stages would help reduce distributional inequities in the shorter term. Higher public expenditures on education and the enhancement of infrastructure are also likely to be helpful in the long run. While these are reasonable hypotheses, whether they hold in a particular case, and the extent to which they do, can only be determined by a comprehensive model such as the one presented in the following chapters.

Thus far we have focused attention on the positive influences of natural resource development. However, rural settings may be especially sensitive to negative impacts. They are characterized by pristine environments, and much of the population has chosen to live there partly because of the associated amenities. At the same time, Warkov (1978) and others have found a distrust of "outsiders" among rural residents. This distrust is a matter not simply of xenophobia, but of concern for the maintenance of the rural lifestyle and avoidance of boomtown effects. However, given that residents of the region may be unable to supply the capital, specialized equipment, and labor needed for development, it must involve nonresidents.

Thus natural resource development impacts are not just a matter of aggregate gains within a region, or relative gains among income groups, but of the number of gainers and losers as well. A policy that promises large gains for a small number of people and little, or possibly even negative, impact for the majority of the population, regardless of their relative income levels, is less likely to be successfully implemented than one with widespread gains and likely accompanying public support.

Several recent studies (see, e.g., Maurer and Napier 1981; Fliegal et al. 1981), suggest that residents of resource-bearing lands have positive attitudes toward large-scale development projects. Residents generally believe that these projects will improve economic prospects for themselves, for other family members, or for other members of the community. Although there is concern about environmental damage and potential boom-town effects, residents and community leaders appear willing to trade these, up to a point, for an improved regional economy.

There is less evidence on attitudes to the distribution of returns of large-scale projects. Rose et al. (1982) note the interest of public officials in the distributional outcome of energy development, but no conclusion is reached as to the weight the officials place on the matter. Ladewig and McCann (1980) test the hypothesis that the distribution of income is an indirect determinant of rural residents' satisfaction with their community and found that a reduction of inequality is positively correlated with an improvement in community satisfaction. No doubt the lack of adequate methods to determine distributional impacts has made it difficult for policy-makers to inform the public of these impacts and to fully gauge public attitudes.

Overview

This study is divided into three main parts. Part I provides the background and conceptual underpinnings of the study. Chapter 2 introduces the input-output modeling approach and explains the reasons for choosing it. The conclusion reached is that I-O is the model framework most compatible with theories of income distribution in the context of natural resource development. Chapter 3 introduces the positive economic emphasis of the study. Three distributional measures are formulated for use in: (1) disseminating information on how individuals are impacted by policy, (2) evaluating how the majority in the community are affected, and (3) interpreting public-participation response.

Part II deals with the construction of a multisector income distribution model of the United States and issues associated with building such models. Chapter 4 explains the innovative concept of the Social Accounting Matrix and shows how our model is a special case of it. The chapter also provides an overview to the construction of the model on a functional income type basis. Chapter 5 focuses on the distribution of wage and salary income as derived from occupation/industry matrices. Chapter 6 focuses on the derivation of a dividend income distribution matrix from primary data obtained from the New York Stock Exchange. In chapter 7 these two factor payments are combined with estimates of the remaining factor payments to arrive at an overall Social Accounting Matrix for income distribution.

Part III pertains to applications of the model. Chapter 8 explains the procedure for applying our methodology to the construction of distributional models at the regional level and summarizes one such application. Chapter 9 is an illustrative case study of the impacts of increased surface mining of coal in the Monongahela National Forest, with an emphasis on the sensitivity of the results with respect to employment practices and absentee ownership of natural resources. Chapter 10 evaluates the incidence of recent tax reform proposals pertaining to the oil and gas industry to determine which income groups bear the burden of the policy once all the general equilibrium effects are taken into account. The final chapter summarizes the study and provides suggestions as to how more extensive data might be obtained to facilitate future research and policy applications.

2 / Input-Output Analysis of Income Distribution Impacts

Economic impact analysis is a well-developed field of inquiry. Numerous studies have explored most of its subtleties, ranging from the dissection of multiplier effects to the dynamics of population migration. A number of valuable empirical methodologies have been adapted to this purpose, most notably input-output, or I-O, analysis (see, e.g., Leontief and Duchin 1986; Miernyk et al. 1970).

One area of impact analysis in which progress has lagged deals with how public policy and other exogenous shocks affect personal income distribution—that is, who gains and who loses as a result of the impact and by what relative amounts. Few operational methodologies exist for this purpose. Some notable examples of I-O–based approaches have been implemented, but the relationship between theories of income distribution and these methods has not been well established.

In this chapter we explore the compatibility of prevailing theories of income distribution and I-O analysis. We then propose that the "institutional" and "structural" theories are crucial to the evaluation of the distribution of policy impacts and are theories consistent with I-O analysis. The chapter concludes with a presentation of an I-O–based income distribution impact framework applicable to natural resources. The case studies of later chapters not only illustrate the model but also serve to examine the relative importance of institutional and structural features by way of sensitivity tests.

The Input-Output Approach to Income Distribution Analysis

In the mid 1970s several researchers independently concluded that I-O could be used for the analysis of personal income distribution (see Miyazawa 1976; Weiskoff 1976; Paukert et al. 1976; Golladay and Haveman 1977; and Rose 1977).[1] The common feature of all of these models was the disaggregation of the payments sector by income class. In previous theoretical and empirical models, income payments were assigned to a vector of value-added terms, or, in a few cases, divided into functional shares (i.e., labor- vs. capital-related income). The new formulation called for translating the vector into an entire matrix that reflected the socioeconomic profile of recipients of payments from each sector of the economy.

A typical version of these I-O–based income distribution models can be illustrated by first defining:

A = the $n \times n$ matrix of technical coefficients $a_{ij} = \dfrac{x_{ij}}{X_j}$

V = the $m \times n$ matrix of income coefficients $v_{ki} = \dfrac{y_{ki}}{X_i}$

X_j = the gross output of industry j
F_j = the final demand for good j
Y_k = the income of the recipient group k
x_{ij} = the amount of output of industry i used in producing good j
y_{ki} = the amount of income received by group k from industry i

The model is one of simultaneous determination of income generation and distribution, where the vector of income by class is given by:

$$Y = VX \tag{1}$$

or, since $X = BF$, where $B = (b_{ij}) = (I - A)^{-1}$, the reduced form equation is:

$$Y = VBF \tag{1'}$$

A development stimulus, for example, would affect income distribution through a change in final demand, ΔF, or the inclusion of a new sector that would yield an augmented inverse of the original transaction table, B^*, thusly:

$$\Delta Y = VB^*\Delta F. \tag{2}$$

A vector representing the distribution of income returns from a unit change in final demand in a given sector, $\Delta f_j = 1$, is given by:

$$\Delta Y_k = \sum_{i=1}^{m} v_{ki} b^*_{ij} \quad k = 1 \ldots m, \tag{3}$$

where the subscript j refers to the sector in which the initial stimulus takes place.

Several important insights can be derived from this common framework. For example, Miyazawa (1976) closes the model to a set of personal consumption vectors, one for each income class. He then derives his "interrelational multipliers," which represent the change in income accruing directly and indirectly to one income class as a result of a unit change in income of another income class. Rose et al. (1982) term the result of equation 3 the "distributional impact vector" and suggest that Gini coefficients could be calculated for all sectors and then ranked in a manner similar to conventional multipliers. In chapter 3 we indicate how the distributional impact vector contains all of the information necessary to yield a measure of how the majority of participants in a public decision would be affected so as to gauge the degree of popular support for a given natural resource policy. In this way the focus on distributional impacts can be shifted from that of normative economics to that of positive economics.

I-O and Alternative Income Distribution Theories

Thus far we have presented a mathematical model, but it seems to lack a theoretical base. The model calls for a mechanical calculation of the income distribution of an economy, but with no direct link to any of the established theories of income distribution. One might ask: if there is no explicit income distribution theory offered, is it because I-O provides one implicitly? The question can be generalized to: does I-O represent a particular theoretical perspective, or is it simply a general framework compatible with any of several different theories?

In broad terms, input-output analysis has often been characterized as being devoid of ideological content, or at least as being ideologically neutral. This conception is supported by the fact that I-O is used extensively in both capitalist and socialist countries, with little modification. Moreover, it does not incorporate any specific behavioral conditions for the individual or the state (e.g., utility or welfare maximization), except that an economy behave in a consistent manner. The ideological leanings of I-O, however, are of less importance to us here than the practical matter of its generality and ability to serve as an unbiased empirical framework that can incorporate alternative theories of income distribution.

Let us begin with the hypothesis that the basic I-O framework contains only one unique feature that affects income distribution, and that otherwise a theory of income distribution must be explicitly built into it. The intrinsic feature is economic structure, which is reflected by sectoral differences in production functions, including primary factors. That is, the distribution of income in an economy at a given point in time is a weighted average of the profile of income returns of each of its various sectors. It appears, however, that this factor, and I-O in general, are compatible with most other income distribution theories, as illustrated below, and that structure is a sufficiently important explanatory factor on its own in a major set of cases relating to natural-resource development.

In reviewing major theories of income distribution, Sahota (1978) notes that most economists believe no satisfactory theory exists. He surveys two sets of theories. The first set consists of partial theories or, more simply, just single determinants of income distribution as follows:

Ability (Pareto 1897; Atkinson 1975; Lydall 1976)[2]
Stochastic (Gibrat 1931; Thurow 1975; Taubman 1976)
Individual choice (Friedman 1953; Reder 1969)
Human capital (Schultz 1961; Mincer 1976)
Educational inequalities (Hunt 1961; Coleman 1966)
Inheritance (Tawney 1931; Meade 1964)[3]
Life cycle[4] (Kuznets 1953; Bronfenbrenner, 1977)
Public expenditure (Kuznets 1955; Stigler 1970)

These factors can be regrouped as follows:

Background (heredity, chance)
Environment (culture, educational inequality)
Demographic (life cycle, migration)
Economic (human capital, public expenditure, individual choice)

Background and environment are essentially noneconomic and do not appear explicitly or implicitly in the standard I-O model; moreover, they are difficult to model and must be taken as given in most frameworks. Some demographic factors, on the other hand, are being successfully integrated into economic models. Still, migration decisions have not been explicitly included in I-O models, and this factor is typically ignored unless labor supply constraints are present. The age profile of income earners is also not incorporated, though it could be with a further disaggregation of the income payments matrix according to age and some transition matrices to take care of dynamics. Few of the economic variables listed have been related to I-O models, though again some potential is there. Microeconomic decisions are typically one step removed from the basic I-O model, though aggregate human capital needs, for example, can be incorporated with a labor investment equation analogous to the capital investment equation of the dynamic I-O model.

The second set of theories discussed by Sahota are more complete and more closely related to I-O, because of the interaction of distributional factors and the workings of the economy (i.e., a general equilibrium setting). Interestingly, Sahota hardly mentions the marginal productivity theory of income distribution which was the dominant theory of distribution for most of this century (Clark 1899; Ferguson 1969).[5] At first glance, this theory may seem incompatible with I-O, because of its emphasis on marginal conditions and factor prices. On the other hand, the constant returns-to-scale nature of I-O production functions is consistent with the product exhaustion requirement of this theory (typically based on Euler's theorem). Also, a more complete theory of income distribution based on factor prices was recently developed in an I-O framework by Leontief (1986). The model makes use of the price/value-added dual of the quantity-based I-O model, but still is capable of explaining changes in input combinations.

Perhaps the approach most compatible with I-O is the Cambridge, or Keynes-Kaldor, model (see Kaldor 1956). Although the Cambridge focus is on functional shares, Miyazawa (1976) has indicated that their model can be transformed to personal income distribution and more than two classes, and has traced its income propagation process within an I-O framework. The Cambridge theory is based on the idea that factor payments and savings (consumption) propensities differ among social classes. This is just a way of extending the point that "structure" matters from the production to the income realm. The dualism theory of distribution (see Ahluwalia and Chenery 1974) is an extension of this concept into the area of broader social accounting, with the distinctions between urban and rural populations, or modern and backward sectors. According to these theories, the accumulation process has the effect of altering input and income coefficients over time. These changes can readily be modeled in a dynamic I-O formulation.

Our final "complete" theory relates to the work of Stiglitz (1969), who examines the effect of complicating factors in what might be called a neoclassical version of the Cambridge model. These factors include nonlinear savings relationships, variable production rates, heterogeneity of labor skills, and alternative tax policies. Several of them correspond to the types of "institutional" and "structural" factors we discuss in the following section.

An Institutional-Structural Theory of Distributional Impacts

A distinction is often made between long-run and short-run theories in economics. Another important, though rarely mentioned, distinction for the matter at hand is, however, the difference between changes occuring during the evolution of a system and changes resulting from departures from its evolutionary trend because of exogenous shocks. Impact analysis is concerned with the ramifications of these exogenous stimuli. One theory may best explain the existing distribution, while another may do best at explaining the effects of policy change. It would appear that I-O is more capable of addressing the latter than other models. This stems from the fact that an I-O model incorporates sectoral distinctions that can more accurately reflect unbalanced growth, and the fact that I-O is less dependent on historical data than, for example, econometric approaches. At the same time the linearity of the "basic" I-O model[6] becomes less reasonable as an approximation of any nonlinearities that may exist as impacts increase.

Basic Considerations

By *institutions* we refer to the category of organizations, information systems, and formalized decision-making processes that arise to facilitate production, consumption, and exchange in an economic system. Markets and prices are institutions, but have come to play a special role as such in economic thought. Either they are the dominant institutions, as in the basic neoclassical model, or they are taken for granted and not considered as uniquely different from the fundamental understanding of economics, as in the institutionalist school.[7]

There are many ways in which institutions affect income distribution impacts. It has long been suggested that union activity and collective bargaining have an important influence on the distribution of income in terms of relative shares between labor and capital (see Levinson 1954 and Bronfenbrenner 1971). In the case of development impacts, labor unions might confine new employment to overtime increments rather than promoting the hiring of previously unemployed workers. Large corporations, as opposed to small local owners, may relocate their own management in a region rather than hiring managers from other companies within the region. Finally, government at various levels affects the net distribution of returns through its regulatory and tax/transfer policies (see, e.g., Reynolds and Smolensky 1978; Danziger et al. 1981).

Attitudes toward dramatic increases in overtime work, the size of the business enterprises undergoing growth, and the size or very existence of a fiscal surplus differ greatly between "impact" and "evolutionary" contexts. Institutional factors are likely to be harder to predict in cases of sudden change, but, paradoxically, the more uncertain the future, the more crucial it becomes to forecast it.

By *economic structure* we refer to the mix of industries in both the qualitative sense of distinctions between primary, secondary, and tertiary sectors, and the quantitative sense of differences in relative input intensities. Sectors differ significantly in their distribution of both wage- and capital-related income.[8] Thus, a structural transformation brought about, for example, by major inroads from foreign competition, or simply the development of a new sector, holds the potential for changing the distribution of personal income. In fact, several empirical studies have found that shifts in relative industry weights can explain a major portion of changes in the labor share of income (see Denison 1954). Findings related to the equality of personal income distribution show a pronounced "U-shape" in relation to economic growth, most cases of which have been of a sectorally unbalanced nature (see Kuznets 1953; Adelman and Morris 1973).

The aggregate neoclassical production function, which is based primarily on historical data and price variables, would not forecast well in the case of these shifts. The technology shift parameter is too general to be of any help in identifying or tracking sector-specific shifts and their second-order repercussions. The input-output model, which can incorporate engineering data on new technologies and adapt data from other regions without a respecification of the entire model, appears to be a worthy alternative.

Income distribution changes can be analyzed further in a structural context with explicit reference to movements within and between functional shares. The neoclassical model emphasizes substitution possibilities among basic factors. The opposite is true in the input-output formulation because of the technological emphasis of the model and the minor role accorded to prices. However, empirical support for the I-O model stems from the fact that there are a finite, and relatively small, number of formal technological processes to produce many goods.[9] Furthermore, optimal scale and adjustment cost factors inhibit input substitution.

The distribution of wage payments is heavily influenced by the occupational structure within each industry. Moreover, I-O offers a legitimate framework for analysis, since most occupations are not readily substitutable for one another, at least not in an efficient manner. Skill levels, or human capital, have a major effect on wage rates, but change little over shorter periods of time (less than five years) and require lead time for attainment. Thus, aside from demographic changes relating to in-migration or labor force participation rates, basic occupational requirements per unit of output are likely to be stable (see Freeman 1980). Changes within and relative to the labor share will arise primarily from changes in the output mix.

Wage rate changes would then depend on the extent of the demand shift for output, the pool of unemployed workers of each skill level, and productivity increases. Demand shifts are well ascertained by the I-O model, while the excess labor pool is taken as a "background" factor in the short run in most models. Productivity increases may not result in wage increases, but when they do, labor income coefficients in the I-O model can be readily adjusted.

The distribution of capital income is also linked to technology and occupation. Profit sharing, stock purchase plans, and various executive perks represent a good deal of the distribution of capital-related income to the middle-income groups. A recent New York Stock Exchange survey, for example, found that one-third of shareowners were enrolled in stock purchase plans with their companies. Stock purchase and profit plans are furthermore often tied to salary levels. To paraphrase a popular saying, it appears that you are (income class-wise) what you do (occupation- and industry-wise).

Natural Resource and Environmental Considerations

The influence of natural resources and the environment on income distribution has increased markedly over time with the greater volume and toxicity of pollutants and higher prices of natural resource commodities, primarily fossil fuels. Of course, these factors will play an even greater role where impacts stem explicitly from resource-development policies.

At the same time, occupation and industry structure can also help explain the workings of resource and environmental influences on income distribution. Emissions of residuals differ markedly between industries on a per unit product basis (see U.S. EPA 1974), and a shift toward industrialization, for example, will almost surely result in an increase in pollution potential. As to job-related health hazards, these are industry- and occupation-linked as well. Moreover, the extent of mitigation of atmospheric and in-plant pollution has depended more on the directives of government institutions than on market decisions (see Rose 1983).

Damages of environmental pollution and related externalities vary significantly across income levels (see Gianessi et al. 1979). Studies have shown that the valuation of amenities is highly and positively correlated with income (see Randall et al. 1976; Loehman 1983). Property damage is positively correlated with income as well.

In terms of the resource base, its geographic distribution is highly uneven, thereby concentrating it in a subset of the world's regions (Rees 1985). Since ownership and income are positively correlated, resource development often results in a high proportion of the gains flowing to a small number of landowners in the form of rents and royalties (see Clawson 1983). Since most resource regions are rural and sparsely populated, most of the resource commodity is exported. Thus offsetting consumption pattern effects (from cheaper coal or oil, for example) in these regions are likely to be very small in relation to the capital income gains.

Resource factors are also strongly affected by institutional considerations such as whether land is held privately or in the public domain, lease bidding arrangements, and tax instruments (see Krutilla et al. 1983). A major new institutional feature is public participation in natural resource policy-making, in which those potentially affected have a major say in the policy outcome.

Implications

To show that the personal income distribution of policy impacts depends on institutional and structural factors represents only part of the necessary conceptual basis for an input-output approach. Ideally, we would like to include an explanation of the genesis of structural and institutional factors. The former is handled adequately by the relationship between interindustry transactions and changes in final demand in an I-O table (see Miyazawa 1976) and by the literature on technological change in I-O models (see Carter 1970; Rose 1984).

Institutional factors, on the other hand, are much more difficult to explain. Numerous scholars have offered important contributions to the field, but the depth of explanation, uniqueness of each institution, the vast number of relevant institutions, and the prominence of noneconomic factors makes a comprehensive model difficult, if not impossible. Moreover, the structure of such a model would not be as tidy or elegant as that of several existing micro-simulation models. In addition to explaining each individual institution, there is the compound task of explaining the interaction among them. Finally, there is the problem of defining and empirically estimating cause-effect relationships that lead to specific outcomes.

There is a parallel to this in the neoclassical literature dealing with the interaction between a single large employer and a union. This case of "bilateral monopoly" yields an indeterminant solution in theory, and in actuality the outcome depends on the relative bargaining strengths of the two parties, a factor that defies specification. Many find the bilateral bargaining model frustrating because of its ambiguous outcome and see it as a failure of the discipline. This attitude is colored by the overemphasis on point estimate predictions by the economics profession. Typically a range of outcomes, which is almost sure to yield the correct one, is deemed inferior to a point estimate almost sure to be wrong. When combined with the methodological approach of sensitivity analysis, an institutional theory can, however, yield some valuable results. The resulting contingent forecasts are not a failing, but a sober realization of the tenuous nature of underlying assumptions and the lack of universality of cause-effect relations.

In a later chapter of this book we employ a sensitivity analysis of the evaluation of income distribution impacts. Major institutional and background conditions included are union policy toward overtime work, degree of absentee ownership, and public ownership of resource-bearing lands. We also show how these factors are likely to be of more importance to the outcome than explanatory factors cited in the mainstream literature.

Income Distribution in the Modern Resource Region

In this section we integrate the various factors underlying the income distribution impact of natural resource policy in the context of what we call the paradigm of the "modern resource region" (MRR). Rose et al. (1978, 1982) have indicated that the MRR is more typical of resource development settings today than the "boomtown" paradigm (see Gilmore 1976). Given the focus on forest areas in this study, we shall use a forest economy as the example.

There are a number of important characteristics common to all forest area economies that help us assess our modeling needs. They represent conditions or implications that our model must be able to take into account, such as:

1. The prevalence of natural amenities; forest areas are more sensitive to environmental damage or opportunity costs associated with mutually exclusive uses than are many other areas. Economic development may offer significant aggregate gains, but negative externalities, even though small, are likely to be widespread. This means that the distribution of net impacts will include all residents, though probably not in a uniform manner.
2. Development efforts are likely to be capital- and land-intensive. Land is plentiful and, for the most part, federally owned, and hence less susceptible to market pressures. Capital is likely to flow in readily in response to significant potential for resource-bearing lands. Thus factor prices are likely to be stable as well.
3. Federal administration; federal custodianship of forest lands results in greater environmental protection than in other "public" areas. Development efforts are likely to be subject to control, making them somewhat evenly paced and not a jolt to the local economy. This contrasts with the boomtown scenario, which manifests itself in general-level price increases owing to shortages or congestion.
4. Mining, logging, and recreation are all relatively risky enterprises. Thus the level and distribution of returns are highly variable and require detailed analysis.
5. The major products of mining, logging, and recreation are primarily exported. These activities are therefore likely to stimulate growth through backward (derived demand) linkages, rather than as more fundamental stimuli working through forward linkages or causing an overall economic or social transformation.

Overall, changes in the distribution of income will stem primarily from the key sector (mining, logging, recreation) through primary and secondary effects on the existing industry mix. This in turn affects the occupational mix, and the allocation of capital. These changes in functional income shares then translate into changes in personal income distribution. Factor prices play a secondary role. Institutional factors relating to labor unions, corporate ownership, public lands policy, and so forth are likely, however, to play a key role.

Given the factors involved in the development of natural-resource areas, the input-output model framework presented at the outset of this chapter looks to be a most promising approach for income distribution analysis. The superiority of other macro models in determining factor price changes is not a major consideration. Moreover, these other models are severely limited in accommodating a new sector and in determining its secondary effects; in most cases structural change, so prominent here, would merely be subsumed under general technological change. Finally, several institutional factors can readily be accommodated within an I-O framework.

A Formal Example

Many of the structural factors we have discussed are incorporated into the basic I-O model, but most of the institutional factors are not. We need to go beyond the simple model presented in equations 2 and 3 to a more comprehensive, formal model. Because of the diverse nature of many of the institutional features involved, the notational representation would be extremely complex. We have therefore chosen to illustrate the direction of the comprehensive model with two examples—unionization and absentee property ownership. At the same time we note the importance of moving toward a comprehensive model in another way—application of structural and institutional features on the consumption side, linked with the payment sector, to yield a complete model of income generation and distribution.[10]

Union hiring practices will greatly influence what percentage of new work opportunities go to those already employed, in the form of overtime, and what percentage go to the unemployed. The policy direction will vary according to the context. For example, where an occupation is partly unionized, as in the case of coal mining, the union may try to prevent "outsiders" from being hired and opt for overtime pay. In locales where the union membership is extensive and a high unemployment rate prevails, the union may press for hiring its unemployed. The model can accommodate either of these extremes as well as combinations in between. The impact of these distinctions on income distribution is that the overtime work option will benefit workers in a proportional manner—that is, average income distribution coefficients can be used. The hiring of new workers, on the other hand, directly benefits only a few and leaves the incomes of the others unchanged, thereby necessitating use of marginal income distribution coefficients.[11] This distinction between marginal and average coefficients has been introduced into the consumption component of I-O models in other contexts (see Miernyk et al. 1967). Carrying through our example, we can suggest that the average propensities to consume various products by a newly employed individual in a low-income bracket will differ from others in that bracket, employed or not. We might think of his consumption pattern being subject to change. On the other hand, an individual in a low-income bracket will differ from others in that bracket, employed or not. On the other hand, an individual receiving only overtime pay (and staying within his original income bracket) will increase his consumption on a proportional basis.

The pattern of capital ownership will determine what percentage of nonwage income is retained and eventually respent in the region. Large corporate involvement, as opposed to small private local ownership, will result in a high proportion of capital income leaking out of the region. Thus capital income coefficients must be adjusted accordingly. In this case, we do not need to distinguish average and marginal coefficients per se; rather we use a proportionality factor to assign capital income retained to the two groups of residents.

A formal presentation of this model is found in equation set 4 below. The equation in the upper partition is the conventional input-output balance equation that allocates the production of goods between intermediate and final uses. In this case, consumption is calculated endogenously on a basis of income class and employment status. In the second partition the income payments quadrant of equation 2 has been divided into three separate components: wage distribution for the continuously employed, wage distribution for the newly employed, and capital distribution.[12] Two additional components apportion the capital income to the two groups of workers. On the consumption side there are only two further subdivisions—the status quo group and the newly employed.[13]

$$
\begin{bmatrix}
I-A & O & O & O & -\bar{c}_{kj} & -c_{kj} \\
-\hat{\rho}_j \bar{w}_{kj} & I & O & O & O & O \\
(1-\hat{\rho}_j)w_{kj} & O & I & O & O & O \\
-d_{kj} & O & O & I & O & O \\
O & I & O & \hat{\gamma}_k & I & O \\
O & O & I & (1-\hat{\gamma}_k) & O & I
\end{bmatrix}
\begin{bmatrix}
\Delta X_j \\
\Delta Y_k^{\bar{w}} \\
\Delta Y_k^{w} \\
\Delta Y_k^{d} \\
\Delta \bar{Y}_k \\
\Delta Y_k
\end{bmatrix}
=
\begin{bmatrix}
\Delta F_j \\
O \\
O \\
O \\
O \\
O
\end{bmatrix}
\qquad (4)
$$

where

A is an $n \times n$ matrix of technical coefficients

X_j is an $n \times 1$ vector of gross outputs in each sector

$Y_k^{\bar{w}}$ is an $m \times 1$ vector of overtime wage income in each income class

Y_k^{w} is an $m \times 1$ vector of new employment wage income in each income class

Y_k^{d} is an $m \times 1$ vector of capital-related income retained within the region by each income class

$\bar{Y}_k$ is an $m \times 1$ vector of total income of the continuously employed for each income class

Y_k is an $m \times 1$ vector of total income of the newly employed for each income class

$\bar{w}_{kj}$ is an $m \times n$ matrix of wage income distribution coefficients for the continuously employed (average coefficients)

w_{kj} is an $m \times n$ matrix of wage income distribution coefficients for the newly employed (marginal coefficients)

d_{kj} is an $m \times n$ matrix of capital-related income coefficients

$\hat{\rho}_j$ is an $m \times n$ diagonal matrix of the proportion of new man-hours to be assigned as overtime in each sector

$\hat{\gamma}_k$ is an $m \times m$ diagonal matrix of the proportion of capital-related income retained within the region that flows to the continuously employed in each income class

$\bar{c}_{kj}$ is an $n \times m$ matrix of personal consumption coefficients for the continuously employed

c_{kj} is an $n \times m$ matrix of personal consumption coefficients for the newly employed

F_j is an $n \times 1$ vector of other final demand

I is the identity matrix

Δ denotes change

The equation set can be solved by the typical inversion and matrix multiplication procedure of input-output analysis. Note that the solution would yield a set of "change" variables—$\Delta \bar{Y}_k$, ΔY_k. These would then be added to baseline values to determine the new income distribution. Alternatively, a set of distributional impact multipliers following Rose et al. (1982) could be calculated directly from the "change" solution.

Another fruitful set of computations would be to calculate income multipliers of the conventional type as well as those suggested by Miyazawa (1976). The multipliers would provide insight into the sensitivity of income formation to key parameters such as ρ and γ, as well as to the marginal propensities to consume. An extensive investigation of this type for economic-demographic models by Batey (1985) has yielded valuable insights.

Again, we emphasize that many other variables can be included in the type of framework represented by equation system 4. These include reductions in income owing to environmental damage, private vs. public resource ownership, tax and transfer payments, population in-migration, and so forth. Overall, if a variable or relationship that bears on income distribution can be quantified and bears either a direct or an indirect relationship to economic activity, it can be included within this framework. The only exception would be cases where strong nonlinearities exist, but even many of these can be included, as in the several examples of wage rate changes discussed in this chapter. Still other elements are also important in examining long-range aspects of income distribution impacts. Many of these can be incorporated into a dynamic I-O framework developed by Leontief (1970) and extended by Duchin and Szyld (1985).

Conclusion

This chapter has endeavored to demonstrate the relationship between fundamental theories of income distribution and input-output analysis and to establish a firm theoretical grounding for the standard I-O income distribution model. We began by pointing out that the only intrinsic distributional feature of the basic I-O model is that *structure matters,* and that any other determinant of income distribution must be expressly built into the model. At the same time we showed that I-O was compatible with several theories of distribution, though not all of them pertained to the resource-development impact analysis that is the focus of this book.

A structural/institutional theory was adopted as being the most consistent with the context of resource-development impacts. This conclusion was supported by the findings of previous I-O and non–I-O studies alike, and will further be supported by the sensitivity tests to be performed in later chapters.

Some readers might be concerned about the characteristic "indeterminacy" of institutional approaches and the gulf between these approaches and the more conventional neoclassical ones. However, this gulf exists only for simple versions of income distribution models. More sophisticated neoclassical models have incorporated complicated factors and, in fact, often refer to them as institutions (see Starrett 1976). At the same time, decades of empirical research on institutions have helped eliminate many of the indeterminacies. It is thus not unrealistic to consider a convergence of the two approaches. The disagreement is primarily a matter of degree over: (1) the prominence of factor and product prices, and (2) the number of institutional considerations that matter.

3 / A Positive Economic Approach to Distributional Analysis

Public ownership and the administered allocation of resources have long been regarded skeptically as market substitutes.[1] A major unanswered criticism of these alternatives is whether they can be democratic or even responsive to consumer preferences in any significant way. Can unelected public officials make allocations on behalf of a constituency that the constituency itself would have chosen? This is an important concern for any nation founded on democratic ideals. Any answer in the affirmative must overcome several major problems. Is it possible for a government agency to provide the data needed by citizens to render an informed judgment? Are the costs of obtaining accurate public feedback prohibitive? Are the institutions for public input unbiased?

This chapter addresses these three problems by formulating three "positive" distributional measures. The analysis is termed "positive" because it is intended to be used to estimate various types of impacts and to use this information to predict policy decisions rather than to make normative judgments on issues of equity, which are usually identified with distributional considerations. The three measures are:

1. The individual impact matrix—a probability distribution of potential impacts for each member of a given socioeconomic group.
2. The community impact index—a tally of how the majority of the public will be affected and the size of the majority.
3. The political articulation index—an indicator of the likely public response, taking into account intensities of preference, attitudes toward risk, political influence, and transaction costs.

Conceptualization

The conceptual basis for our positive distributional measures emanates from a utility function approach to the decision-making process in a participatory setting, such as the one surrounding the U.S. Forest Service. The measures are presented in a sequence that allows us to illustrate how each builds on the information content of its predecessor.

The Individual Impact Matrix

Cost-benefit analysis (CBA) is the most prevalent, standardized evaluation method applied to public projects today. CBA is, however, only a net aggregative measure, and some economists (see Herfindahl and Kneese 1974) argue that distributional information is a useful supplement in project evaluation. The environmental impact statement (EIS) has more recently been used to supplement CBA's by identifying the diversity of impacts of public projects. In many cases the EIS identifies affected parties, but usually in an imprecise and aggregative manner (e.g., "Residents along Highway 101 will experience a tenfold increase in automobile traffic"). Typically, the rationale for any disaggregation of costs or benefits is vaguely stated (e.g., "Special attention should be given to define who or what will be benefited, and by how much"; U.S. EPA 1975). The level of detail and accuracy needed are never spelled out. Also, how this finding is supposed to affect a final decision on the project is rarely specified.

Where efficiency considerations are paramount, and the manner in which decisions are reached is not important, the undetailed EIS is no hindrance to policy-formation. However, where the decision process itself is important, as in a participatory democracy, knowledge of the distribution of potential impacts is crucial to affected citizens and policy-makers. In the absence of an extreme degree of altruism, voters would have to know how the proposed policy would affect them individually, over and above the net impact on the community, in order to render an informed judgment.

The resources expended in obtaining detailed information such as this are one form of the "costs of collective action" and can be exorbitant. Even when individual-based data are available, one can conceive of relying on a more aggregated vector of impact distribution. This would be the case where the policy entails an efficiency gain, but the costs of perfect information about the effects of the policy on each participant in the collective choice process exceed the efficiency gain from the policy itself.

Public participation brings together two sets of decision-makers: (a) affected citizens and (b) public officials. For now, let us couch the analysis in terms of income/utility levels with a minimum loss of generalization.[2] On the basis of prior work,[3] each individual, i, is assumed to receive utility in the following form:

$$U_i = f \text{ (individual gain, net aggregate gain, equity of gains)} \tag{1}$$

Individual gain unambiguously represents the pursuit of self-interest and subsumes personal gains from the environment and other less tangible goals. Net aggregate gain refers to the overall good of the community, while equity is concerned with how evenly gains are distributed across income groups.[4]

Assuming the same utility function for every individual within an income class, but allowing for differences over classes, or simply expressing gains in income terms, a single individual can represent each group if individual gains within the group are equal. More likely, there will be an entire distribution of impacts in each group, and our first measure becomes an "individual impact matrix."

The Community Impact Index

The individual impact matrix contains a great deal of information and serves a useful purpose on that score alone from the standpoint of the parties at interest in Forest Service policies. However, forest managers need a way of sifting through the matrix and arriving at a summary judgment. There are a number of alternatives. For one, there is the summation of individual net gains in dollar terms, though it leads us right back to the benefit-cost criterion. The summation of individual net utility changes is merely a "weighted" form of this criterion. Both of them correspond to the "dollar voting" of well-functioning markets.

Actually, both income and utility aggregates are weighted versions of individual votes—that is, the "one-person-one-vote" condition of most formal elections and many types of representation. In the context of the previous section, the individual voter approach would mean transforming the distributional impact matrix so that each cell entry represented the number of individuals in a given income group and a net gain/loss category. The summary measure, which we refer to as the "community impact index," would then be the aggregation of the matrix into a scalar that represented the net number of gainers or losers. That is, it would convey how the majority of the relevant population were qualitatively affected.

The discussion thus far indicates that the "weighted" (dollar-vote) and "individual" (one-person-one-vote) measures can conflict. Net dollar gains to the community may be positive, but a majority of the population may still incur net losses. Thus, one of the indices can in no way be considered a good proxy or substitute for the other. Which of these two impact measures to use in our analysis depends on the decision-making process of forest managers and participants.

Studies of Forest Service decision-making bring out some very interesting points. Culhane and Friesema (1981) found that managers:

1. have definitely been influenced by public participation;
2. are skeptical of special interests and more likely to listen to a participant who represents interests broader than his or her own;
3. have an easier time dealing with information than with preferences or group pressures (coalitions);
4. resent vote-counting implications of public participation to the extent that they encroach on sound forest management principles.

These conclusions support our construction of a model with the following characteristics of the manager's decision function:

1. that it take into account impacts of policies on individuals and that it be at least in part individualist, i.e., an aggregation of individual utility functions;
2. that it contain elements of broader community interests;
3. that it contain professional objectives.[5]

Thus, we express the forest manager's decision function as:

$$U_m = g \text{ (aggregate gains, distribution of gains, professional objectives)} \qquad (2)$$

Hence, forest managers will be able to utilize the information provided by the community impact index in policy assessment. This utility function is markedly different from that describing the self-interested bureaucrat (Niskanen 1971), although arguments for the manager's utility function that would be important from the self-interest viewpoint could be subsumed within other professional objectives. Hence, this utility function does not conflict with the self-interest hypothesis, nor is it intended to imply that the forest manager is a completely neutral party in the decision-making process.

Political Articulation Index

The utility framework also serves as a basis for political expression of forest area residents' preferences. Continuing to assume that residents are motivated by rational self-interest, then:

Political Activity $= h$ (expected net benefits)[6] (3)

Many analysts have suggested that individuals consider benefits and costs in attempting to influence the policy-making process. An individual's interest in influencing policy may stem from private benefits because of net income gains or it may stem from distributional consequences that are perceived as desirable. The output or goal of political activity is to alter policy decisions. Since this output is uncertain, individuals attach some rough probabilities to the effects their activity will have on policies chosen. In a similar vein, much political activity may be seen as changing the probability of particular policy outcomes rather than affecting the policy itself.

Political activity will also be affected by the value of resources expended to influence policy decisions. Participation in the Forest Service planning process depends on the costs of political contributions, organizing interest groups, letter-writing, meeting with Forest Service personnel, travel, participation in lawsuits, and so on. The effectiveness of attempts to change policy is greatly influenced by accessibility to policy-makers (Culhane 1981), an important determinant of the costs of political activity. As suggested by Nowack et al. (1982), the individual's status and interpersonal skills influence the level of political activity. Hence, the magnitude and type of political response to the Forest Service planning process is jointly determined by the expected benefits of given types of political activity, political influence, and the associated opportunity costs incurred by participation.

The Forest Service has several avenues for public participation in the planning process (Friesema and Culhane 1979; Culhane 1981). The most frequently used process is the public hearing. Interested parties are invited to attend and submit short verbal statements on the issue being considered; written statements are also solicited by the Forest Service, either at the time of the hearing or at a later date. Since alternative policies are rarely voted upon in local referenda, this is often the most important outlet for expression of preferences by residents.

Interestingly, public hearings do not draw a large (relative to the population) number of participants. One explanation, offered by Olson (1965), is that group activity for collective ends is stifled by public goods aspects, such as the free-rider problem and the inconsequentiality of individual actions. A group will be more successful in attracting members to its cause if it offers attainment of one or more private goods. Of the three utility function arguments in equation 1, only net individual gain is a private good. In Olson's framework, however, if the group is to be successful, it should be able to control the distribution of most, if not all, policy benefits. Obviously, this is unlikely to occur in general, and in the context of forest land-use policy in particular. We suggest that several other well-established explanations for nonparticipation, such as transactions costs, are more useful in this context. For example, suppose there are a large number of losers as a result of a given policy option, but with relatively small losses, or weakly negative utility. If the opportunity costs of participating in a public hearing are positive, and generally exceed losses, very few of these potential losers will actually participate. Thus, a public hearing may indicate widespread support or opposition to a given policy, but this may be misleading because those who weakly oppose or support a policy are unlikely to participate.

Since costs and benefits of the act of participating are important, two indices of political response can be constructed. The first is a zero-opportunity cost measure of preferences. If a referendum could be held for which the opportunity cost of voting were zero (or trivial), and if local citizens had perfect information and the decision criterion was majority rule (preferences are given equal weight), the outcomes would simply be given by the "community impact index" of the previous section.

In practice all these assumptions may be violated. Perfect information is not available, but the agency proposing the policy can partially rectify this problem by providing additional information. Although majority rule is used in most referenda decisions, it cannot measure intensity of preferences, and may be replaced by a decision rule having this property. Most important, the opportunity costs of voting (and of casting an informed vote) are not zero.[7]

Since costs of preference determination are important from the perspective of allocative efficiency, policy-makers may find another index useful. A "political articulation index" may be constructed from preferences revealed at a public hearing, for example. Public hearings are not a costless method of determining preferences, but are probably less costly than holding a referendum. This second index thus accounts for positive opportunity costs of preference articulation. It can be constructed by multiplying all income/utility indices for impacted citizens by a political activity scale. This preserves the ordering of the income/utility scale, since someone who opposes the policy initially will also be so ranked in the overall index. However, preferences would be weighted by the expected net benefits of appearing at the public hearing. The overall index indicates who is most likely to appear at a public hearing and whether they will support or oppose the policy proposal.

Considering pure self-interest as a motivation, an appearance at a public hearing implies that expected benefits exceed costs. This is most likely to be true for community leaders, since Friesema and Culhane note that status affects the weight policy-makers attach to testimony. As shown by Culhane (1981), representatives of business or citizens interest groups with large constituencies are also likely to have more influence than an individual citizen. On the other hand, some individuals at the meeting may have low status but very strong preferences and/or low opportunity costs of attending.

The Forest Service can clearly improve its understanding of preferences to the extent that it can get individuals to reveal them. Although little has been said about coalitions, they do lower the cost of participating in public hearings or in other forms of political activity. Groups such as the Sierra Club and trade associations have nominal membership fees, which are lower than the cost of personally appearing at meetings or lobbying. The group instead sends a spokesperson who is knowledgeable, and carries the influence of large numbers. Typically, interest groups represent a larger constituency than the local population. Whether the Forest Service gives more weight to current residents' preferences or to outsiders, it is important for it to know whose interests are being represented.

Individual Policy Impact Information in Economic Models

Most policy-impact models have been oriented toward the determination of aggregate measures such as net benefits, employment, and fiscal balance (see Krutilla et al. 1977; Isserman and Merrifield 1987). Public participation, however, requires the dissemination of data on the impact on individuals rather than on the community as a whole. Acknowledging the limitations of data and modeling capabilities, it may only be feasible to provide information on groups. This will be useful if the groupings are defined so that the individual can make the necessary association and the variation of impacts within groups is low relative to that of the population as a whole. Otherwise, the distribution of impacts within the group must be known so that an "expected value" of impacts can be calculated.

Choosing the most appropriate grouping is thus important. A recent major study of Forest Service decision-making by Culhane (1981) delineates constituent groups in terms of major interests: economic, environmental, recreational, and other (schools, government, professional, etc.). While this categorization is convenient because it pertains to formal visible organizations, it is not clear that it yields the greatest information per group (or per dollar expended on information gathering) for the purpose of the participants or forest managers themselves.

We suggest that income or utility (I/U) levels are superior because:

1. I/U levels are unique for each individual (i.e., alternative constituent groupings involve overlaps, as an individual may simultaneously be an employee of a recreation company, an environmentalist, and a member of a professional group).
2. I/U levels represent a common denominator for comparing impact types (e.g., wages, property value increases, disamenities).
3. I/U levels facilitate the calculation of second-order impacts (e.g., the direct impacts on owners of lodging places may be small in comparison to the indirect impacts of increased economic activity).
4. I/U levels facilitate the calculation of normative indices of the distribution of impacts, or equity.
5. I/U levels facilitate the incorporation of important principles of the theory of consumer choice.

Another reason for choosing I/U levels is that they are the units of analysis for the majority of a new generation of economic models that focus on distributional impacts. These range from input-output approaches (see, e.g., Golladay and Haveman 1977; Rose et al. 1982) to micro-simulation models (see, e.g., Scarf and Shoven 1984; Hazilla and Kopp 1984). An important feature of these new models is that they have been able to overcome the long-standing obstacle of lack of data, and are thus operational.

The capabilities of these models can serve as the basic information requirement for public participation. This is the approach taken in devising the model presented in this book. The core of the modeling system is the multisector income distribution matrix, which disaggregates the direct income payments from each sector of the economy by income class of recipient. In a policy simulation, the model's solution yields the following income distribution impact matrix:

$$\Delta Y = [\Delta y_{kj}] \tag{4}$$

where Δy denotes a change in income, k represents income class, and j represents the sector from which the change in income emanates.

For example, a policy to allow mining in a given National Forest will stimulate mining activity directly and economic activity elsewhere in the region through multiplier effects. It may at the same time cause a decrease in some recreational activity or generate water pollution affecting the entire population of the area. Some of these effects may have to be calculated separately, but the analysis is facilitated if they are translated into dollar terms and eventually combined.

A hypothetical example of an income distribution impact matrix is presented in table 3.1 below for an economy divided into five sectors and five income groups. Keep in mind that the numbers represent the distribution of increments to income, and may differ from the distribution of baseline income. For purposes of simplification we assume an equivalence between these marginal and average distributions in all but one important case. The relative proportions in each column except mining are representative of empirical findings in the next part of this book.

Table 3.1. Income Distribution Impact Matrix (1,000 dollars)

Income Class of Recipient, k	Sector, j					
	Forestry	Mining	Manufacturing	Trade	Service	Total
0–9,999	50	5,000	500	300	200	6,050
10,000–24,999	200	1,000	1,200	900	700	4,000
25,000–49,999	300	1,000	1,600	1,200	800	4,900
50,000–99,999	400	1,000	400	500	200	2,500
100,000 +	50	2,000	300	100	100	2,550
Total income gain	1,000	10,000	4,000	3,000	2,000	20,000
Total externality loss	200	8,000	3,000	600	200	12,000

The unrepresentative distribution in the leading sector, mining, arises because institutional factors come into play. An increase in economic activity can in general be attained by existing employees working overtime, by hiring additional employees, or by some combination of the two. In the case of a large increase in mining activity, however, the overtime work option may be limited by labor union policy or physical constraints. Thus, the high proportion of returns in mining flowing to the 0 to $10,000 income group[8] represents exclusive reliance on hiring previously unemployed workers.[9]

The last row in table 3.1 represents a hypothetical set of income losses associated with various types of externalities (pollution, disamenities, loss of recreational opportunities) generated in each sector. The emission flows underlying these damages can be calculated with an I-O model by utilizing the concept of a pollution coefficient (see, e.g., Leontief 1970). In order to simplify the example, and because of the difficulty of ascribing, say, air or water pollution damages to any single source, we have not shown the distribution of damages from each sector. It suffices for our purpose to consider an aggregate vector of damages and refer to related work by Randall et al. (1978), Gianessi et al. (1979), and Loehman and De (1983) to acknowledge that the overall distribution of environmental damage can differ across income groups.

Specification of Positive Measures of Income Distribution

Based on the decision-making context and modeling capability discussed above, we proceed to the formal specification and illustration of the use of the three positive measures of income distribution impacts.

The Individual Impact Matrix

As would be the case for any resource-development scenario, our example indicates a differential impact across sectors as well as income groups. An individual's relative gain will depend on his or her association with a given sector as an employee, and possibly with several sectors as a dividend, interest, rent, or royalty earner. Those associated with the focal point of development will stand to gain the most, and gains will decline as linkages with the key sector become weaker. Nearly all individuals will suffer externality losses (e.g., pollution, congestion, disamenities), and market transmitted losses will take place in those sectors displaced by the development effort (e.g., decreased recreational activity when land is shifted to mining).

Table 3.2. Individual Impact Matrix

Income Class of Recipient, k	Net Income Change Class, r				
	−999 to 0	0 to 999	1,000 to 4,999	5,000 +	Total
0–9,999	500 (.50)	200 (.20)	100 (.10)	200 (.20)	1,000 (1.0)
10,000–24,999	750 (.33)	750 (.33)	500 (.22)	250 (.11)	2,250 (1.0)
25,000–49,999	1,400 (.70)	300 (.15)	200 (.10)	100 (.05)	2,000 (1.0)
50,000–99,999	50 (.10)	250 (.50)	100 (.20)	100 (.20)	500 (1.0)
100,000 +	0 (.00)	100 (.40)	100 (.40)	50 (.20)	250 (1.0)
Total	2,700 (.45)	1,600 (.27)	1,000 (.17)	700 (.12)	6,000 (1.0)

In our example, an individual miner may have a good idea of his new employment prospects, but other members of the community may be uninformed about their future, since they are impacted through indirect economic effects and externalities. The information contained in equation 4 above can be rearranged, however, to provide more insight. The necessary computations begin by calculating the average gain or loss per person in every cell of table 3.1 to reveal the range of individual impacts. The range is then split into appropriate "income change" categories, r, which become the column dimension of a new matrix, replacing the sector designation, j. We are moving toward grouping together all individuals who receive the same level of gain or loss, regardless of where their payments originate. Moreover, the focus is shifted to impacted individuals rather than total income flows.

This is the basis for our individual impact matrix presented in table 3.2 above. The numbers not in parentheses in the body of the table represent the number of individuals, n, in each income class, k, who receive gains or losses in each size class, r. We then standardize this matrix by dividing each cell entry in a given row by its corresponding row sum (see the results in parentheses in table 3.2). Our individual impact matrix, I, is thus

$$I = \frac{(n_{kr})}{(n_k)} \tag{5}$$

Continuing with our example to illustrate these points, we first observe in table 3.2 that there are a total of 6,000 affected citizens grouped into the same five income classes as before and whose income changes are grouped into four size classes, one of which is negative. For the lowest income group, for example, the entries in parentheses mean that an individual originally in that group has a 50 percent chance of a loss between −$999 and 0, a 20 percent chance of a gain between 0 and $999, a 10 percent chance of a gain between $1,000 and $4,999, and a 20 percent chance of a gain greater than $5,000. The two hundred individuals in the first row of column 4 of table 3.2, who together stand to reap earnings greater than $5,000 are two hundred formerly unemployed miners now scheduled to earn $25,000 annually (refer back to the $5 million gain from mining to the lowest income bracket in table 3.1). Other gross gains and gross losses are combined in the other entries of the table. We might note that the groups with the highest probability of a loss are those in the lowest and middle-income groups. Again this is intended to reflect real world conditions, where environmental damage tends to be spread more evenly than personal income, and higher income groups are better able to avoid damage (e.g., they live farther away from polluted areas or visit alternative recreation areas farther away). For the case of a lower income household, this means that if it incurs the same damage as a higher income household, it is more likely to suffer a net loss, because its gross personal income gain is likely to be smaller than that of the higher income household. Our result for the middle-income group is, on the other hand, contrived to illustrate the possibility of a disproportionate share of losses falling on one neighborhood. More will be said about the important implications of this prospect below.

In effect, the fact that the "I matrix" gives an individual in a given group the range of individual impacts or the entire distribution should prove more valuable than the mere expected value to those individuals who have more complex attitudes toward risk (e.g., the Savage minimax regret criterion). These attitudes can be more formally incorporated into the analysis with the measure presented below in connection with the political articulation index.

The Community Impact Index

As mentioned previously, the individual impact matrix contains considerable information of interest to all groups concerned with Forest Service policies. However, a single statistic may also be of use to policy-makers and citizens. An obvious choice is an aggregation of net dollar gains/losses.

In a public participation setting, dollar weights may be inappropriate. We see as more relevant a "community impact index" that conveys how the majority of the relevant population are affected qualitatively. This index is simply the aggregation of the individual impact matrix into a scalar that represents the net number of gainers or losers.

Let us define the number of people with net gains, G, as

$$G = \sum_k \sum_g n_{kg} \tag{6}$$

where g denotes the subset of r corresponding to positive income change categories. The community impact index, C, can then be defined as:

$$C = \frac{G}{n} \qquad\qquad 0 \leq C \leq 1 \tag{7}$$

In our example, there are 3,300 who stand to gain from the increased mining activity and 2,700 who stand to lose from it, so $C = .55$. The low value of the index arises in part from the concentration of gains. The two hundred newly employed mine workers (3.33 percent of the region's workforce) would receive $5 million (25 percent of the gross gain and 50 percent of the net gain).

We refer to the value of C as low because gross gains are twice the size of gross losses. The combination of these aggregates, or the net benefits of the development effort to the community, can be expressed as:

$$N = \sum_k \sum_r \Delta y_{kr} \tag{8}$$

We reiterate that C and N can be of opposite signs if gains or losses are even more heavily concentrated than in our example.

Recall also that C and N, as well "professional" objectives, are likely to be arguments in the forest manager's decision function. To the extent that C measures the preferences of affected residents, the index will also be quite useful to policy-makers where the size of the winning margin is an important guide to policy (see Russell 1979). Note also that if the well-being of any subgroup of the population is considered to be of relatively greater importance than that of the others, weights can be attached to the "n" values of the former. This differs from the dollar weighting of N (e.g., higher weighting of low-income individuals) and represents another way of incorporating equity into the analysis.

The Political Articulation Index

Though the previous index represents an ideal standard of majority rule, its direct application may be unlikely. First, forest managers may not have the resources to calculate it. Second, it does not represent active participation of citizens in the decision-making process. Forums for public opinion and participation, however, can serve as the basis of a substitute—the political articulation index. This index may be calculated, for example, from the results of a public meeting on a given policy.

In essence, the political articulation index is a type of "revealed" impact measure that also takes into account people's intensity of preference, political influence, attitudes toward risk, and transactions costs. Each of these factors can serve to weight individual impacts, with the overall weight in each case indicating an individual's or group's probability of active political participation. For example, a person with $50,000 to gain from a given policy would be more likely to attend and speak out at a public hearing than one who stands to gain only $5. Furthermore, if we assume asymmetry of the utility function stemming from risk aversion, a $5,000 gain would not give rise to the same fervor as a $5,000 loss, and would result in a higher probability of participation for a $5,000 gain on the part of a poor person than for a wealthy person.

A hypothetical weighting matrix, W, that follows up on our mining development example is presented in table 3.3 below. The relative ranking of weights is to a great extent owing to the attributes of utility functions mentioned in the previous paragraph, though the absolute levels are arbitrary. There may, however, be some interesting exceptions. Note that the probability that a person in the lowest income group will attend a public hearing is .90, while the probability of participation for a middle-income person is .97. Lower-income individuals may feel they have less political influence than those in other groups, and therefore that their vote carries less weight. They may also be stifled by transaction costs (travel expenses, hiring a babysitter, etc.). On the other hand, the relatively high probability of attendance by middle-income individuals who stand to bear losses is more than just the wielding of individual influence. Recall in our reference to the individual impact matrix (see table 3.1) that a very high proportion of the people who stood to lose from increased mining (1,400 of a total population of 6,000) were in the $25,000 to $50,000 income bracket. This could stem from the not unlikely situation where damages are concentrated in a single, socioeconomically uniform neighborhood or small community. This could result in a coalition that is buoyed by its strength in numbers, and may translate into a high probability of success in influencing the outcome, thereby overriding transaction cost obstacles for group members.

Other kinds of W matrices may be useful, since the row categories may change depending on the group characteristics of interest to policy-makers (e.g., age and ethnic or interest group). For any given group characteristic, a separate W matrix would be desirable for each argument in the utility function of equation 1 (individual net gain, aggregate net gain and equity).[10] Even with the valuable insight into several of the factors that might comprise W by Culhane (1983) and others, we acknowledge the difficulty in its empirical estimation with the current data available from public hearings. First, analysis of the distribution of policy impacts has been skimpy at best. Second, very little data exist on income, age, perceived size of gain or loss from a given policy, and access to policy-makers—that is, factors that would affect preferences for the policy and participation.

Table 3.3. Weighting Matrix

Income Class of Recipient, k	Net Income Change Class, r			
	-999 to 0	0 to 999	$1{,}000$ to $4{,}999$	$5{,}000 +$
0–9,999	.90	.70	.95	.99
10,000–24,999	.95	.60	.90	.95
25,000–49,999	.99	.50	.80	.90
50,000–99,999	.75	.25	.40	.67
100,000	.40	.10	.20	.33

Subjective judgment by the policy-maker may have to play a major role in the meantime. The political articulation index, A, can now be defined as:[11]

$$A = \sum_k \sum_g (w_{kg} \otimes n_{kg}) / \sum_k \sum_r (w_{kr} \otimes n_{kr}) \qquad\qquad 0 \le A \le 1 \qquad (9)$$

The index, in effect, modifies the passive community impact measure to yield an active intensity of preference measure.

Interestingly, a favorable majority score on the community impact index (7) can turn into an opposing majority on the political articulation index (9), or vice versa. Such a reversal takes place in our mining development example because of the concentration of a sizable portion of total gross gains among a small number of mine workers and the concentration of losses among a large block of individuals in middle-income brackets. The application of the weighting matrix in table 3.3 to the individual impacts of table 3.2 yields an A index of 0.46.[12] This contrasts sharply with the value of $C = .55$ calculated in the previous section.

Prior to recent distributional impact models, the Forest Service did not have the means to calculate the community impact index and of necessity placed significant emphasis on preferences expressed at public hearings, as well as written testimony. Now policy-makers have a choice. If forest managers are relatively sensitive to the actual welfare of a forest community, they will tend toward incorporating equation 7 into their decision-making function. To the extent that they are influenced by public action, they will make use of equation 9. Which measure is most appropriate is largely a normative question, and need not be resolved here.

Conclusion

Distributional ramifications of public policy are often neglected. One reason is that they are often viewed as necessitating normative judgments. On the other hand, more commonly used efficiency-based assessments, such as cost-benefit analysis, are viewed as objective and straightforward. However, in cases involving public participation in decision-making, a positive net benefit result may clash with citizen preferences. If a majority of the affected population incur net losses, their support of the policy could only be motivated by a level of altruism that cannot be justified theoretically or empirically. In the context of public participation in natural resource policy, overriding public sentiment places an efficiency objective in a clearly paramount position, which is a normative judgment in its own right. This is not to say that the popularity of a policy should be the only criterion, or that the trade off between efficiency and participatory democracy cannot be bridged by some redistribution. It is to say that the issues raised in this chapter are complex and can never be resolved if not properly addressed. Our intended contribution has been to specify positive measures of the distribution of economic impacts, to offer an operational methodology by which they can be calculated, and to illustrate their role in the context of natural resource policy. These measures will be applied in a case study presented in chapter 9.

II / CONSTRUCTION OF THE MODEL

4 / A Social Accounting Matrix of Income Distribution

This chapter presents the framework for our empirical model and an overview of how it will be constructed. Our inclusion of the socioeconomic variable—income category—transforms the input-output framework into a special case of a Social Accounting Matrix, or SAM. In the following section we introduce the SAM concept and show how its incorporation of a broader set of economic interactions, outside the realm of standard economic models, can improve the accuracy of estimates of important economic variables such as aggregate output, employment, and income.

The dearth of available data on the distribution of personal income by both sector of origin and income bracket of recipient make the estimation procedure difficult. In subsequent sections we explain our approach of converting data on individual functional income payment categories into an overall matrix of personal income distribution.

Economic and Socioeconomic Accounts

Economic accounts serve as the empirical foundation for economic analyses at the regional and national levels. A leading authority on the subject, John Kendrick (1972), has gone so far as to propose that "much of the success of economics in recent decades has been due to the development of economic accounts," (p. vii). This would not appear to be an exaggerated claim, since economic accounts represent the major step in rendering theoretical advances operational.

Economic accounts are typically comprehensive tabulations of transactions between economic entities. They have many of the valuable features of business accounts, such as double entries, but differ primarily by including flows or end-of-period balances for all economic units as a group. There are many important examples, the most prominent of which include the U.S. National Income and Product Accounts (NIPA) and the United Nations System of National Accounts (SNA). Input-output tables are also examples of economic accounts, with the advantage of showing explicitly the origins and destinations of transactions.

Social Accounting Matrices

The SAM format does not differ from the standard I O version, except for expansion of entities to include socioeconomic institutions, such as households, government, unions, etc. A further delineation is often made along such lines as urban/rural, black/white, or rich/poor. Analysis of the size distribution of personal income is typically undertaken in terms of a further disaggregation of the latter categories according to income bracket.

The SAM concept was pioneered by Nobel laureate Richard Stone (1961) and, in its ultimate form, represents a generalization of the relations between producers of the I-O model to include disaggregated payment/spending relations among all relevant institutions or entities having the legal right of ownership and hence, the ability to accumulate and to provide services. This reformulation strengthens the link between input-output tables and national or regional income accounting and significantly increases the range of applications.

A schematic diagram of a comprehensive, but somewhat aggregated, SAM is presented as Figure 4.1. The single disaggregated feature in the figure is the set of "interindustry transactions" among production units—a conventional input-output table at the core of the SAM. While the SAM concept is consistent with even an aggregate (single) production entry, most researchers have included the interindustry detail as the primary effort at disaggregation. Placing the research in this book in perspective, we seek to disaggregate the value-added entry in figure 4.1 by socioeconomic group. In actuality this will be done for all entries in the factors-of-production row. We leave to future researchers the specification and disaggregation of the remaining elements of the scheme, which should prove very valuable. As Miernyk et al. (1967) and others have shown, the disaggregation of personal consumption by demographic or income category can improve the accuracy of estimates of the impacts of increases in consumer spending. When the disaggregated consumption vectors are combined with our disaggregated payments sector, the two components yield a comprehensive general equilibrium model of income formation and distribution as put forth in theory by Miyazawa (1976).[1]

Very few social accounting matrices have been constructed, and with a few noteworthy exceptions (see, e.g., Smith 1980; Juster and Land 1981) most work has been done outside the United States (see, e.g., Pyatt and Roe 1979; Bell et al. 1982; Bulmer-Thomas 1982). In addition there have been some successful attempts at extending the concept even further to include demographic-economic linkages, most notably by Batey and Madden (1983). The major effort at developing a social accounting model for the United States and its subregions has just been started (see, e.g., Despotakis 1985). This model is an outgrowth of the "Impact Analysis System for Planning," or IMPLAN, which represents a major socioeconomic data base and the means for constructing input-output models for regions as small as individual counties (see Alward et al. 1985). The data and model presented in this book will be incorporated into this ambitious effort as well.

Admittedly, our model is not a complete SAM, but it does have many of the SAM's capabilities. It is, however, the first multisector model ever to trace all of the individual types of income payments from producers to recipients, disaggregated according to income level. It also represents the most extensive use to date of primary data for the compilation of a multisector personal income distribution matrix.

Methods of Accounting

The major impetus to economic accounting in the "modern era" started in the midst of the Great Depression. In the United States, Simon Kuznets, in cooperation with the Department of Commerce, began compiling annual estimates of national income. A few years later, James Meade and Richard Stone, with guidance from John Maynard Keynes, compiled national income estimates for Great Britain (Kendrick 1972). During that period, Wassily Leontief published his first input-output tables for the United States. After World War II,

		Production accounts		Institutions accounts	
		Production activities 1	Factors of production 2	Current 3	Capital 4
1	Production activities	Interindustry transactions	0	Consumption expenditure	Investment expenditure
2	Factors of production	Value added	0	0	0
3	Current	0	Factor payments	Current transfers	0
4	Capital	0	0	Savings	Capital transfers

Source: Pyatt and Roe (1977). Copyrighted by and reprinted with permission of Cambridge University Press.

Figure 4.1. An Aggregated Social Accounting Matrix Embracing Input-Output Transactions

Kuznets spearheaded efforts at establishing economic accounts throughout the world. Various types of regional accounts received their major impetus in the 1950s, led by Werner Hochwald, Frederick Moore, and others (see Polenske 1980).

A methodological core was established by these various pioneers and their followers (see Jaszi 1955 and 1986). This included establishment of important economic categories, the definition and classification of economic units, and informal criteria of evaluation. Economic accounting can be characterized as "deterministic," or based on a tabulation of the universe of data, with no inherent stochastic properties assumed. This theme is extended to samples of data, which are typically "scaled-up" to known universe levels (control totals) or unknown universe levels (estimates). This is in contrast to the inferential statistic, or econometric, approach that has come to dominate quantitative economic analyses in recent years.

The rationale for the deterministic approach is that there is nothing as reliable as primary data, even acknowledging measurement error or reconciliation problems (where separate origin and destination accounts are kept). A major impetus for this approach is the extensive collection of data by governments at all levels expressly for adaptation to economic accounts, (see Ruggles and Ruggles 1970; Kendrick 1972).

The econometric approach to empirical model building has gone through a more rapid period of methodological advance than has economic accounting. The econometric approach also appears to offer a definite step-by-step procedure for implementation and objective criteria for measuring the reliability of the results. These features should not be taken to imply that this approach is superior to economic accounting. Also, the two approaches need not always be viewed as competitors, but rather as complementing each other in empirical model building.

The lack of a set method for many of its applications may, in fact, render economic accounting as challenging to implement as econometric methods. In addition, economic accounting often represents the pioneering step, as in defining and operationalizing a new concept. For example, we now take gross national product (GNP) as an obviously worthwhile economic indicator, but the reader would have great difficulty finding a reference to it before the 1930s and should realize that it took several years to develop an operational definition and to compile the first reliable estimates. Finally, we note that economic accounting methods are the most prevalent approach to tabulating the data upon which most time-series analyses are based.

The major common features of economic accounting methodologies can be summarized as:

1. Use of economic principles to define and delineate basic concepts,
2. Emphasis on primary data,
3. A bottom-up aggregation of composites,
4. Use of control totals as checks of accuracy or as the basis for making adjustments,
5. A double-entry balancing where possible,
6. Use of analogue, historical, biproportional matrix, or statistical methods to compensate for data omissions or problems.

This summarizes the methodology we apply to the estimation of a multisector income distribution model in the chapters ahead. It is part of a general approach that has proven successful in many areas of quantitative economics thus far, such as the estimation of GNP and national income. Also, it is being used to advance the frontier of model construction in areas such as gross state product (GSP) accounting (see, e.g., Weber 1979) in addition to our efforts in the areas of national and regional income distribution.

A Classification Scheme for Income Flows and Receipts

Recall from chapter 2 that our ultimate aim is to construct a multisector distributional matrix defined as:

$$V = v_{kj} = \frac{y_{kj}}{X_j}$$

where v_{kj} is the coefficient representing the cents worth of income received by income class k per dollar of output of good j, y_{kj} represents its "flow" counterpart, and X_j represents the total gross output of sector j. A schematic depiction of this matrix is presented in figure 4.2. To our knowledge no such matrix has ever been compiled for the U.S. economy, least of all one using primary data for each income type. Given the realities of data availability, our strategy will be to construct this matrix from the "ground up"—that is, by aggregating submatrices for each component of national income.

We begin by examining the income payments by producers, as exemplified by the manufacturing sectors of the U.S. economy in table 4.1. The table provides an itemization of all capital-related payments except rental income. These "other value-added" components (including those taxed away) together comprise 12.3 percent of total net revenue (gross output). Only about two-fifths of this is paid to households, since major portions are taxed away, reinvested, or set aside for amortization. Overall, however, the ratio of nonwage to wage income is small in manufacturing and for the economy as a whole.

Even more illuminating is an inspection of the $1,915.9 billion of *income payments*

	Sector, i			
Income Class, k	Livestock . . . Coal Mining . . . Lumber Products . . . Transportation			
<$5,000				
$5,000–9,999				
$10,000–14,999				
$15,000–19,999		$\{v_{ki}\}$		
$20,000–24,999				
$25,000–34,999				
$35,000–49,999				
$50,000–74,999				
$75,000–79,999				
$100,000>				

Figure 4.2. Schematic Depiction of the Multisectoral Income Distribution Matrix

Table 4.1. Income Statement for Manufacturing, 1982
(corporations with assets of $25 million or more)

Conventional Account Category	Amount		Input-Output Account Category	Amount	
	Level[a]	% of Gross Income		Level[a]	% of Other Value-added
Net Revenue	1,672.0		Gross Output	1,672.0	
Net operating revenue	1,619.1				
Misc. operating income	18.5				
Net Nonoperating revenue	33.4				
Net Expenses	1,514.1		Intermediate Input,	1,467.5	
Operating expenses	1,467.3		Wages/Salaries and Rental		
Misc. net expenses	.2		Payments		
Nonoperating expenses[b]	46.6				
Gross Income	158.7	1.000	Other value-added[c]	205.3	1.000
Taxes	30.2	.190	Taxes	30.2	.147
Depreciation and depletion	64.4	.406	Depreciation and		
Retained earnings	24.9	.157	depletion	64.4	.314
Dividends	39.2	.247	Retained profits	24.9	.121
			Distributed profits	39.2	.191
			Interest	46.6	.227

Source: Federal Trade Commission 1983.

[a]In billions of dollars.
[b]Primarily interest payments.
[c]Other value-added plus wages/salaries and rental payments equals total value-added.

Table 4.2. Types of Adjusted Gross Income, 1982

Income Type	Billions of Dollars	% of AGI	Multisector Data Availability
Wage and salary	1,565.0	81.7	Refined occupation/ industry matrix
Pension and annuity	60.1	3.1	Unknown
Dividend[a]	54.0	2.8	Refined NYSE data
Interest	157.0	8.2	Unknown
Business and professional income	50.6	2.6	Unknown
Partnership income	−0.9	b	Unknown
Small corporation income	−0.8	b	Unknown
Sale of property	0.6	b	Unknown
Farm income	−9.8	−0.5	IRS data
Farm rental income	2.2	0.1	IRS data
Royalty income	6.3	0.3	IRS data
Sale of capital assets	34.4	1.8	IRS data
Rental income	−8.5	−0.4	IRS data
Estate income	5.7	0.3	IRS data
Total reported gross income	1,915.9	100.0	

Source: IRS 1984a.

[a]Includes $1.7 billion dividend exclusion.
[b]Less than 0.05%.

received by households in 1982 in table 4.2. The table lists fourteen "types" of personal income, though it is evident that most of them are a small percentage of total adjusted gross income (eight of the categories each comprise less than 1 percent of AGI).[2] Clearly wage and salary income dominates. Interest income is the next major contributor to personal income, after wages and salaries, accounting for 8 percent of AGI. Dividend income is only 2.8 percent of the total. Note also the income losses associated with partnership, farm, small business, and rental income for households in the United States. Farm losses in 1982 amounted to almost $10 billion, and rental income losses totaled $9 billion.

Of course, the average proportion of each income type in total AGI conceals the very aspect we are interested in—variations across income classes. The distributional data presented in table 4.3 reveal these important distinctions. For households in the $0–$14,999 income class, wage and salary income is a rather significant percentage of total AGI. In contrast, for high income households, $100,000 and over, wage and salary income accounts for slightly over 50 percent of total AGI. The proportions, though certainly not the magnitudes, are reversed in the case of dividend income. While accounting for only 3 percent of the total AGI for all households collectively, 12 percent of AGI for high-income households is attributable to dividend income.

As indicated in the final column in table 4.2, we have obtained primary data for wage/salary and dividend income types. Another six income components, comprising 15.5 percent of total AGI, can be modeled readily by combining generalizations of these results and IRS data, as also indicated in table 4.2. The process is facilitated by the fact that several categories of income do not emanate from the intermediate sectors of the economy, but rather from household financial activities. For example, income from rent, the sale of capital assets, or estates emanates primarily from transactions between individuals and does

Table 4.3. Comparison of Wage/Salary and Dividend Income by Income Class, 1982

Income Class	Wages & Salaries per Household (000 dollars)	Dividends per Household (000 dollars)	Wages & Salaries as a Percentage of Adjusted Gross Income	Dividends as a Percentage of Adjusted Gross Income
Under 14,999	7.1	1.4	90.1	2.0
15,000–19,999	16.6	1.7	84.5	1.6
20,000–24,999	21.6	1.6	87.3	1.3
25,000–34,999	29.0	1.8	89.7	1.5
35,000–49,999	37.5	2.3	89.4	1.9
50,000–99,999	56.7	5.2	78.1	4.8
100,000 and over	128.8	29.8	52.8	12.0

Source: IRS 1984a.

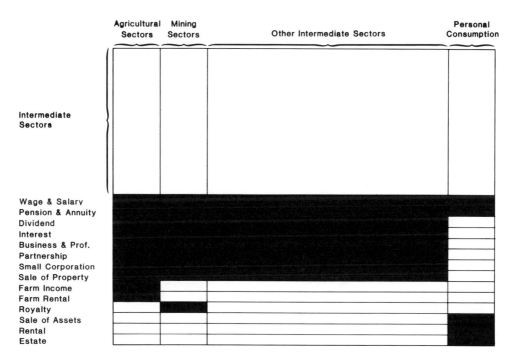

Figure 4.3. Personal Income Types by Sector of Origin

not involve any multisectoral data needs. The reader is referred to the schematic depiction of income category flows in figure 4.3.

Construction of the Model

A flow chart of the steps involved in the construction of our income distribution matrix is presented as figure 4.4. First, two sets of primary data,[3] one relating to wage income and the other to dividend income, are refined into multisector distributional matrices at the national level. These matrices are then combined with IRS data to complete the estimation of other

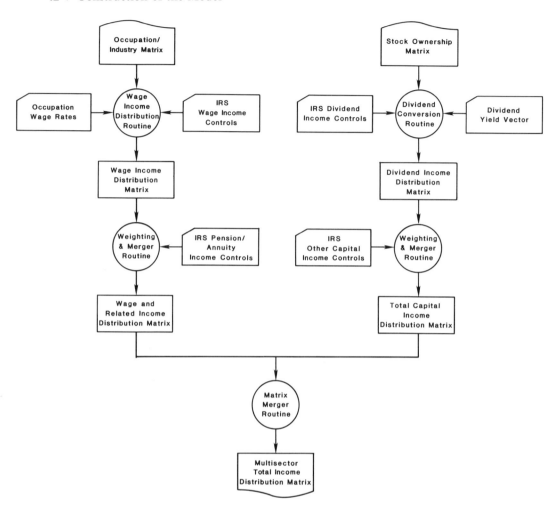

Figure 4.4. Income Distribution Matrix Development

income types. Finally, all of the various submatrices are merged to form a total income distribution matrix. A similar procedure is followed at the regional level, though more nonsurvey data are utilized in the latter.[4]

The wage and salary component will be estimated with the aid of an occupational category matrix, a useful tool that disaggregates employment totals according to occupation by sector. Chapter 5 shows how this matrix can be converted into the required income class counterpart by simply aggregating all those occupations that have the same mean annual salary and multiplying each cell of the aggregated matrix by the appropriate income. The occupational category matrix serves another useful purpose in resource-development policy since a version of it representing baseline conditions can be compared with one corresponding to a development target, with the difference indicating employment opportunities and manpower training requirements.

While multisectoral wage and salary income distributions have been estimated before (see, e.g., Golladay and Haveman 1977), the estimation of a multisectoral capital-related income distribution matrix is a pioneering contribution of this study. Chapter 6 presents a detailed account of how New York Stock Exchange survey data were refined to yield a dividend distribution matrix. Several other types of capital income, such as interest and business and professional income, were patterned after the dividend results. The distribution of other types of property income unique to a given sector (i.e., farm income, royalty income) or associated with household financial activities were readily obtained from the Internal Revenue Service (1984a). These estimates are presented in chapter 7.

Note that the analyses of the following chapters represent the before-tax/transfer distribution of impacts. In addition to normal local government fiscal impacts associated with resource development, large sums of money may flow to the federal government when mining and timbering are encouraged. In the case of National Forests, federal law calls for a portion of this money to be returned to the host area and it is likely that the distribution of the benefits of this "reinvestment" will not be uniform across income groups. While no empirical analysis of this aspect of natural resource policy is undertaken here, our general conceptual framework can readily serve as a basis for future examination of the distribution of federal spending in these areas.

Conclusion

Given the realities of data availability, our income distribution matrix is compiled from data on individual factor payments. Each of these "submatrices" is useful in analyzing the structure of income and represents an important direct link between functional and personal distribution. Furthermore, the submatrices can aid policy-makers in pursuing goals related to income distribution and other areas, such as manpower training and investment incentives.

Our model can be incorporated into sophisticated versions of the I-O framework that overcome inherent limitations such as fixed, scale-determined input requirements, absence of joint products, and exclusion of production externalities. These restrictive assumptions of I-O pertain only to the simple static form of the model, and great strides have been made in recent years in giving I-O greater flexibility (see, e.g., Hudson and Jorgenson 1974; Leontief 1986). Several of these modifications are applicable to a multisectoral income distribution matrix as well. In any case, the "fixity" of income distribution coefficients, and conventional input requirements coefficients for that matter, is basically an empirical question. Several studies, as well as our findings in the following chapters, indicate a relatively stable distribution of several types of income. Where variability is an important feature, our results can serve as an important input in building an even more flexible model.

5 / The Wage and Salary Income Distribution Matrix

This chapter explains the method used to construct a multisector model of wage and salary income distribution, and presents the results for the U.S. economy. This income type is the most prominent of all, constituting over 80 percent of total national personal income in 1982. This average, however, should not obscure the fact that the proportion of wages and salaries varies significantly across income classes.

Though no direct data on the multisectoral distribution of wages and salaries exist, a model can be constructed by refining an existing survey-based data set, rather than collecting primary data anew. The data set is a matrix of occupational requirements by sector, or "occupation/industry" matrix, that is well established in the literature both in terms of its conceptual soundness and accuracy (see, e.g., Miernyk et al. 1970; Freeman 1980). The use of data from this matrix has proven successful in earlier work on income distribution by Golladay and Haveman (1977). Our method of model construction, however, differs significantly from theirs.

In the following section we establish the conceptual basis for our use of an occupation/industry matrix. Subsequent sections discuss the basis for choosing among several data sources, describe supplementary data needed, present the basic wage and salary income matrix for individuals in occupational groupings, and present and analyze the wage and salary matrix for households.

Conceptual Framework

We seek to construct a matrix that represents the amount of wage and salary income flowing to each income class from each sector. Schematically, the matrix would appear as:

Income Class	Sector		
	agriculture . . . mining . . . manufacturing . . .		
< $5,000			
5,000–9,999			
.			
.			
.			
100,000+			

44

Although no such data exist in ready form, the similarity between the desired matrix and an occupation/industry matrix of the form below is apparent:

	Sector		
Occupation	agriculture . . . mining . . . manufacturing . . .		
Farmer			
Technician			
.			
.			
.			
Manager			

All that is necessary to make the transformation is to substitute the average annual earnings per worker for the occupational labels at the left of the second of the two schematic diagrams above, and rearrange the resulting income rows in ascending order. If wages and salaries for any given occupational group are normally distributed around their mean, the result will be perfectly accurate. In actuality, wage and salary distributions are often modestly skewed above the mean, and there will be some, though not necessarily a significant, inaccuracy.[1] The options are to live with the small error or to incorporate the distribution of earnings into the analysis. The second alternative is just a generalization of the original occupation/industry matrix and our original transformation step. It involves further subdividing occupations by earnings categories as an intermediate step. Its disadvantages are that it yields a three-dimensional matrix and makes coefficient changes more difficult to implement.

In either case the result is a tabulation of "flows" of wage and salary income for a given year. To transform the matrix into a useful model, we need to hypothesize a functional relationship between wage and salary income and some explanatory variables. Referring back to the base data matrix, we invoke the standard I-O assumption that there is a fixed proportional requirement of labor by occupation per unit of output produced in each sector. That is, if two engineers are required to produce one ton of steel, then four engineers are required to produce two tons of steel. No other occupational skill can be substituted for engineers, or any other occupations for that matter. Freeman (1980) has conducted a thorough empirical test and found the U.S. occupation/industry coefficients to be rather stable over the short run.

In addition to fixed skill requirements, one other assumption is inherent in our initial analysis—wage and salary rates are fixed in the short run. The dollar flows of our matrix are, of course, the disaggregated "wage bill," or the wage rate times person-years in each occupation and industry.

While the basic matrices are constructed in conformance with these restrictive assumptions, as noted in chapter 2, I-O analysis is more flexible than typically assumed. Following the methodologies developed in recent years (see, e.g., Hudson and Jorgenson 1974; Rose et al. 1982), substitution of nonlabor for labor inputs and changes in wage rates can be incorporated into the analysis.

Data

Since several sets of reliable data pertinent to our study are available, the first step is to evaluate them for compatibility with our needs. Three criteria are employed to assess data compatibility: (1) data aggregation and disaggregation levels among occupation and industry categories, (2) temporal dimensions of data collection and dissemination, and (3) overall consistency in data reporting units.

Three governmental entities, under the auspices of two different departments, are delegated responsibility to collect, analyze, and publish statistics on labor employment in the United States. Two of the entities, the Bureau of the Census (BOC) and the Bureau of Economic Analysis (BEA), are under the purview of the U.S. Department of Commerce. The Bureau of Labor Statistics (BLS) has as its parent agency the Department of Labor. The availability of occupation- and industry-specific data from each merits some brief discussion.

A U.S. occupation/industry matrix is available through the Bureau of the Census on computer tape. In its most disaggregated form, the matrix contains 503 occupations and 231 industries; also, it is aggregated to the 134 × 51 level. Occupation/industry matrices for states, on the other hand, are unavailable on computer tape, but exist in hard copy format (U.S. Bureau of the Census 1983).

A Bureau of the Census data source, *Summary Tape File 4* (*STF 4*), provides occupation and industry control totals for state and county levels for 70 occupational and 49 industrial classifications (U.S. Bureau of the Census 1984). Data are reported for the number of people sixteen years of age and older employed in select occupations and sectors of employment. *STF 4* also facilitates the further adaptation of either U.S. or state occupation/industry matrices through the availability of control totals on persons employed by occupation and sector at the county level.

Another source for industry classifications is the U.S. Bureau of Economic Analysis (BEA), which generates input-output tables for the U.S. economy (see, e.g., U.S. BEA 1984). One noteworthy contrast between data published by the Bureau of Economic Analysis and the Bureau of the Census is the level of industry aggregation. Data presented by the Bureau of the Census are more highly disaggregated by major industry group than the data contained in the I-O tables from the Bureau of Economic Analysis.

Another source for employment and industry-related data is the *Current Population Survey* (CPS), a monthly survey of labor force statistics (U.S. Department of Labor 1982). Statistics published in the CPS include estimates of total employment and unemployment, age, sex, race, education level, and marital status of labor force participants. Also included are data for the distribution of workers by hours worked, occupation, and industry of employment.

Weekly earnings of wage and salary workers are published quarterly in the BLS publication, *Employment and Earnings*. One limitation of the data contained in this publication is the exclusion of the farm sector of the economy, the self-employed, proprietors, and domestic workers in private homes. Industry data are typically provided for major labor areas, usually restricted to Metropolitan Statistical Areas (MSA).

An occupation/industry matrix is available through the U.S. Bureau of Labor Statistics for 1982 (U.S. BLS, 1982b). The matrix provides data on 700 occupations and 378 industries. In general, only occupations with 5,000 workers or more are included.

Reconciliation of these various data bases is not easily accomplished. The most difficult problem in reconciling the data is the aggregation of industry and occupation categories in accordance with the Bureau of the Census control totals available from *STF 4* (Bureau of the Census 1984).

Unfortunately, no single data source fulfills all data needs. The advantages of data available through the Bureau of Labor Statistics appear to be twofold. The frequency of data updates is superior to that for data generated by the Bureau of the Census. Census data are available on a decennial basis, while the occupation/industry matrix of the Bureau of Labor Statistics is updated every two years. Second, the business survey method should, in practice yield more reliable results than the household-based survey method of the Bureau of the Census. However, BLS data have some serious disadvantages as well. The industry occupation matrix of the BLS generally includes only occupations with 5,000 or more workers, a possible drawback if one attempts to capture small occupation categories.[2] Also, although BLS data are highly detailed in matrix form, as represented by the (700 × 378) dimensions of the matrix, aggregating the occupational categories to conform to the Census control totals may prove cumbersome. Reconciling the industry classifications, however, appears to be less problematic.[3]

Bureau of the Census matrices for the United States and individual states most readily conform to the Census control totals as provided in *STF 4*. The occupation/industry matrix is available for all states in a 134 × 44 format, as aggregated from 503 occupations and 231 industries. Its conformity must be judged superior to that of the Bureau of Economic Analysis, which aggregates 85 industries to 10 industrial categories. Moreover, Census data are classified according to place of residence, not place of employment. Consistency is further assured in using Census data bases in that the methodologies for data collection, analysis, and reporting are similar to those used for the control totals used to adapt the matrix to individual regions.

Overall, U.S. Bureau of the Census data were deemed best for occupation/industry matrix development for the reasons cited above. Census data are not available for as many years as those provided by the Bureau of Labor Statistics. However, conformity to the control totals in terms of industry and occupation aggregation is a more important consideration.

Average wage and salary levels for approximately 58 occupations are available from a Bureau of the Census publication, *Money Income of Households, Families, and Persons in the United States: 1982* (1984a). Average wage rates are presented by occupation for male and female workers twenty-five years of age and older, and conform to the occupation categories of other Census publications.

The Basic Wage and Salary Income Distribution Matrix

Construction of the Matrix

The steps employed to create the U.S. wage and salary income distribution matrix are as follows:

1. The U.S. Bureau of the Census computerized occupation/industry matrix is accessed. The matrix covers employment in 1980 for persons sixteen years of age and older by occupation and sector of employment at the 503 occupation and 231 industry levels.

2. The dimensions of the occupation/industry matrix are reduced through automatic aggregation of the BOC classification codes to a matrix of dimensions 134 × 52.

3. The matrix is further aggregated to a 59 × 41 version to conform to the regional

control totals for occupation and industry employment available on *STF 4* (U.S. Bureau of the Census 1984).

4. The wage and salary income distribution matrix for individuals is generated by multiplying cell entries of the above matrix by average wage and salary levels (U.S. Bureau of the Census 1984) for each occupation. The resulting cell entries of the new matrix depict total wage and salary earnings by occupation, as designated by the row headings, resulting from employment in a given sector, designated by the column headings. Cell entries are the wage and salary payments to each occupation from each industry. Column sums of the matrix represent the total wage and salary payments to all individuals employed by each respective sector. Row sums depict the total wage and salary income received by given occupations across all sectors of employment.

Discussion of the Results

Limitations of space do not enable us to show the U.S. occupation/industry matrix, but we can briefly summarize it. The matrix reveals that the sectors of greatest employment are the educational service, construction, and public administration sectors, comprising nearly 20 percent of the nation's employment. Among the sectors with the lowest employment are textiles, railroads, and the paper and allied products industries. In terms of occupation, officials and administrators, administrative support personnel, and machine operators and tenders are most prevalent nationally. These occupations include nearly 20 percent of the nation's total labor force. Officials and administrators, comprised of managers of various specialties, are well represented across all sectors. Other occupations, such as machine operators and tenders, are most concentrated among the manufacturing sectors.[4]

Table 5.1 is the wage and salary income distribution matrix for individuals as generated by the aforementioned procedure. Wage payments by the public administration sector comprise almost 20 percent of the nation's entire wage bill going to individuals. The textile mill products, apparel, railroads, repair, and personal service sectors have the lowest wage bills. In terms of occupations, officials and administrators dominate the total wages received by individuals, with 12 percent of the wages paid to individuals accruing to them. Conversely, among the least represented occupations in terms of the total individual wage bill are surveyors and mapping scientists and the sales-related occupations (outside of finance, business, and retail trade).

The Wage and Salary Income Distribution Matrix for Households

Construction of the Matrix

Thus far, the distribution of wage and salary income has been computed on an individual basis. However, we consider household units to be a superior basis for our Social Accounting Matrix. To transform our preliminary results to a wage and salary income distribution matrix for household units, we used the following procedure:

1. The U.S. Bureau of the Census (1984a) compiles an occupation/income class matrix on the basis of the person in longest employ in a household unit. Data are reported on the number of households within forty-five occupations and twenty-one income classes. This matrix reflects differences in income within an occupation, accounts for multiple-wage-earner families, and includes nonwage income.

Table 5.1. U.S. Wage/Salary Income Distribution Matrix for Individuals (millions of 1982 dollars)

	AGRICULTURE, FORESTRY, FISHERIES	MINING	CONSTRUCTION	FOOD & KINDRED PRODUCTS	TEXTILE MILL PRODUCTS	APPAREL	PRINTING & PUBLISHING	
01 PUBLIC ADMINISTRATORS AND OFFICIALS	0.1	0.3	0.0	0.6	0.0	1.0	0.1	1
02 OTHER ADMINISTRATORS AND OFFICIALS	884.5	2554.8	233.0	3863.4	788.0	1015.3	3964.5	2
03 MANAGEMENT RELATED	152.5	1016.5	1323.0	843.1	155.1	148.1	408.6	3
04 ARCHITECTS	400.3		7412.6					4
05 ENGINEERS	94.8	1778.1	2126.7	474.0	166.1	73.7	124.8	5
06 SURVEYORS AND MAPPING SCIENTISTS	15.1	82.1	82.9				0.7	6
07 OTHER SCIENTISTS AND MATHEMATICIANS	453.1	1358.2	143.5	302.6	45.0	15.2	89.4	7
08 DOCTORS AND OTHER DIAGNOSTICIANS	1112.6			15.8				8
09 OTHER HEALTH, INCLUDING NURSES	10.9	5.2	7.0	29.3	11.2	10.8	3.9	9
10 ELEMENTARY AND SECONDARY TEACHERS	0.9			7.5	15.2	1.6	7.0	10
11 OTHER EDUCATION RELATED	5.2	13.0	7.9			15.1	30.8	11
12 SOCIAL SCIENTISTS AND URBAN PLANNERS	2.7	20.0	19.8	37.0	4.0	3.1	3.4	12
13 SOCIAL, RECREATION AND RELIGIOUS	5.7	9.9	9.8	5.0			2.6	13
14 LAWYERS AND JUDGES	136.7	122.2	216.1	33.9	3.8	3.1	23.8	14
15 ARTISTS, ENTERTAINERS, AND ATHLETES	52.7	50.2		61.7	44.3	115.7	2789.8	15
16 HEALTH TECHNOLOGISTS AND TECHNICIANS							0.5	16
17 LICENSED PRACTICAL NURSES								17
18 OTHER TECHNOLOGISTS AND TECHNICIANS	266.7	1035.3	1767.5	605.1	204.1	500.2	386.2	18
19 SUPERVISORS AND SALES, SELF-EMPLOYED	91.5	20.7	94.0	143.3	15.7		125.3	19
20 SUPERVISORS AND SALES, SALARIED	175.1	20.0	840.0	1713.0		50.2	1955.8	20
21 SALES, FINANCE, AND BUSINESS SERVICES		331.4	440.7	1526.6	237.6	40.3	993.7	21
22 SALES REPRESENTATIVES, NON-RETAIL								22
23 OTHER SALES, RETAIL AND PERSONAL				24.8	0.2	458.1		23
24 CASHIERS	3.1	3.1	6.1				1.0	24
25 SALES RELATED						2.7		25
26 SUPERVISORS AND ADMIN SUPPORT	43.4	219.0	281.9	308.0	84.3	108.3	323.6	26
27 COMPUTER EQUIPMENT OPERATORS	212.2	29.6	2.7	100.3	29.0		127.4	27
28 SECRETARIAL RELATED	218.2	666.5	1425.1	532.8	14.6	120.9	744.3	28
29 ACCOUNTANTS AND AUDITORS	13.7	237.1	821.5	96.3	152.5	95.1	318.6	29
30 OTHER FINANCIAL RECORDS PROCESSING		55.1	135.8		38.5	51.8	84.8	30
31 MAIL AND MESSAGE DISTRIBUTING	45.2		273.6	688.7			353.4	31
32 SHIPPING, RECEIVING, AND OTHER CLERKS	183.3	2127.5	606.0	519.7	250.4	303.6	399.4	32
33 OTHER ADMINISTRATIVE SUPPORT		390.4		118.0	197.0	205.6	1124.2	33
34 PRIVATE HOUSEHOLD	31.5				49.0			34
35 GUARDS	18.1	370.0	97.5	95.1	4.3	23.5	41.3	35
36 OTHER PROTECTIVE SERVICES		10.2	10.7					36
37 FOOD PREPARATION AND SERVICE	76.9	11.3	1.2	447.1	2.0	1.8	6.1	37
38 NURSING AND OTHER HEALTH ASSISTANTS	16.9							38
39 CLEANING AND BUILDING SERVICES	35.1	127.0	217.1	13.3	108.2	65.2	108.8	39
40 PERSONAL SERVICES	272.4					3.6		40
41 FARMING, FORESTRY, AND FISHING	11215.9	6.7	1.8	1495.2	2.4		1.3	41
42 AUTO MECHANICS AND REPAIRERS	38.6	2888.0	49.2	268.3	90.6	208.0	210.5	42
43 OTHER MECHANICS AND REPAIRERS	13.0	2147.0	2102.1		107.0	1.1	233.6	43
44 CARPENTERS	82.1	852.3	2888.0	2791.6			110.8	44
45 OTHER CONSTRUCTION TRADES	28.0	3956.7	9715.3	2976.8	991.5	27.6	69.6	45
46 EXTRACTIVE OCCUPATIONS	153.0	676.6	1278.0	144.4	154.8			46
47 SUPERVISORS AND PRODUCTION	16.7	516.2	1162.6	3667.0	3914.7	944.8	1585.3	47
48 PRECISION PRODUCTION	354.8	1206.7	2134.0	2601.4	430.3	644.8	626.7	48
49 PLANT AND SYSTEM OPERATORS	131.3	2383.2	2134.3	2224.0	222.3		22.0	49
50 MACHINE OPERATORS	15.1	253.2	4321.2	963.8	215.8	6657.9	4708.9	50
51 FABRICATORS AND ASSEMBLERS	39.2	333.2	728.4	92.3		161.8	161.8	51
52 PRODUCTION INSPECTORS AND RELATED	221.0	362.2	5009.4	2498.7	272.6	453.8	148.3	52
53 MOTOR VEHICLE OPERATORS						57.5	356.1	53
54 OTHER TRANSPORTATION OPERATORS								54
55 MATERIAL MOVING EQUIPMENT OPERATORS						148.8	169.2	55
56 CONSTRUCTION LABOR							55.7	56
57 FREIGHT AND MATERIAL HANDLERS								57
58 CRAFT AND PRODUCTION						59.0	62.3	58
59 OTHER HANDLERS AND MISCELLANEOUS			39.1			312.9	255.0	59
60 TOTAL	17756.0	31072.2	79138.6	30327.5	10111.2	12673.8	23130.7	60

49

Table 5.1. U.S. Wage/Salary Income Distribution Matrix for Individuals (millions of 1982 dollars) *(cont.)*

	CHEMICALS & ALLIED PRODUCTS	PAPER & ALLIED PRODUCTS	PETROLEUM & COAL	FURNITURE, LUMBER, & WOOD	PRIMARY METALS	FABRICATED METALS	MACHINERY EXCEPT ELECTRICAL	
01 PUBLIC ADMINISTRATORS AND OFFICIALS	3319.3	1521.1	247.2	1682.3	1620.7	3466.2	5987.2	1
02 OTHER ADMINISTRATORS AND OFFICIALS	992.6	40.2	697.3	294.2	530.0	775.4	155.4	2
03 MANAGEMENT RELATED		49.2		177.2				3
04 ARCHITECTS	208.4		1067.6		1048.6	1373.7	468.9	4
05 ENGINEERS	1600.0	17.3	33.2	83.1	203.0	144.1	1060.6	5
06 SURVEYORS AND MAPPING SCIENTISTS	83.2	14.5	16.2	3.6	32.7	20.8	38.1	6
07 OTHER SCIENTISTS AND MATHEMATICIANS	50.2	2.8	9.1	1.8	5.2	20.0	32.3	7
08 DOCTORS AND OTHER DIAGNOSTICIANS	21.0	16.0	2.7	2.5	12.2	20.5	5.2	8
09 OTHER HEALTH INCLUDING NURSES	79.9	10.8	25.7	6.2	20.3	21.0	105.2	9
10 ELEMENTARY AND SECONDARY TEACHERS								10
11 OTHER EDUCATION RELATED	108.1	15.0	51.6	5.2	20.3	21.0	62.3	11
12 SOCIAL SCIENTISTS AND URBAN PLANNERS	132.4	7.5	59.7	5.0	38.1	82.7	36.7	12
13 SOCIAL RECREATION AND RELIGIOUS	133.5		95.7	15.2				13
14 LAWYERS AND JUDGES			45.2			21.0		14
15 ARTISTS, ENTERTAINERS, AND ATHLETES	2101.3	435.7	748.7	155.2	646.8	909.8	2814.8	15
16 HEALTH TECHNOLOGISTS AND TECHNICIANS	90.8	29.1	59.7	9.7	28.0	54.8	180.0	16
17 LICENSED PRACTICAL NURSES	110.3		4.1					17
18 OTHER TECHNOLOGISTS AND TECHNICIANS	1810.3	689.2	728.3	473.1	492.4	916.8	1709.5	18
19 SUPERVISORS AND SALES, SELF-EMPLOYED								19
20 SUPERVISORS AND SALES, SALARIED	4.7	4.7	0.8	1.0	6.1	15.0	4.5	20
21 SALES, FINANCE, AND BUSINESS SERVICES		0.1	0.8	0.7	1.3	2.5	5.2	21
22 SALES REPRESENTATIVES, NON-RETAIL	321.4	176.0	265.1	114.0	235.3	303.2	518.3	22
23 OTHER SALES, RETAIL AND PERSONAL	118.7	24.5	87.0	22.9	364.9	584.7	25.4	23
24 CASHIERS	867.8	286.3	446.4	229.7	346.0	583.1	1167.7	24
25 SALES RELATED	213.4	102.6	80.6	36.9	114.6	246.5	37.7	25
26 SUPERVISORS AND ADMIN SUPPORT	51.0	58.5	53.0	285.2	93.8	104.2	1429.9	26
27 COMPUTER EQUIPMENT OPERATORS	611.0	378.1	530.8	285.2	602.3	727.3	1468.0	27
28 SECRETARIAL RELATED	58.3	27.5	432.3	180.6	358.5	456.2	94.1	28
29 ACCOUNTANTS AND AUDITORS	13.5		9.6	83.4	145.7	105.1	13.3	29
30 OTHER FINANCIAL RECORDS PROCESSING	122.1	57.2	11.8	111.0	119.5	118.8	14.9	30
31 MAIL AND MESSAGE DISTRIBUTING	11.6		1.2	1.0	5.6	1.6	13.8	31
32 SHIPPING, RECEIVING, AND OTHER CLERKS	25.2	126.6	195.4	109.4	217.1	201.1	28.5	32
33 OTHER ADMINISTRATIVE SUPPORT	6.8	1.6	3.3	3.3	21.3	1.3		33
34 PRIVATE HOUSEHOLD	13.8	1.3	3.3	479.2	38.0	39.5	105.5	34
35 GUARDS	300.2	181.3	1145.5	558.0	1878.8	1233.9	266.8	35
36 OTHER PROTECTIVE SERVICES	135.1	109.5	438.5	323.4	858.7	480.0	40.0	36
37 FOOD PREPARATION AND SERVICE	515.5	26.4	418.2	230.4	943.3	736.4	64.5	37
38 NURSING AND OTHER HEALTH ASSISTANTS	643.9	35.2	228.8	1462.6	2625.7	2902.4	157.6	38
39 CLEANING AND BUILDING SERVICES	270.4	146.2	916.9	1408.1	1212.0	2461.5	3805.8	39
40 PERSONAL SERVICES	350.1	295.4	425.5		148.3	84.0	6330.4	40
41 FARMING, FORESTRY, AND FISHING	36.5	161.9	545.1	3012.7	4476.1	5002.8	514.3	41
42 AUTO MECHANICS AND REPAIRERS	3467.6	369.0	978.2	1328.7	1174.0	3045.0	5805.0	42
43 OTHER MECHANICS AND REPAIRERS	655.4	348.9	680.3	1337.2	552.2	695.8	4475.1	43
44 CARPENTERS	309.7	265.0	306.2	582.2	337.5	369.7	1195.1	44
45 OTHER CONSTRUCTION TRADES	38.0	345.4	99.4		146.2		34.1	45
46 EXTRACTIVE OCCUPATIONS	53.5	67.5	515.6	683.9	1527.7	746.6	10.0	46
47 SUPERVISORS AND PRODUCTION	34.2	73.8	49.6	35.6	167.2	80.5	78.1	47
48 PRECISION PRODUCTION	11.7		19.2		207.2		73.1	48
49 PLANT AND SYSTEM OPERATORS	123.6	135.4	134.5	272.0	203.4	120.2	19.0	49
50 MACHINE OPERATORS	60.1	60.4	765.5	514.2	885.4	654.0	925.5	50
60 TOTAL	28066.7	15039.0	23080.6	15538.1	23374.3	29018.7	51510.0	60

50

Table 5.1. U.S. Wage/Salary Income Distribution Matrix for Individuals (millions of 1982 dollars) *(contd.)*

#		ELECT MACH EQUIP	MOTOR VEH EQUIP	OTHER TRANSPORT EQUIP	MISC MANUFACTURING	RAIL ROADS	TRUCKING & WAREHOUSING	OTHER TRANSPORT SERVICE
01	PUBLIC ADMINISTRATORS AND OFFICIALS	4491.6	119.2	223.1	4433.0	114.2	2934.5	225.0
02	OTHER ADMINISTRATORS AND OFFICIALS	1325.5	573.9	954.5	866.8	250.9	307.2	2917.2
03	MANAGEMENT RELATED	5637.6	1461.7	5568.9	1922.6	218.0	68.8	525.6
04	ARCHITECTS		0.5					9.1
05	ENGINEERS	5637.6	1519.2	625.5	411.0	58.9	25.1	455.8
06	SURVEYORS AND MAPPING SCIENTISTS	567.2	21.9	12.1	26.1	0.7	1.8	106.1
07	OTHER SCIENTISTS AND MATHEMATICIANS	8.1	7.0	40.3	23.7	2.3	3.2	64.5
08	DOCTORS AND OTHER DIAGNOSTICIANS	35.9	13.3		54.3	1.9	3.5	48.8
09	OTHER HEALTH, INCLUDING NURSES	14.1	10.5	34.6	54.3	0.6	0.5	17.4
10	ELEMENTARY AND SECONDARY TEACHERS	85.8	102.2		41.8	32.6	13.2	38.6
11	OTHER EDUCATION RELATED	31.6	2.8	236.2	350.0	30.5	1.0	13.6
12	SOCIAL SCIENTISTS AND URBAN PLANNERS	60.2	45.7		38.5			89.8
13	SOCIAL, RECREATION AND RELIGIOUS	35.1		1491.0	1358.5	100.0	57.5	1140.3
14	LAWYERS AND JUDGES	7.5	4.7		119.2	0.5	4.6	57.6
15	ARTISTS, ENTERTAINERS, AND ATHLETES	3012.7	30.2	30.2	119.2	88.5	516.0	74.6
16	HEALTH TECHNOLOGISTS AND TECHNICIANS	101.7		196.7	1705.0	0.3	1.2	1306.2
17	LICENSED PRACTICAL NURSES	103.8	25.7		15.3	1.1	26.9	19.4
18	OTHER TECHNOLOGISTS AND TECHNICIANS	1010.0	401.1	9.7	3.3	15.9	16.1	84.9
19	SUPERVISORS AND SALES, SELF-EMPLOYED	29.0	4.1					
20	SUPERVISORS AND SALES, SALARIED	5.2	2.8	230.3	355.0	116.0	218.3	863.2
21	SALES, FINANCE AND BUSINESS SERVICES	44.5	17.4	110.9	118.2	160.1	56.8	376.0
22	SALES REPRESENTATIVES, NON-RETAIL	185.3	60.2	543.4	772.0	125.9	283.3	196.0
23	OTHER SALES, RETAIL AND PERSONAL	253.7	257.5	74.7	309.2	149.5	212.0	79.0
24	CASHIERS	100.1	74.7	1054.0	1015.3	95.1	212.0	6118.0
25	SALES RELATED	118.0	41.0		855.0	82.1	855.0	673.3
26	SUPERVISORS AND ADMIN SUPPORT	876.2	413.8	828.3	698.6	527.0	555.0	10880.8
27	COMPUTER EQUIPMENT OPERATORS	143.1	279.6	502.2	98.5			137.0
28	SECRETARIAL RELATED	14.2	107.9	128.0	11.3	87.6	65.0	347.0
29	ACCOUNTANTS AND AUDITORS	10.2	18.5	7.3	9.0	10.5	3.0	21.0
30	OTHER FINANCIAL RECORDS PROCESSING	212.0	7.7	112.2	235.8	44.9	85.4	234.0
31	MAIL AND MESSAGE DISTRIBUTING	3.3	2.1	2.1	6.0	2.1	3.1	345.1
32	SHIPPING, RECEIVING, AND OTHER CLERKS	28.3	2.5	392.1	1442.0	1163.8	284.0	148.1
33	OTHER ADMINISTRATIVE SUPPORT	1864.9	468.1	1792.5	503.6	671.8	1214.2	1771.8
34	PRIVATE HOUSEHOLD	31.0	107.1	1141.7	2813.2	47.1	42.1	175.3
35	GUARDS	47.2	27.2	1307.0	2814.2	111.5	983.2	265.1
36	OTHER PROTECTIVE SERVICES	3087.7	1714.5	2065.9	1314.0	484.1	84.6	161.9
37	FOOD PREPARATION AND SERVICE	3221.7	1116.5	2514.1	1689.8	111.4	61.9	105.2
38	NURSING AND OTHER HEALTH ASSISTANTS	3826.0	2372.2	1689.8	4326.9	258.0	101.6	105.2
39	CLEANING AND BUILDING SERVICES	5426.0	3617.2	2076.4	3024.9	484.6	1018.7	339.7
40	PERSONAL SERVICES	1165.8	786.1	602.3	991.2	134.2	573.5	1018.0
41	FARMING, FORESTRY, AND FISHING	432.3	252.7	611.9	749.2	134.8	1255.9	1253.8
42	AUTO MECHANICS AND REPAIRERS	27.4	13.6	36.2	717.0	5009.1	459.8	13.7
43	OTHER MECHANICS AND REPAIRERS	164.8	51.7	51.7	124.7	21.3	16.4	394.4
44	CARPENTERS	1845.5	225.7	225.7	169.1	21.8	993.1	203.3
60	TOTAL	42109.4	19006.7	27281.8	33433.3	12185.7	24460.7	25379.7

51

Table 5.1. U.S. Wage/Salary Income Distribution Matrix for Individuals (millions of 1982 dollars) *(contd.)*

	COMMUNICATIONS	UTILITIES	WHOLESALE TRADE	GEN MERCH STORES	FOOD/DAIRY STORES	AUTO DEAL SERVICE STATIONS	EATING & DRINKING PLACES	
01 PUBLIC ADMINISTRATORS AND OFFICIALS	4785.4	1895.7	2111.2	4510.6	4239.1	5052.1	0.3	1
02 OTHER ADMINISTRATORS AND OFFICIALS	920.3	805.0	3954.9	1638.3	522.9	40.2	7148.5	2
03 MANAGEMENT RELATED	2540.1	1951.8	1099.6	31.8	2.0	3.1	18.2	3
04 ARCHITECTS		23.2	14.3	33.4	3.0	3.5		4
05 ENGINEERS	2540.7	383.7	664.9	68.8	26.1	2.0	8.0	5
06 SURVEYORS AND MAPPING SCIENTISTS							7.3	6
07 OTHER SCIENTISTS AND MATHEMATICIANS	395.1	7.1	311.1	8.8	26.3	2.3	0.9	7
08 DOCTORS AND OTHER DIAGNOSTICIANS	16.9	28.0	311.1	54.6	23.6	2.8	2.8	8
09 OTHER HEALTH, INCLUDING NURSES	12.6	9.3	21.6	15.6	26.6	8.7	4.0	9
10 ELEMENTARY AND SECONDARY TEACHERS	39.5	32.1		3.6	3.7	8.1		10
11 OTHER EDUCATION RELATED			155.5	8.2	3.9	1.0	2.0	11
12 SOCIAL SCIENTISTS AND URBAN PLANNERS	40.5		21.8	2.0	1.9	6.7	3.6	12
13 SOCIAL, RECREATION AND RELIGIOUS	105.9	170.2	81.2	26.6	57.3	2.3		13
14 LAWYERS AND JUDGES	276.4	116.0	447.6	406.2	5.0	23.7	66.5	14
15 ARTISTS, ENTERTAINERS, AND ATHLETES	2139.8	20.6	147.5	40.5	4.6	0.5	16.1	15
16 HEALTH TECHNOLOGISTS AND TECHNICIANS	22.3					1.3		16
17 LICENSED PRACTICAL NURSES			1321.0	145.5	163.0	1200.0	16.1	17
18 OTHER TECHNOLOGISTS AND TECHNICIANS	205.5	1022.2	1637.3	374.2	5386.0	1180.9	181.7	18
19 SUPERVISORS AND SALES, SELF-EMPLOYED			3446.2	466.8	160.7	3366.5	1.0	19
20 SUPERVISORS AND SALES, SALARIED	82.8	37.4	11.5		16.9	26.4	18.0	20
21 SALES, FINANCE, AND BUSINESS SERVICES	1454.2	244.9	29799.2	1140.3	1633.0	577.0	8.1	21
22 SALES REPRESENTATIVES, NON-RETAIL	547.8	11.5	1154.6	1181.0	441.9	317.5	223.2	22
23 OTHER SALES, RETAIL AND PERSONAL	39.5	9.5	156.3				661.3	23
24 CASHIERS	28.9	37.1						24
25 SALES RELATED			1498.2	619.7	385.2	141.5	4.6	25
26 SUPERVISORS AND ADMIN SUPPORT	257.2	372.6	589.7	100.6	46.0	14.1	85.2	26
27 COMPUTER EQUIPMENT OPERATORS	257.9	94.3	332.6	389.6	198.5	553.3	15.2	27
28 SECRETARIAL RELATED	964.0	569.5	2576.7	538.3	514.7	1000.1	7.6	28
29 OTHER FINANCIAL RECORDS PROCESSING	21.8	228.7	117.2	179.3	30.5	64.0	6.0	29
30 ACCOUNTANTS AND AUDITORS	166.5	117.2	203.9	1532.6	948.5	241.0	43.8	30
31 MAIL AND MESSAGE DISTRIBUTING	587.8	852.4	3104.0	1691.5	546.4	292.0	85.1	31
32 SHIPPING, RECEIVING, AND OTHER CLERKS	547.0	939.3	3221.3			590.0	0.4	32
33 OTHER ADMINISTRATIVE SUPPORT	4495.8		148.3	418.8	7.0	26.9	32.4	33
34 PRIVATE HOUSEHOLD		124.0	19.6	235.3	351.2	19.3	715.3	34
35 GUARDS	51.5	16.2	65.7	314.2	250.8	166.7	18.7	35
36 OTHER PROTECTIVE SERVICES		3.1	432.3	28.8	11.1	2.7	237.7	36
37 FOOD PREPARATION AND SERVICE	10.1	256.6	571.3	309.0	30.0	63.9	241.7	37
38 NURSING AND OTHER HEALTH ASSISTANTS		3.6					2.9	38
39 CLEANING AND BUILDING SERVICES	11.7	14.5	671.7	506.7	1510.0	6327.9	3.2	39
40 PERSONAL SERVICES			119.2	812.3	34.8	1679.2	36.0	40
41 FARMING, FORESTRY, AND FISHING	55.5	1734.1	974.9			59.2	14.0	41
42 AUTO MECHANICS AND REPAIRERS	870.8	172.1	4229.0	846.3	770.2	518.3	0.8	42
43 OTHER MECHANICS AND REPAIRERS	25.7	2787.3	1630.8	325.9	4518.0	276.6	8.8	43
44 CARPENTERS	11.8	11.8	174.2	22.1	118.5	219.7	0.6	44
45 OTHER CONSTRUCTION TRADES	270.8	1940.4	1847.0	35.4	134.8	234.3	28.6	45
46 EXTRACTIVE OCCUPATIONS	78.4	1240.0	928.8	81.2	89.6	100.0	8.8	46
47 SUPERVISORS AND PRODUCTION	240.0	1787.2	654.7		737.2	513.0	188.2	47
48 PRECISION PRODUCTION	1787.2	431.7	7995.6	199.2	150.8	808.3	0.6	48
49 PLANT AND SYSTEM OPERATORS	431.1	252.7					1.3	49
50 MACHINE OPERATORS	252.2	147.7	1464.7	99.7	73.2	43.7	0.2	50
51 FABRICATORS AND ASSEMBLERS	69.5	878.3	83.7			5.8	3.3	51
52 PRODUCTION INSPECTORS AND RELATED	147.5	398.6	24.8	6.8		62.5	1.2	52
53 MOTOR VEHICLE OPERATORS	32.4	68.8	856.0	636.5	4298.2	62.5	19.7	53
54 OTHER TRANSPORTATION OPERATORS	878.3	109.7		308.8	963.6	3539.4	50.5	54
55 MATERIAL MOVING EQUIPMENT OPERATORS	33.9	461.7						55
56 CRAFT AND PRODUCTION	398.6							56
57 CONSTRUCTION LABOR	7.0							57
58 FREIGHT AND MATERIAL HANDLERS	68.8							58
59 OTHER HANDLERS AND MISCELLANEOUS	18.9	76.2	3157.7					59
60 TOTAL	34828.4	22358.0	110386.2	33205.8	33205.8	33206.8	17141.6	60

52

Table 5.1. U.S. Wage/Salary Income Distribution Matrix for Individuals (millions of 1982 dollars) (*contd.*)

		OTHER RETAIL TRADE	BANKS, CREDIT AGENCIES	INS. REAL-ESTATE FINANCE	BUSINESS SERV	REPAIR SERV	OTHER PERS. SERV	RECREATION SERV	
01	PUBLIC ADMINISTRATORS AND OFFICIALS	0.2	0.5	2.2	1.9	0.1	1.0	0.9	1
02	OTHER ADMINISTRATORS AND OFFICIALS	5378.8	5434.5	14726.7	9053.2	1506.1	6995.8	3202.6	2
03	MANAGEMENT RELATED	817.4	4638.6	3345.7	5049.5	86.2	521.7	315.7	3
04	ARCHITECTS	9.3	8.9	88.6	28.1	1.0	5.4	4.6	4
05	ENGINEERS	52.0	24.7	323.5	1791.7	36.8	45.7	79.4	5
06	SURVEYORS AND MAPPING SCIENTISTS	0.2	0.4	11.5	9.1	0.2	0.9	0.7	6
07	OTHER SCIENTISTS AND MATHEMATICIANS	78.5	238.0	886.7	2463.4	6.4	21.5	27.2	7
08	DOCTORS AND OTHER DIAGNOSTICIANS	77.2	5.5	66.6	58.1	0.3	15.2	31.0	8
09	OTHER HEALTH, INCLUDING NURSES	749.0	10.1	82.0	413.8	0.4	132.8	17.9	9
10	ELEMENTARY AND SECONDARY TEACHERS	80.2	10.2	17.6	67.2	3.1	216.2	686.2	10
11	OTHER EDUCATION RELATED	17.7	12.5	58.1	101.7	2.0	24.9	37.0	11
12	SOCIAL SCIENTISTS AND URBAN PLANNERS	15.2	75.1	131.9	286.0	1.8	16.0	12.0	12
13	SOCIAL, RECREATION AND RELIGIOUS	4.4	6.4	53.8	51.0	0.2	39.6	84.2	13
14	LAWYERS AND JUDGES	9.1	94.3	549.5	113.2	3.8	11.3	19.2	14
15	ARTISTS, ENTERTAINERS, AND ATHLETES	846.1	82.6	247.3	2779.3	12.0	751.6	2556.3	15
16	HEALTH TECHNOLOGISTS AND TECHNICIANS	10.2	2.4	10.2	41.8	0.5	5.9	2.8	16
17	LICENSED PRACTICAL NURSES	0.9	1.4	6.8	120.0	0.1	120.3	1.0	17
18	OTHER TECHNOLOGISTS AND TECHNICIANS	152.0	293.7	1267.8	3788.3	98.5	137.7	155.4	18
19	SUPERVISORS AND SALES, SELF-EMPLOYED	992.6	0.2	73.9	21.7	22.2	25.1	4.2	19
20	SUPERVISORS AND SALES, SALARIED	3372.5	47.3	420.5	311.7	138.6	116.2	50.6	20
21	SALES, FINANCE, AND BUSINESS SERVICES	39.5	367.7	33519.9	3183.9	179.3	201.8	245.8	21
22	SALES REPRESENTATIVES, NON-RETAIL	14.2	0.5	14.4	42.9	3.3	10.3	0.3	22
23	OTHER SALES, RETAIL AND PERSONAL	10199.7	6.2	192.7	219.9	143.9	830.0	172.8	23
24	CASHIERS	519.5	68.1	66.1	29.7	26.0	149.3	231.7	24
25	SALES RELATED	42.3	3.0	29.3	88.2	0.4	3.8	0.8	25
26	SUPERVISORS AND ADMIN SUPPORT	294.1	1092.8	2201.3	984.9	40.5	150.1	87.6	26
27	COMPUTER EQUIPMENT OPERATORS	64.5	310.3	419.9	641.1	8.2	24.8	14.4	27
28	SECRETARIAL RELATED	559.1	1417.0	5378.5	2595.7	184.5	399.9	277.0	28
29	ACCOUNTANTS AND AUDITORS	833.7	985.3	1214.6	612.2	205.9	320.8	146.0	29
30	OTHER FINANCIAL RECORDS PROCESSING	77.5	288.8	502.8	141.4	12.0	45.2	17.2	30
31	MAIL AND MESSAGE DISTRIBUTING	94.9	223.8	403.7	428.3	8.1	32.6	22.5	31
32	SHIPPING, RECEIVING, AND OTHER CLERKS	639.6	118.6	276.6	548.0	69.6	158.1	78.9	32
33	OTHER ADMINISTRATIVE SUPPORT	828.3	5503.1	5734.8	3110.8	149.1	1432.3	302.9	33
34	PRIVATE HOUSEHOLD	0.0	0.0	0.0	0.0	0.0	1124.6	0.0	34
35	GUARDS	55.8	151.0	312.2	2766.1	8.3	202.3	264.8	35
36	OTHER PROTECTIVE SERVICES	6.0	9.2	31.8	185.8	1.1	21.7	19.1	36
37	FOOD PREPARATION AND SERVICE	55.4	12.5	38.1	30.7	1.5	1022.0	455.4	37
38	NURSING AND OTHER HEALTH ASSISTANTS	55.6	2.5	15.1	169.8	0.2	270.9	6.2	38
39	CLEANING AND BUILDING SERVICES	139.2	166.7	1274.2	2337.9	41.2	2443.5	380.8	39
40	PERSONAL SERVICES	17.4	4.1	71.1	76.4	2.8	4852.3	531.6	40
41	FARMING, FORESTRY, AND FISHING	32.3	2.6	213.1	25.8	8.7	168.2	241.2	41
42	AUTO MECHANICS AND REPAIRERS	47.3	2.5	17.8	54.9	4101.5	18.9	23.5	42
43	OTHER MECHANICS AND REPAIRERS	1079.8	37.7	319.5	1198.0	2990.3	276.8	414.2	43
44	CARPENTERS	92.2	6.1	142.5	51.2	12.5	68.7	53.6	44
45	OTHER CONSTRUCTION TRADES	571.3	21.3	512.0	457.6	112.7	196.6	92.8	45
46	EXTRACTIVE OCCUPATIONS	3.0	0.4	3.5	7.3	1.6	0.7	1.5	46
47	SUPERVISORS AND PRODUCTION	699.6	52.9	192.1	434.9	126.9	318.4	84.4	47
48	PRECISION PRODUCTION	925.8	5.6	31.3	212.8	592.6	999.1	46.0	48
49	PLANT AND SYSTEM OPERATORS	10.2	14.1	145.7	90.2	5.2	121.5	15.1	49
50	MACHINE OPERATORS	311.1	49.4	166.7	886.9	325.8	2382.2	220.9	50
51	FABRICATORS AND ASSEMBLERS	149.5	4.7	20.2	365.1	558.6	35.1	16.7	51
52	PRODUCTION INSPECTORS AND RELATED	38.6	7.0	22.0	111.2	8.6	85.3	3.9	52
53	MOTOR VEHICLE OPERATORS	1220.9	45.3	89.7	505.0	454.3	621.7	109.9	53
54	OTHER TRANSPORTATION OPERATORS	3.0	0.8	3.4	9.1	2.6	8.9	10.0	54
55	MATERIAL MOVING EQUIPMENT OPERATORS	133.4	8.2	41.5	127.4	19.9	19.3	22.6	55
56	CRAFT AND PRODUCTION	12.7	0.7	8.5	16.5	75.2	14.9	4.7	56
57	CONSTRUCTION LABOR	7.2	0.8	19.2	15.5	2.3	11.0	6.0	57
58	FREIGHT AND MATERIAL HANDLERS	305.0	3.8	15.1	45.5	6.0	25.4	41.2	58
59	OTHER HANDLERS AND MISCELLANEOUS	364.2	11.0	161.0	400.7	338.3	239.7	77.4	59
60	TOTAL	33206.8	21993.2	76193.1	49810.3	12750.0	28513.6	12030.4	60

Table 5.1. U.S. Wage/Salary Income Distribution Matrix for Individuals (millions of 1982 dollars) *(contd.)*

		HOSPI-TALS	HEALTH SERV	EDUCA-TION SERV	SOCIAL SERV	LEGAL & OTHER SERV	PUBLIC ADMINIS-TRATION	TOTAL WAGE INCOME	
01	PUBLIC ADMINISTRATORS AND OFFICIALS	132.1	688.0	1730.8	548.9	989.1	28277.2	28554.2	1
02	OTHER ADMINISTRATORS AND OFFICIALS	308.7	808.8	177.0	742.5	989.6	143822.1	186242.1	2
03	MANAGEMENT RELATED	56.7			748.7	2180.6	30398.5	719261.5	3
04	ARCHITECTS	56.9	131.5	50.1	112.3	1816.3	10485.1	21255.9	4
05	ENGINEERS	200.2		129.8	1091.5	333.2	10398.3	52663.9	5
06	SURVEYORS AND MAPPING SCIENTISTS		475.4		115.1	12.2	1525.0	2577.4	6
07	OTHER SCIENTISTS AND MATHEMATICIANS	280.2	399.3	418.0	380.0	128.8	1866.9	24900.9	7
08	DOCTORS AND OTHER DIAGNOSTICIANS	603.4	8655.8	640.0	2040.0	101.3	1853.0	46220.8	8
09	OTHER HEALTH, INCLUDING NURSES		256.8	2292.3	5610.0	72.8	1853.5	119119.0	9
10	ELEMENTARY AND SECONDARY TEACHERS	80.6	273.3	257.4	2872.5	108.8	10742.5	10742.5	10
11	OTHER EDUCATION RELATED	108.9	83.1		757.8	694.7	11994.5	11285.3	11
12	SOCIAL SCIENTISTS AND URBAN PLANNERS	205.8	1321.7	123.1	757.8	5142.7	2299.4	12836.2	12
13	SOCIAL RECREATION AND RELIGIOUS		495.7	131.7	206.1	694.7	443.2	19337.2	13
14	LAWYERS AND JUDGES	159.7	3120.0		23.3	1226.0	108.8	20149.8	14
15	ARTISTS, ENTERTAINERS, AND ATHLETES	168.0	240.7	403.5	8.0	1.8	16236.5	6028.5	15
16	HEALTH TECHNOLOGISTS AND TECHNICIANS		114.2	40.7	2.3	613.0	214.8	3665.8	16
17	LICENSED PRACTICAL NURSES		13.0	20.1	8.4	610.3	32.3	49112.0	17
18	OTHER TECHNOLOGISTS AND TECHNICIANS		88.7	19.3	185.1	212.5	355.4	22356.1	18
19	SUPERVISORS AND SALES, SELF-EMPLOYED	27.4	85.7	25.3			35.0	45236.7	19
20	SUPERVISORS AND SALES, SALARIED			71.9	24.8	150.1	12570.5	42735.7	20
21	SALES, FINANCE, AND BUSINESS SERVICES	250.2	624.7	35.3	244.1	1383.0	1685.1	33978.2	21
22	SALES REPRESENTATIVES, NON-RETAIL		378.8	766.2	244.4	339.0	18126.0	8411.2	22
23	OTHER SALES, RETAIL AND PERSONAL	876.5	1062.2	18.4	358.8	18.2	2697.5	335.1	23
24	CASHIERS		80.7	34.3	97.7	428.5	1067.0	30210.3	24
25	SALES RELATED	209.0	148.7	34.3	1145.3	325.8	3398.2	56431.3	25
26	SUPERVISORS AND ADMIN SUPPORT	107.1	404.8	903.0			20675.0	52844.3	26
27	COMPUTER EQUIPMENT OPERATORS			99.2	127.9	38.0	4707.0	55284.8	27
28	SECRETARIAL RELATED	139.9	97.5	275.3	339.7	2.7	503.2	5168.0	28
29	ACCOUNTANTS AND AUDITORS	236.5		213.0	174.0	30.8	588.7	10293.3	29
30	OTHER FINANCIAL RECORDS PROCESSING	1995.6	1154.5	489.7	824.8	30.0	3230.2	25205.3	30
31	MAIL AND MESSAGE DISTRIBUTING	622.3	441.2	190.7	1099.3	12.6	1107.7	68137.7	31
32	SHIPPING, RECEIVING, AND OTHER CLERKS	11.3	31.1	124.8	42.6	1.2	1303.5	11823.3	32
33	OTHER ADMINISTRATIVE SUPPORT	131.3	137.8	103.6	15.7	39.5	6445.0	14936.8	33
34	PRIVATE HOUSEHOLD	135.1	29.8	125.0		3.7	50.3	12493.0	34
35	GUARDS	14.6	111.9	81.5	57.0	3.4	2928.0	11823.3	35
36	OTHER PROTECTIVE SERVICES	14.0		27.3	15.7		4670.0	14943.0	36
37	FOOD PREPARATION AND SERVICE	601.1		273.1		21.6	503.2	14936.8	37
38	NURSING AND OTHER HEALTH ASSISTANTS	407.5	1563.1	489.7	983.3	322.5	1514.7	18877.7	38
39	CLEANING AND BUILDING SERVICES	589.6		52.8	202.8	36.1	3230.2	85151.1	39
40	PERSONAL SERVICES	218.0	399.7		142.6	17.1	1639.2	14979.3	40
41	FARMING, FORESTRY, AND FISHING	8.7	210.3	348.2	231.8	13.3	1646.7	13887.0	41
42	AUTO MECHANICS AND REPAIRERS	56.7	29.6		236.3	2.2	398.1	116113.8	42
43	OTHER MECHANICS AND REPAIRERS					17.6	2524.1	43781.8	43
44	CARPENTERS	8.2	10.9		21.6	2.8	1082.3	72040.2	44
45	OTHER CONSTRUCTION TRADES	6.6	19.1	18.1	6.9	1.7	150.2	20640.4	45
46	EXTRACTIVE OCCUPATIONS	4.8	2.1	4.0		6.8	178.0	25820.7	46
47	SUPERVISORS AND PRODUCTION	1.9	71.1	19.8	11.9	1.3	199.3	5682.9	47
48	PRECISION PRODUCTION					1.2	1893.6	10945.2	48
49	PLANT AND SYSTEM OPERATORS							24203.0	49
50	MACHINE OPERATORS								50
51	FABRICATORS AND ASSEMBLERS AND RELATED								51
52	PRODUCTION INSPECTORS AND RELATED								52
53	MOTOR VEHICLE OPERATORS								53
54	OTHER TRANSPORTATION OPERATORS								54
55	MATERIAL MOVING EQUIPMENT OPERATORS								55
56	CRAFT AND PRODUCTION								56
57	CONSTRUCTION LABOR								57
58	FREIGHT AND MATERIAL HANDLERS								58
59	OTHER HANDLERS AND MISCELLANEOUS								59
60	TOTAL	20750.5	93820.8	155518.0	27204.7	16443.1	298733.3	1564995.2	60

54

2. We then extract the information on wage and salary differentials from this household distribution matrix by adjusting for the two other variables. This is done indirectly by calculating wage/salary to total income ratios, based on economywide averages for each income class. The result is used to calculate a set of weights for the wage and salary distribution across income classes for each occupational group.

3. These weights are used to distribute the wage income of individuals to households on a sectoral basis by multiplying the figures in table 5.1 by them.

4. The original twenty-one income classes are aggregated to ten by adding the corresponding cell entries, thus arriving at an income class matrix that is compatible in size with the results of the following chapters.

5. A biproportional matrix "balancing" routine (see Bacharach 1972) adjusts the matrix to conform to control totals for wage and salary income by income class from the IRS (1984a) and by sector from the U.S. Bureau of Economic Analysis (1984b).

The total dollar wage and salary earnings by occupation for a given sector of employment are thus distributed according to the U.S. distribution of total wage income by occupation. One assumption inherent in this procedure is that the distribution of income for a given occupationally designated household is the same among all industries. As with many of our simplifying assumptions, this one is invoked for lack of better data.

Overall, we have not addressed many of the complexities associated with the definition and use of the household unit (see Medoff 1975; Danziger and Taussig 1982). Many of these pertain to demographic features, such as age and family size (see Kuznets 1976), for which we have few data as well. Another consideration is the fact that the household formation issue is only one of dozens that had to be addressed in this study, and further attention to it at the expense of others was seen as involving very high opportunity costs. In any case, we have endeavored to present our results in stages (as in the individual wage and salary matrix vs. the household one) and carefully to cite our data sources. Thus, the reader able to obtain superior data will be able to perform calculations that can modify our results.

Presentation of the Matrices

The wage and salary income distribution matrix for households is presented in table 5.2. Occupation headings are replaced with income class categories to denote the rows of the matrix. Sectors are still denoted for forty-one SIC categories, following the previous methodology adopted for Bureau of the Census control totals. To facilitate a compact presentation of the results, however, the matrix has been transposed.

The wholesale trade, public administration, and health services and hospital sectors were responsible for almost 32 percent of the total wage and salary bill paid in 1982. At the other end of the spectrum were the textile mill products and entertainment and recreation services sectors, together comprising only 1 percent of the total wage and salary disbursements in 1982.

Table 5.3, the wage/salary income coefficient matrix, depicts the proportion of each sector's wage and salary bill paid to household income classes. For example, within the agriculture, forestry, and fisheries sector, almost 63 percent of wages and salaries went to households with incomes of less than $25,000. In contrast, 53 percent of the wage and salary bill paid by the legal and professional service sector accrued to household income classes of $35,000 or more. For all sectors collectively, the $20,000 to $50,000 household

Table 5.2. U.S. Wage/Salary Income Distribution Matrix for Households (millions of 1982 dollars)

	UNDER $5000	5000-9999	10000-14999	15000-19999	20000-24999	25000-34999	35000-49999	50000-74999	75000-99999	OVER 100000	TOTAL
01 AGRICULTURE AND RELATED	2154.3	3730.4	3291.5	3085.0	2349.1	3313.3	2684.0	1235.3	431.1	817.2	23091.2
02 MINING	281.9	328.9	319.8	394.4	342.8	740.3	708.4	566.3	531.5	1007.5	3990.2
03 CONSTRUCTION	2292.3	2952.9	3906.2	3519.4	3421.8	7409.3	7788.1	5956.6	1199.7	2266.7	83677.9
04 FOOD AND KINDRED	839.5	2667.3	3215.7	3259.1	3421.5	3788.8	3760.5	3260.6	504.2	957.0	3686.7
05 TEXTILES	288.6	845.3	1207.7	1259.1	1382.5	2719.0	2197.1	679.6	120.3	228.1	10954
06 APPAREL	366.0	1501.0	1577.8	1621.3	1833.5	3477.2	2138.5	811.5	149.3	283.1	3892.3
07 PRINTING AND PUBLISHING	545.5	1201.7	2195.4	2305.0	2544.0	5142.6	4880.1	2129.0	621.3	1185.0	23108.3
08 CHEMICALS	380.8	1435.6	2318.4	2559.7	3005.4	6267.4	6456.7	5713.0	656.5	1244.6	21798.2
09 PAPER AND PRODUCTS	372.9	1097.6	1612.1	1707.7	1701.6	3804.8	3328.6	1153.3	238.1	451.4	15734.0
10 PETROLEUM REFINING	573.8	1196.8	2375.7	1775.4	2075.8	5795.0	5182.4	1832.7	376.0	712.8	2890.7
11 LUMBER AND FURNITURE	485.5	1290.9	2513.8	1893.3	3091.1	4042.5	3496.4	1716.2	417.8	589.0	16697.7
12 PRIMARY METALS	612.3	1968.9	2917.6	2689.0	2638.0	6285.2	6677.7	2310.7	349.0	905.7	26620.8
13 FABRICATED METALS AND PRODUCTS	1056.9	2862.0	3603.7	3909.8	5825.3	7813.0	9986.5	4627.4	998.3	1893.6	29901.2
14 MACHINERY, EXCEPT ELECTRICAL	890.6	2367.0	3667.4	3907.1	4737.3	9813.9	8360.3	6842.9	842.4	1593.8	50528.2
15 ELECTRICAL MACHINERY EQUIPMENT	991.8	1363.0	2135.7	2133.0	2847.0	9099.7	4301.3	4456.7	567.2	1495.7	51471.7
16 MOTOR VEHICLES	491.7	1150.2	2036.4	2436.5	2847.0	6029.7	6980.3	2452.1	517.5	1057.7	11986.5
17 OTHER TRANSPORTATION EQUIPMENT	344.1	838.4	3281.6	3184.7	1683.6	3215.1	2697.3	843.9	658.8	3013.1	26183.1
18 MISCELLANEOUS MANUFACTURING	743.2	1742.3	1381.2	3495.1	1685.5	6566.5	5492.1	2853.0	461.7	575.4	12649
19 RAILROADS	741.7	1742.3	2609.1	3289.5	3526.3	6165.5	5600.8	2048.6	373.9	875.4	3884.0
20 TRUCKING AND WAREHOUSING	529.2	1352.3	2038.5	2024.9	2590.0	7103.4	8400.4	1947.5	601.8	1614.5	26258.9
21 OTHER TRANSPORTATION	2301.3	1130.0	8450.3	2024.9	1090.7	5293.3	5320.4	1945.5	851.0	4614.5	26621.8
22 COMMUNICATION	1830.7	3335.4	3428.0	3842.4	3730.7	7638.4	6492.2	1285.3	709.9	6499.8	3243.3
23 UTILITIES	1402.7	2258.5	2973.4	3814.8	3845.7	8291.8	7117.6	2251.3	601.8	1338.0	10542.3
24 WHOLESALE TRADE	1346.0	2285.6	2499.3	3790.2	3848.4	8788.7	7177.6	2778.6	611.8	1171.0	50527.2
25 GENERAL MERCHANDISE RETAIL	1528.0	3141.5	2499.3	2793.3	1853.5	3193.7	3169.0	4564.2	617.8	898.9	34151.5
26 FOOD AND MERCHANDISE RETAIL	1645.8	3141.5	3359.4	3624.9	3693.5	7549.3	6962.2	2952.0	764.9	1450.0	35093.7
27 SERVICE STATIONS	1476.0	2861.0	1826.4	3953.8	2197.1	4438.8	4418.9	2385.1	305.2	1146.2	20080
28 EATING AND DRINKING PLACES	1477.4	2682.8	5158.7	5995.3	6371.7	13438.8	16559.7	8734.2	300.1	5695.7	69232.1
29 OTHER RETAIL	2280.4	4723.0	1113.5	3245.8	4624.4	9307.3	4840.4	5357.0	158.3	2799.2	47771.4
30 BANK AND CREDIT INSTITUTIONS	2692.0	4489.5	4375.1	3245.8	3612.4	3407.9	3043.9	2158.8	601.9	1304.2	13049.2
31 INSURANCE AND REAL ESTATE	2692.0	913.4	4375.1	1375.1	3612.4	5871.7	5280.3	1275.8	601.9	1803.6	3490.2
32 BUSINESS SERVICE	830.7	913.4	1164.0	1138.0	1112.4	2235.4	2429.8	2727.9	603.2	1803.6	1193.0
33 AUTO REPAIR AND SERVICES	3486.0	705.1	1096.0	691.3	2977.0	12974.4	1406.2	1705.4	6593.4	1326.8	2663.5
34 OTHER REPAIR AND PERSONAL SERVICES	449.0	799.1	824.6	7653.3	7897.4	12974.4	3742.1	9104.4	298.6	12498.8	8967.5
35 RECREATION	959.0	1767.0	2514.5	1687.5	1674.2	3196.2	6114.4	1651.2	566.1	566.0	1545.5
36 HOSPITALS	235.5	523.7	1514.5	2597.5	2471.2	4746.4	6112.4	3062.9	795.6	566.0	2652.7
37 HEALTH SERVICES			1103.0	1043.3	2636.0	2636.0	3566.0	2137.5	675.6	1280.7	1414.7
38 EDUCATION											
39 SOCIAL SERVICES											
40 LEGAL AND OTHER SERVICES											
41 PUBLIC ADMINISTRATION	235.5	523.7	1103.0	1043.3	1215.4	6413.4	3566.0	2137.5	675.6	1280.7	1414.7
42 TOTAL	45553.1	102616.7	145516.2	153368.5	172852.8	340299.0	338750.2	145721.7	41203.7	78107.6	1564995.2

56

Table 5.3. U.S. Wage/Salary Income Coefficient Matrix for Households, 1982

	UNDER $5000	5000-9999	10000-14999	15000-19999	20000-24999	25000-34999	35000-49999	50000-74999	75000-99999	OVER 100000	TOTAL
01 AGRICULTURE AND RELATED	0.093	0.162	0.143	0.134	0.102	0.143	0.116	0.053	0.019	0.035	1.000
02 MINING	0.026	0.065	0.106	0.108	0.125	0.232	0.213	0.080	0.080	0.031	1.000
03 CONSTRUCTION	0.027	0.071	0.100	0.114	0.121	0.239	0.213	0.074	0.014	0.027	1.000
04 FOOD AND KINDRED	0.026	0.072	0.101	0.115	0.132	0.248	0.191	0.074	0.016	0.030	1.000
05 TEXTILES	0.026	0.077	0.114	0.117	0.100	0.250	0.237	0.062	0.011	0.021	1.000
06 APPAREL	0.021	0.081	0.095	0.094	0.110	0.223	0.217	0.058	0.011	0.020	1.000
07 PRINTING AND PUBLISHING	0.024	0.054	0.085	0.094	0.124	0.232	0.217	0.092	0.027	0.051	1.000
08 CHEMICALS	0.025	0.065	0.102	0.106	0.125	0.243	0.215	0.099	0.024	0.046	1.000
09 PAPER AND PRODUCTS	0.024	0.070	0.099	0.102	0.121	0.247	0.204	0.073	0.015	0.029	1.000
10 PETROLEUM REFINING	0.029	0.068	0.107	0.105	0.126	0.240	0.220	0.077	0.013	0.030	1.000
11 LUMBER AND FURNITURE	0.025	0.077	0.098	0.112	0.114	0.247	0.238	0.067	0.013	0.025	1.000
12 PRIMARY METALS	0.023	0.062	0.086	0.105	0.125	0.236	0.217	0.070	0.016	0.024	1.000
13 FABRICATED METALS AND PRODUCTS	0.021	0.066	0.087	0.096	0.118	0.247	0.217	0.077	0.020	0.030	1.000
14 MACHINERY, EXCEPT ELECTRICAL	0.021	0.056	0.100	0.096	0.132	0.237	0.255	0.091	0.021	0.037	1.000
15 ELECTRICAL MACHINERY EQUIPMENT	0.024	0.057	0.078	0.107	0.123	0.248	0.222	0.073	0.020	0.038	1.000
16 MOTOR VEHICLE EQUIPMENT	0.021	0.069	0.095	0.089	0.108	0.244	0.208	0.093	0.013	0.025	1.000
17 OTHER TRANSPORTATION EQUIPMENT	0.019	0.050	0.118	0.095	0.116	0.233	0.185	0.104	0.021	0.040	1.000
18 MISCELLANEOUS MANUFACTURING	0.028	0.063	0.095	0.115	0.105	0.237	0.255	0.084	0.012	0.036	1.000
19 RAILROADS	0.028	0.028	0.076	0.109	0.132	0.248	0.237	0.065	0.011	0.021	1.000
20 TRUCKING AND WAREHOUSING	0.018	0.083	0.099	0.096	0.108	0.233	0.231	0.059	0.018	0.023	1.000
21 OTHER TRANSPORTATION	0.018	0.041	0.086	0.103	0.105	0.239	0.196	0.078	0.016	0.033	1.000
22 COMMUNICATION	0.024	0.051	0.124	0.107	0.092	0.249	0.221	0.108	0.018	0.018	1.000
23 UTILITIES	0.022	0.051	0.096	0.114	0.125	0.158	0.204	0.087	0.033	0.033	1.000
24 WHOLESALE TRADE	0.052	0.093	0.087	0.104	0.094	0.213	0.199	0.107	0.027	0.038	1.000
25 GENERAL MERCHANDISE	0.040	0.081	0.089	0.093	0.119	0.194	0.239	0.072	0.018	0.062	1.000
26 FOOD AND DAIRY, RETAIL	0.038	0.135	0.126	0.087	0.088	0.254	0.233	0.079	0.020	0.037	1.000
27 SERVICE STATIONS	0.076	0.100	0.092	0.124	0.114	0.188	0.153	0.073	0.022	0.038	1.000
28 EATING AND DRINKING PLACES	0.047	0.090	0.105	0.112	0.084	0.189	0.204	0.084	0.024	0.033	1.000
29 OTHER RETAIL	0.023	0.041	0.092	0.096	0.094	0.145	0.189	0.114	0.022	0.045	1.000
30 BANKS AND CREDIT INSTITUTIONS	0.021	0.056	0.079	0.101	0.112	0.129	0.153	0.126	0.029	0.041	1.000
31 INSURANCE AND REAL ESTATE	0.022	0.044	0.077	0.035	0.110	0.183	0.145	0.112	0.031	0.055	1.000
32 BUSINESS SERVICES	0.078	0.077	0.095	0.098	0.094	0.226	0.249	0.062	0.055	0.082	1.000
33 AUTO REPAIR AND SERVICES	0.040	0.082	0.085	0.072	0.084	0.217	0.247	0.107	0.017	0.059	1.000
34 OTHER PERSONAL SERVICES	0.038	0.053	0.093	0.086	0.088	0.145	0.232	0.079	0.012	0.023	1.000
35 RECREATION	0.030	0.067	0.092	0.099	0.094	0.179	0.216	0.102	0.036	0.037	1.000
36 HOSPITALS	0.036	0.036	0.077	0.031	0.112	0.183	0.207	0.115	0.032	0.033	1.000
37 HEALTH SERVICES	0.016	0.048	0.085	0.072	0.084	0.247	0.232	0.148	0.074	0.061	1.000
38 EDUCATION	0.020	0.066	0.093	0.086	0.110	0.226	0.216	0.110	0.020	0.067	1.000
39 SOCIAL SERVICES	0.029			0.035					0.030	0.139	1.000
40 LEGAL AND OTHER SERVICES									0.047	0.057	1.000
41 PUBLIC ADMINISTRATION									0.028	0.089	1.000
42 TOTAL								0.093	0.026	0.050	1.000

57

income classes received approximately the majority, or about 54 percent, of the total wage and salary payments in 1982. About 29 percent of the total wage and salary bill accrued to household income classes of $20,000 or less, while about 17 percent accrued to household income classes of $50,000 or more.

Conclusion

The matrix generated thus far represents only the total dollar flows resulting from wage and salary income for employed persons sixteen years of age and older. The Social Accounting Matrix presented in chapter 7 merges income distribution matrices computed from all sources of income (i.e., wages and salaries, dividends, rents, royalties, etc.). The distribution of many of these payments is much more skewed than that of wages and salaries for most sectors. The reader is thus asked to place the inferences derived from this chapter in the broader perspective of the chapters that follow.

6/ The Dividend Income Distribution Matrix

The major obstacle to the implementation of a complete multisectoral income distribution model is the lack of primary data for capital-related income. The major analyses to date have been limited to wage and salary income alone (see, e.g., Golladay and Haveman 1977) or have been forced to invoke several tenuous assumptions in adapting secondary data for this purpose (see Rose et al. 1982).

This chapter presents the first multisectoral dividend distribution matrix generated from primary data. The data base is the 1983 New York Stock Exchange Survey of shareholders (NYSE 1984a), which we have refined from a stockholdings to a dividend payments basis. While analogous primary data sets were not available for other property income types, the dividend-distribution results serve as the most solid foundation to date for estimating the distribution of property income as a whole (see chapter 7).

The following section presents the underlying assumptions of our multisector dividend-distribution matrix and a discussion of previous research relevant to its estimation. Subsequent sections describe the NYSE data base and other data bases used, the derivation of a stockownership matrix, and the modifications necessary to translate the stocks to annual returns. The final section offers an interpretation of the results. While the analysis confirms many established hypotheses, our empirical model should add a new sense of precision to previous assessments of the distribution of property income and should greatly increase the scope of issues that can be analyzed in the future.

Basic Hypotheses

As presented in chapter 2, the V matrix is specified in terms of fixed coefficients. The reasonableness of the fixed-coefficients assumption ultimately must be determined by empirical test. As noted in chapter 5, Freeman (1980) has shown it to be reasonable for manpower-requirements matrices over time, thus indicating that it would be reasonable for wage and salary income. The assumption, however, may be more tenuous for capital-related income. Some nonlabor functional payments are likely to be stable—for example, royalties are typically associated with long-term contracts and many rental agreements are long-term as well. On the other hand, interest rates have been subject to major fluctuations. In general, both normal and economic profits are typically volatile. That portion of profits paid out as dividends, however, is likely to be more stable given long-run motivations (e.g., enhancing the firm's reputation) associated with paying a dividend.[1] Also, dividends are paid on a per share basis and the number of shares outstanding does not fluctuate significantly from year to year in most sectors. Finally, even if there are fluctuations, the object of distributional analyses is relative differences rather than absolute levels.[2] We therefore invoke the fixed-coefficient assumption as a reasonable approximation.[3]

One major implicit assumption of our analysis is that the personal income distribution of stock dividends differs significantly between sectors. That is, some sectors are characterized by a relative preponderance of wealthy stockholders, while others may be held on equal footing by the spectrum of stockholding income groups. This assumption will be considered a hypothesis subject to formal test in this chapter. If it is refuted, a multisectoral analysis would be superfluous and the specification of the necessary vector could readily be compiled from published data on annual dividend returns by income class, aggregated across all sectors (e.g., IRS 1984a).

Previous studies are mixed with regard to this hypothesis, though none has performed an in-depth analysis. Friend and his associates were able to gain access to data on individual tax returns from the IRS to compile their matrix in two separate studies (see Crockett and Friend 1966; Blume, Crockett, and Friend 1974).[4] Actually, the IRS data yielded only information on dividend payments, to which the authors had to apply price-dividend ratios by income class and make several other very thorough adjustments.[5] The tabulations were done at a highly aggregated level (I. Friend, pers. com., 1984) and were never published as such, although reference is made to some implications in Blume, Crockett, and Friend's 1974 paper. The authors state: "An analysis of this distribution reveals a remarkable similarity in the percentages of each industry held across AGI [adjusted gross income] classes. The only major differences across AGI classes occurred in the telephone and communication industry and in the utilities. Both of these industries tended to be a much more important part of the portfolios of lower income filers than the upper income filers" (p. 31).

Again, we emphasize that the income class/sector results of neither study were published, and it is thus difficult to interpret "remarkable similarity."[6] In addition, the situation may have changed. The authors do, for example, note some significant changes between 1960 and 1971 in the income profile of utility and communication industry stockholders.

The Data Base

The 1983 New York Stock Exchange survey of stockowners (NYSE 1984a) was the major source for constructing a data base that would be compatible with an input-output methodology (i.e., one that contained characteristics on a multisectoral level). The survey covered the period mid 1981 to mid 1983, and we have taken the results as representative of the year 1982. The survey included questions about age, income, economic outlook, willingness to assume risk, size of stock portfolio, education, and industry in which the individual or household was a shareholder. For our purposes, the most useful information was contained in the responses concerning income, size of stock portfolio, and sector(s) of holding(s). The survey breakdown included thirteen stock portfolio size classes, ten income classes, and over a hundred potential three-digit SIC designations.[7]

For each income bracket, the raw data were tabulated in a matrix with stock portfolio size class as the row designation and industry of ownership as the column designation. Individual cell entries indicated the number of individuals reporting shareholdings in a given industry. Thus, the basic data may best be interpreted as a frequency distribution of

Table 6.1. Supplementary Data on Stock and Dividend Characteristics, 1982

Sector	Annual Dividend Yield[a,b,c] (% of stock value)	Mutual Funds Diversification[d] (% of fund-held stock)	Outstanding Stock Composition[a] (% of total stock)
Agriculture and forestry	3.883	2.576	.158
Mining	4.350	.543	2.523
Petroleum extraction	2.700	1.535	3.326
Construction	3.304	.400	2.665
Food and tobacco	4.398	5.042	6.222
Textiles	4.492	.616	.705
Lumber and furniture	4.269	7.447	.158
Paper	3.424	3.490	2.800
Chemicals	4.054	13.518	10.852
Petroleum refining	7.192	5.139	11.136
Rubber, stone, and glass	3.336	1.550	.476
Fabricated metals	3.239	1.625	.158
Machinery	3.843	1.433	2.169
Electric equipment	2.729	11.213	5.518
Transportation equipment	3.080	4.537	3.947
Miscellaneous manufacturing	1.350	2.576	.347
Transportation	3.192	3.289	2.498
Communication	5.156	2.474	.157
Utilities	9.352	8.414	15.619
Wholesale and retail trade	3.274	7.964	5.596
Finance	5.225	9.227	9.185
Miscellaneous services	2.726	2.806	13.955
Lodging and meals	1.743	2.576	.830
Total		100.000	100.000

[a]New York Stock Exchange 1984b.
[b]Standard and Poor's Corporation 1984.
[c]Value Line, Inc. 1984.
[d]Investment Company Institute 1983.

stockownership for each stock portfolio class. Initially, ownership of mutual fund shares was treated as a separate industry. The survey responses thus yielded ten matrices, one for each income class.

Additional data series were needed to translate equity holdings (stock) into dividends (annual income flows). *Shareownership, 1983,* the annual New York Stock Exchange fact book (NYSE 1984b), provided data on total cash dividend payments and total stock values for thirty-two sectors, the basis for the calculation of the price-dividend ratios in column 1 of table 6.1. Not all NYSE data corresponded precisely to the twenty-three sector designations of the two-digit SIC classifications. Although some sectors were directly comparable, others had to be aggregated and assigned to their appropriate counterparts by the research team. For the few remaining sectors, the *Value Line Investment Survey* and *Standard and Poor's Industry Surveys* were used as supplemental sources to derive a sample from which sectoral dividend yields could be inferred.

Sector-by-sector investment returns to mutual fund portfolios could not be ascertained, and it was decided to use the same dividend-price ratio for a given sector's stock held by a mutual fund as for the sector's stock held outright. The average dividend rate for mutual funds was, in fact, higher than for NYSE listings in 1982. Our use of the same dividend-price ratio for both categories implicitly ascribes the higher mutual fund return to the selective mix of sectors, rather than to any gain within a sector from the selective mix of individual stock issues by fund managers.

The Stock Ownership Matrix

Refinement of NYSE Data

In order to develop a stock ownership matrix by sector and income class, four basic steps were necessary:

1. The NYSE data were tabulated into a frequency matrix, depicting the number of stockholders within each sector for each of the stock portfolio size classes for a given household income bracket.
2. Individual stockholder portfolios were then distributed equally among the sectors in which they reported stockholdings. Hence, an individual with a portfolio of $1,000 holding stock in four distinct sectors is assumed to invest $250 in each of the sectors.[8]
3. Total dollar holdings for each portfolio size class were distributed across sectors by multiplying the respective mean portfolio values by the total number of individuals reporting stock ownership within each portfolio size class.
4. The matrix for each income class was then collapsed to a vector by summing the total dollar holdings for each sector across all portfolio size classes.

The vectors derived following this procedure represent total dollar shareholdings for a given income class distributed over all sectors of the economy. Repeating the procedure for all income classes develops the complete sample stock ownership matrix aggregated to the 24-sector level, with the last sector representing mutual funds.

Mutual funds were then distributed to sectors according to data for 1982 presented in the *Mutual Fund Fact Book* (Investment Company Institute 1983). These data disaggregate mutual fund portfolios into holdings in twenty-nine industry categories. This classification scheme was transferred to the 23-sector designation used in this chapter on the basis of industry similarities. The refined data are presented in column 2 of table 6.1.

Further Refinements

The data base compiled thus far simply represents a sample and needs to be scaled up to yield a complete stockownership matrix for the United States. Not only is the NYSE survey data a subset of total NYSE listings, it is also a subset of the broader category of all domestic stock issues. The latter includes stocks listed on other exchanges and traded over the counter and unlisted issues such as mutual funds and bank stocks. A complete tabulation of the market value of all domestic issues by market type and ownership group is presented in table 6.2. Direct sources for the more important items of the table—NYSE issues and mutual funds—were available for 1982. The other entries are estimated by using percentages presented in a similar table in Blume et al. (1974). The results contain inaccuracies to the extent that there have been unaccounted-for shifts in stock categories. Note that NYSE-listed stocks represent 62 percent of the total value in table 6.2 and that another 30 percent is attributed to the "other unlisted" category for which few data exist. Hence, our assumption

Table 6.2. Ownership of Domestic Stock Issues, 1982
(billions of 1982 dollars)

Type of Stock	Individual		Nonprofit Institution	Domestic Corporation	Foreign-held	Total
	Direct	Beneficiary				
Listed	565	256	241	246	46	1,355
NYSE, domestic and foreign	—	—	—	—	—	1,305[a]
Other, domestic and foreign	—	—	—	—	—	96
Less: foreign	—	—	—	—	—	45
Unlisted	438	75	32	211	5	761
Mutual funds	42	—	—	—	—	49[b]
Banks and insurance companies	58	—	—	—	—	73
Other	338	—	—	—	—	639
All domestic	1,003	331	273	457	51	2,116[c]

[a]New York Stock Exchange 1984b.
[b]Investment Company Institute 1983.
[c]All other: see p. 62.

that the NYSE distribution is representative of stockownership as a whole may not be excessive.

The procedure for scaling up the sample matrix was as follows:

1. Control totals for the universe of stockholdings in each sector were calculated by applying the sectoral distribution of NYSE listings (in the form of weights) to the overall total holdings by individuals ($1,334 billion, as indicated in columns 1 and 2 of table 6.2).
2. For each sector a "scale-up" factor was formed by dividing the control total for the sector by the corresponding column sum of the relevant sector in the sample matrix.
3. The scale-up factor for each sector was then used to multiply each element in the corresponding column of the sample matrix.
4. The matrix yielded from the first three steps automatically conformed to the column control total (total stock issues by sector). However, summing across the rows, we obtain the total stock holding by income class, for which there is no explicit control total. As a proxy we used the relative proportions from the distribution of dividends in the annual *Statistics of Income: Individual Income Tax Returns* (IRS 1984a).
5. A biproportional matrix method (see Bacharach 1972) was used to "balance" the matrix to conform to both control totals simultaneously. This balancing routine had the beneficial effect of compensating for poor coverage of the lower and upper income groups in the sample.

Presentation of the Stock Ownership Matrix

A 23 × 7 matrix of the distribution of equity ownership by sector and income class of the economy for the United States in 1982 is presented as table 6.3. A given cell of the table represents the total value of stock in a sector, as designated by the row headings, held by households within an income class, as designated by the column headings. Each row sum

Table 6.3. U.S. Stock Ownership Distribution Matrix, 1982
(millions of 1982 dollars)

Sector	Under 15,000	15,000– 19,999	20,000– 24,999	25,000– 34,999	35,000– 49,999	50,000– 99,999	Over 100,000	Total
Agriculture and forestry	473[a]	137	36	144	255	840	116	2,001
Mining	5,993[a]	2,967	1,157[a]	1,547	2,215	2,810	15,232	31,921
Petroleum extraction	1,042	1,035	739	4,231	4,145	4,178	15,655	31,025
Construction	5,962	2,881[a]	1,291[a]	2,027	2,855	5,284[a]	13,407[a]	33,707
Food and tobacco	18,194[a]	5,387	1,523	5,965	10,150	32,902	4,588	78,709
Textiles	1,453[a]	2,034	1,098	301	202	906	2,922[a]	8,915
Lumber and furniture	372[a]	178[a]	50	169	421	459[a]	352	2,001
Paper and printing	7,016[a]	515	394	2,680[a]	1,395	9,704	13,720[a]	35,424
Chemicals	27,345[a]	12,009[a]	2,982	17,032	19,712	14,961	43,236	137,276
Petroleum refining	8,450	6,504	7,713	7,614	19,966	19,293	82,365	151,906
Rubber, stone, and glass	1,186[a]	356	113	351	458	1,006	2,545	6,015
Fabricated metals	9	17	30	50	348	434[a]	1,112	2,001
Machinery	1,351	2,936[a]	526	6,356	2,232	12,893	1,145	27,440
Electric equipment	510	2,401	1,928	5,551	6,452	13,693	39,265	69,799
Transportation equipment	230	1,746	590	2,929	7,677	11,249	25,505	49,925
Miscellaneous manufacturing	870[a]	373[a]	84	591	288	688	1,494	4,388
Transportation	6,398	1,047	3,859	1,979	4,699	10,996	2,626	31,603
Communication	203	178	29	439	372	457	305	1,983
Utilities	15,517	11,019	17,617	28,905	29,331	30,219	64,970	197,579
Trade	10,436	9,117	4,376	12,126	11,651	15,311	7,766	70,782
Finance	962	2,806	6,628	23,104	10,398	53,157	75,432[a]	172,537
Miscellaneous services	41,702[a]	5,996	11,924	11,348	43,777	36,143[a]	25,634	176,524
Lodging and meals	2,149[a]	138	416[a]	1,172	970	1,509	4,144[a]	10,498
Total	157,823	71,774	65,104	136,611	179,969	279,092	443,585	1,333,957

[a]Cell entries are based on interpolated data.

represents the total equity in a given sector held by individual households. Each column sum is the total equity owned by members of a given household class. The column sums appear puzzling at first glance in that stockownership by the Under $15,000 income class is more than twice the amount owned by either of the next two higher brackets. However, this is because of the fact that the lower bracket includes several times as many households as either of the other two, or as any of the other higher brackets. On a per household basis, the distribution of stock ownership follows the expected J shape—that is, the value of stock-ownership per household increases exponentially with income.

An analysis of table 6.3 supports our earlier hypothesis that the income distribution of stock ownership varies significantly across sectors and that a multisectoral analysis of stockownership and its associated dividend income flow is therefore warranted. Several sectors are characterized by a relatively even distribution of returns (see, e.g., communications and retail/wholesale trade). Several other sectors are characterized by concentration of ownership by the higher income groups (see, e.g., petroleum extraction, petroleum refining, fabricated metals, electrical equipment, and transportation equipment).[9]

The Dividend-Flows Matrix

Construction of the Matrix

The dividend-flows matrix was constructed as follows:

1. The stock ownership matrix was premultiplied by a diagonal matrix of price-dividend ratios (see table 6.1, column 1). This yielded a preliminary dividend-flows matrix.

2. The preliminary matrix was then balanced by the biproportional matrix adjustment method. Control totals for column elements were taken from the Internal Revenue Service's *Statistics of Income* table of dividends by adjusted gross income (IRS 1984a). Row control totals were derived by combining the NYSE stock value weights (see table 6.1, column 3) with the price-dividend ratios.

The total dividends calculated in the preliminary matrix were $66 billion, compared with the $54 billion sum of row control totals (recall table 4.2). The difference between the two figures is owing to a combination of underreporting[10] of income for tax purposes and errors caused by assumptions on our part such as the representativeness of NYSE listed stocks. Note also that the matrix adjustment computation was minimized by the fact that row and column control totals of the stock and dividend matrices were directly comparable.

Table 6.4. U.S. Dividend Distribution Matrix, 1982
(millions of 1982 dollars)

Sector	Under 15,000	15,000– 19,999	20,000– 24,999	25,000– 34,999	35,000– 49,999	50,000– 99,999	Over 100,000	Total
Agriculture and forestry	18	4	1	4	8	28	3	68
Mining	259	104	37	53	81	106	507	1,148
Petroleum extraction	28	23	15	89	94	98	324	670
Construction	196	77	31	52	79	152	339	925
Food and tobacco	796	192	49	205	373	1,261	155	3,031
Textiles	65	74	36	11	8	35	100	329
Lumber and furniture	16	6	2	6	15	17	12	73
Paper and printing	239	14	10	72	40	289	359	1,023
Chemicals	1,101	394	89	539	667	528	1,341	4,658
Petroleum refining	604	379	407	428	1,200	1,208	4,535	8,760
Rubber, stone, and glass	39	10	3	9	13	29	65	168
Fabricated metals	0	0	1	1	9	12	28	52
Machinery	52	91	15	191	72	431	34	885
Electric equipment	14	53	39	118	147	326	821	1,518
Transportation equipment	7	44	13	70	198	302	602	1,235
Miscellaneous manufacturing	12	4	1	6	3	8	15	50
Transportation	203	27	90	49	125	306	64	864
Communication	10	7	1	18	16	21	12	85
Utilities	1,442	834	1,208	2,111	2,292	2,462	4,652	15,001
Trade	339	241	105	310	318	436	194	1,944
Finance	50	119	254	944	454	2,422	3,023	7,266
Miscellaneous services	1,132	133	239	242	999	860	536	4,139
Lodging and meals	37	2	5	16	14	23	55	153
Total	6,659	2,832	2,649	5,544	7,224	11,361	17,776	54,045

Table 6.5. U.S. Dividend Coefficient Matrix, 1982

Sector	Under 15,000	15,000–19,999	20,000–24,999	25,000–34,999	35,000–49,999	50,000–99,999	Over 100,000	Total
Agriculture and forestry	.268	.063	.015	.064	.121	.417	.051	1.000
Mining	.226	.091	.032	.046	.070	.093	.442	1.000
Petroleum extraction	.042	.034	.022	.133	.141	.147	.483	1.000
Construction	.211	.083	.034	.056	.085	.164	.366	1.000
Food and tobacco	.263	.063	.016	.068	.123	.416	.051	1.000
Textiles	.197	.225	.110	.032	.023	.108	.305	1.000
Lumber and furniture	.217	.085	.022	.077	.206	.235	.158	1.000
Paper and printing	.233	.014	.010	.070	.039	.283	.351	1.000
Chemicals	.236	.085	.019	.116	.143	.113	.288	1.000
Petroleum refining	.069	.043	.046	.049	.137	.138	.518	1.000
Rubber, stone, and glass	.234	.057	.016	.054	.076	.174	.387	1.000
Fabricated metals	.006	.008	.014	.024	.181	.236	.531	1.000
Machinery	.058	.103	.017	.215	.081	.487	.038	1.000
Electric equipment	.009	.035	.025	.078	.097	.215	.541	1.000
Transportation equipment	.006	.035	.011	.057	.160	.244	.487	1.000
Miscellaneous manufacturing	.235	.082	.017	.126	.066	.163	.311	1.000
Transportation	.235	.031	.104	.057	.145	.353	.074	1.000
Communication	.122	.087	.013	.208	.188	.241	.141	1.000
Utilities	.096	.056	.081	.141	.153	.164	.310	1.000
Trade	.174	.124	.054	.159	.164	.224	.100	1.000
Finance	.007	.016	.035	.130	.063	.333	.416	1.000
Miscellaneous services	.273	.032	.058	.058	.241	.208	.129	1.000
Lodging and meals	.244	.013	.035	.104	.092	.150	.362	1.000
Total	.123	.052	.049	.103	.134	.210	.329	1.000

Presentation of the Matrix

A 23 × 7 matrix of the distribution of stock dividends by sector and income class of the economy is presented as table 6.4. A given cell of the table represents the total dividend paid out by a sector, as designated by the row headings, to a household income class, designated by the column headings. Row sums represent the total dividend payout by each of the twenty-three sectors, and column sums represent the total dividends received by each of the seven household income classes.

The relative proportions between cells in a given column are similar to those in table 6.3, because of the similarity of the relative proportions of the control totals between the two tables. This means that our major hypothesis about significant intersectoral differences in stockholdings holds for annual dividend payments as well. We can illustrate this point more clearly by translating table 6.4 into a standarized, or structural, coefficient table. The result of dividing each cell in a given row by the respective row's sum is presented as table 6.5.[11] From the table we can readily see, for example, that around 50 percent of the dividends from sectors such as petroleum extraction and electrical equipment flow to the highest household income bracket. Also, a comparison of tables 6.4 and 6.5, reveals that while the flow of dividends to households in the $15,000–$19,999 bracket is almost three times greater from food and tobacco than from the textile sector, the payout as a proportion of each sector's total dividends is more than four times greater from the textile sector than from food and tobacco.

Interpretation of the Results

Gini Coefficients

Various statistical measures have been formulated for characterizing distributions, though none is without its shortcomings (see, e.g., Atkinson 1975; Speaker 1985). We utilize two types of Gini coefficient (a one-parameter measure of income distribution that indicates the degree of income inequality on a scale of zero to one), acknowledging the inherent limitations of one-parameter measures. The first is based on a plotting of the cumulative percentage of dividend income against the cumulative percentage of stockholding households. The second plots the percentage of dividend income against the cumulative percentage of all income-earning households.

The first set of Gini coefficients may seem to be the more appropriate of the two at first glance, but it can be misleading. For example, assume that the only stockholders in a given sector are ten millionaires, who each receive $100,000 per year of dividends from that sector's earnings. The corresponding Gini coefficient would be equal to zero, reflecting the perfect equality of returns (to stockholders). At the same time, one can justifiably characterize the ownership of the sector in question as being dominated by the upper income classes and the situation as anything but egalitarian. The second measure reflects this high degree of concentration. For example, if the total number of income earners in the population were 1,000, the second Gini measure would reflect the fact that 1 percent of the relevant households received 100 percent of the dividend income.

The results of the Gini calculations are presented in table 6.6. The first pair of

Table 6.6. Gini Coefficients for the Distribution of Dividend Income

Sector	Stockholder Base Gini		Total Population Gini	
	Value	Rank	Value	Rank
Agriculture and forestry	.370	6	.464	3
Mining	.497	17	.524	10
Petroleum extraction	.452	15	.799	19
Construction	.346	5	.541	12
Food and tobacco	.375	8	.470	4
Textiles	.378	10	.417	1
Lumber and furniture	.423	12	.504	9
Paper	.534	19	.580	14
Chemicals	.420	11	.479	5
Petroleum refining	.505	18	.771	18
Rubber, stone and glass	.448	14	.542	13
Fabricated metals	.764	23	.912	23
Machinery	.225	3	.679	17
Electrical equipment	.546	20	.872	21
Transportation equipment	.592	22	.881	22
Miscellaneous manufacturing	.445	13	.492	8
Transportation	.083	1	.484	6
Communcation	.230	4	.596	15
Utilities	.377	9	.656	16
Wholesale and retail trade	.140	2	.486	7
Finance, insurance, and real estate	.556	21	.864	20
Miscellaneous services	.372	7	.445	2
Lodging and meals	.466	16	.531	11

columns pertain to the value and rank order respectively of Gini coefficients calculated on the basis of stockholders only. The second pair represent the corresponding information for calculations based on the entire income-earning population.

The lowest four stockholder Gini coefficients are for transportation, trade, machinery, and communication, and range from .083 to .230 in value (see columns 1 and 2 of table 6.6). Total population Ginis (column 3 of table 6.6) increase substantially in each case and there is a significant change in rank order for these four sectors. On the other hand, the rank order changes are minimal between the highest four Ginis in each category (i.e., the fabricated metals; transportation equipment; finance, insurance, and real estate; and electrical equipment sectors). The size of the coefficients does, however, change significantly from a range of .546 to .764 to a range of .864 to .912.

Note that for each sector, the second Gini coefficient has a higher value than the first. This is owing to the fact that lower income groups generally make up a relatively much larger proportion of the total population.[12] Accordingly, dividend returns are more concentrated in the context of the total population, though to different degrees across sectors. The reader can verify this by noting how the size of the increases in Gini coefficients is strongly influenced by the proportion of dividend income paid to lower income groups when one shifts from the stockholder base to the total base (compare the transportation sector with the paper sector).

The superiority of one Gini coefficient over the other appears to depend on the context. The stockholder Gini would be the most useful in predicting how stockholders in a given company might vote in a particular proxy battle. For example, given that socioeconomic background influences attitudes toward risk and return, a sector dominated by relatively low-income shareholders would be more prone to resist a major takeover effort. On the other hand, for an analysis of the impacts of government policies on national or regional income distribution, the total population Gini coefficient would be more appropriate. For example, expansion of sectors with relatively high Ginis would skew overall income distribution more.

Evaluation

Two ways to evaluate our results are to compare them with our prior expectations of the distribution of dividend returns and to examine the reasonableness of the assumptions invoked during the computational procedure. On both scores, the results appear to stand up well.

One would expect that sectors that offer stable low-risk returns would be attractive to lower income groups. From tables 6.3 through 6.5, we see that sectors such as transportation and trade have a fairly even distribution across income groups, which means that they are relatively skewed toward lower income groups in relation to the distribution of returns over all stocks (see the "Total" for rows of tables 6.4 and 6.5). On the other hand, one would expect that sectors that offer attractive capital-gain opportunities, but at some significant risk, or those sectors that offer tax advantages, would attract relatively more well-to-do investors. This is borne out by the mining, petroleum extraction, and the petroleum refining sectors in the tables. Some sectors, such as utilities, attract both types of investors owing to their stability and tax advantages, hence the distribution of their returns is bimodal.

Not surprisingly, we also find a strong correlation between Gini coefficients for income payouts (table 6.6) and industrial concentration as measured either by the market share of the eight largest firms in a sector or indices such as Gini coefficients for firm size distributions. For example, fabricated metals, transportation equipment, and finance have very high income-distribution Ginis, while the textile, food and tobacco, and trade Ginis rank relatively low. Distributional dynamics indicate a relatively greater accumulation of wealth over time by investors in sectors with higher than normal returns—that is, sectors composed of firms with significant market power.

Many of the assumptions invoked during the course of the computations were made on the basis of necessity, formal tests, or implicit "cost-benefit" analyses of improvements in accuracy that additional efforts to lessen the restrictiveness of the assumptions might yield. For example:

1. AGI was used as a proxy for household income for lack of a better substitute. In spite of its limitations, however, related studies using AGI have been rather successful (see Blume, Crockett, and Friend 1984).

2. The assumption regarding the allocation of missing stock values for diversified portfolios was chosen after comparing it with several other "weighting" schemes and finding little significant difference in the results.

3. The assumption regarding the equality of price-dividend ratios for stocks held outright vs. stocks held through mutual funds does not appear to warrant modification in light of the low proportion of mutual fund equity holdings in relation to total equity outstanding—less than 4 percent.

Thus, while our results are based on a limited sample and some restrictive assumptions, they are consistent with several prior hypotheses and represent as far an advance in the state of the art as the data allow. Those who are skeptical about the use of the fixed coefficient matrix (table 6.5) for predictive purposes should be comfortable with the stock and flow matrices (tables 6.3 and 6.4), which provide considerable insight into personal investment practices in the United States in 1982. We caution the reader to view the results "holistically" within a sector rather than to focus on any single cell entries, especially those based on interpolated data.

Conclusion

Our results indicate significant differences in the relative proportions of dividends going to various income classes across sectors. The results are generally consistent with a priori expectations, given differences in risk and return across sectors and differences in attitudes toward risk and return across income groups. But even though they are not surprising, the results offer a substantial improvement in precision over the "general tendencies" typically noted in the literature until now. The quantification of the distribution of dividend income will enable researchers to make stronger comparisons between sectors and to determine the extent to which the impacts of broad-based policies offset one another.

7 / The Total Income Distribution Matrix

This chapter is the culmination of the construction of a multisectoral model of income distribution. It presents the procedures used to construct the overall model and an analysis of the results at the national level for 1982. Much of the basis of the matrix of total income flows by sector of origin and income class of recipient stems from the wage and salary distribution presented in chapter 5 and the dividend distribution presented in chapter 6. These two submatrices must be merged and reconciled, however, and the remainder of the income payments must be added to them. The end-product of our empirical work represents one form of a Social Accounting Matrix (SAM), as discussed in chapter 4.

The following section provides a discussion of data and is brief because it depends primarily on data sets discussed in the previous two chapters. The subsequent sections establish control totals for property-type income by sector and show how the dividend matrix of chapter 6 can be used as a basis for distributing other components of capital-related income. The next section establishes control totals for wage/salary and pension/annuity income, and shows how the occupational category analysis of chapter 5 can be used to distribute these income types among household income classes and sectors. The wage and property components are then combined and the results presented as a distributional version of a national Social Accounting Matrix in the final section.

Data

Most of the data that go into the construction of our overall model are carried over from chapters 5 and 6. Thus the fact that the dividend and wage/salary distribution matrices are based on survey data provides a solid foundation for the SAM. The major additional data used to complete the model are primary data control totals for the several income types not yet estimated. In cases where an income type emanates from a single sector, as in the case of farm rental and mineral royalties, or stems from household financial activities, as in the case of asset sales and estate income, these control totals are all that is needed. For several other income types, further estimation is required.

Income bracket control totals were obtained from the *1982 Statistics of Income: Individual Income Tax Returns*, or *SOI* (IRS 1984a). Economic sectoral control totals for selected income types were obtained from the *1982 Statistics of Income: Corporation Income Tax Returns* (IRS 1984b). These publications are produced annually by the Internal Revenue Service from a large sample of tax returns. We, therefore, consider them the most accurate data on income received that is presented according to the income bracket of the recipient.

Property Income Distribution Matrices

Estimation

Property income types other than dividends can be divided into three groups on the basis of their role in an I-O table (recall table 4.2 and figure 4.3). The first, and most straightforward to estimate, are income payments associated with household financial activities, which include sales of capital assets, rental income, and estate income. This is not to say, for example, that every rental payment in the economy is included in this category, but only those payments flowing to individual (nonbusiness) landlords. Rental payments from one business to another or from a consumer to a business are not a part of personal income. They are simply business (intermediate sector) revenues. There are, of course, direct rental payments from business to individuals, but they are likely to be a very small portion of the total rental payments.[1] A similar pattern holds for income derived from the sale of capital assets. No further estimation is necessary for the income distribution of these payments, because a single vector, consisting of payments of each income type is available in IRS (1984a).

The second subcategory of property income pertains to payments from individual sectors. The two most obvious ones are farm income and farm rental income. Again, single vectors for each are available from the *SOI*. Since there are four agricultural sectors in the IMPLAN classification, the $9.8 billion of farm losses and $2.2 billion of farm rental income were further apportioned on the basis of weights calculated according to relative levels of preliminary estimates of 1982 gross outputs (Bureau of Labor Statistics 1985). Royalty income was assigned to the six mining sectors in the same manner. Note, of course, that a small proportion of royalty income emanates from publishing and some from various other sectors in payment for access to inventions. These income payments can be separated out at a later date if data become available.

The final subcategory includes interest income and income from business and professions, partnerships, and small corporations. In the absence of other information on indi-

Table 7.1. Household Financial Activities Income Distribution Matrix, 1982
(millions of 1982 dollars)

Income Class	Sale of Capital Assets	Rental Income	Estate Income	Total Income
Under 5000	2,816	−2,485	157	488
5,000–9,999	573	−408	193	358
10,000–14,999	863	−431	247	679
15,000–19,999	544	−680	202	66
20,000–24,999	574	−1,352	234	−544
25,000–34,999	1,647	−1,784	550	413
35,000–49,999	2,369	−1,196	845	2,018
50,000–74,999	2,947	−790	773	2,929
75,000–99,999	2,040	−208	496	2,327
Over 100,000	20,030	856	2,052	22,937
Total	34,404	−8,478	5,746	31,672

vidual sectors at this time, these income types, which amounted to only 11 percent of AGI in 1982, are distributed *across income groups* in the same proportions as dividend income. The distribution of interest income *across sectors,* however, is based on primary data (IRS 1984b). The sectoral distribution for the three other categories is equivalent to that of dividends owing to lack of other reliable data. It is difficult to assess the direction of any biases introduced by our procedures.

Presentation of the Results

The distributions of the various capital-related income payments other than dividends are found in tables 7.1, 7.2, and 7.3. Table 7.1 contains the individual distribution vectors for the household financial activity payments, and clearly shows a significant difference between the three categories. Table 7.2 gives the industry specific payments for agriculture and mining. Note that several of these payments result in net losses for certain income classes. Not surprisingly, losses are typically, though not universally, incurred by lower income groups.

In table 7.3, the relative proportions of income within a given sector are the same as for the dividend income data upon which they are based. Again, for the purpose of exposition, the rows and columns of table 7.3 are a transposed version of our previous format (i.e., rows are sectors and columns are income classes). The sector designations have been expanded to conform to the IMPLAN sectoring scheme,[2] and the number of income categories has been increased from seven to ten.

Table 7.4 shows the distribution of total capital-related income. The overall capital payments of the farm sector are dominated by farm and farm rental income and are rendered somewhat more equal than previously on a total flow per income class basis. On a per household basis however, farm rental and farm income collectively are relatively concentrated in the middle to higher income levels. The distribution of capital-type income returns in mining is highly influenced by royalties, since their $6.3 billion sum represents more than 52 percent of the total capital-related income emanating from the mining industry. This influence causes an even more pronounced skewness toward higher income groups in the sector, with the brunt of the effect in the $100,000 + bracket (see also table 7.2). Finally, the payments associated with household financial activities contain some interesting anomalies with regard to the bottom income bracket's rather sizeable sale of capital assets, the negative total for the fifth bracket, and the sizeable total for the tenth bracket.

Table 7.2. Farm, Farm Rental, and Royalty Income Distribution Matrix, 1982
(millions of 1982 dollars)

Income Class	Farm Income	Farm Rental Income	Royalty Income
Under 5000	−7,867	−67	252
5,000–9,999	−433	136	142
10,000–14,999	−416	359	227
15,000–19,999	−161	178	210
20,000–24,999	−201	220	261
25,000–34,999	−75	445	347
35,000–49,999	126	574	705
50,000–74,999	31	139	746
75,000–99,999	19	65	370
Over 100,000	−859	129	3,059
Total	−9,834	2,178	6,319

Table 7.3. All Other Capital-Related Income Distribution Matrix for the United States, 1982 (millions of 1982 dollars)

		UNDER $5000	5000-9999	10000-14999	15000-19999	20000-24999	25000-34999	35000-49999	50000-74999	75000-99999	OVER 100000	TOTAL
01	LIVESTOCK PRODUCTS	12	147	171	61	13	66	66	66	31	68	604
02	OTHER AGRICULTURAL PRODUCTS	16	186	217	77	17	87	87	87	33	81	765
03	FORESTRY AND FISHERY PRODUCTS	1	315	35	12	1	3	13	13	3	1	761
04	AGRICULTURAL SERVICES	1	30	24	9	1	13	14	8	3	19	123
05	IRON AND FERRALLOY MINING	-168	227	252	128	003	1062	148	647	317	1	1
06	NONFERROUS METAL MINING	-208	279	310	138	103	476	517	557	311	316	95
07	COAL MINING	-223	421	345	231	115	425	127	127	87	236	195
08	OIL AND GAS EXTRACTION	-122	588	345	148	105	314	103	153	803	431	1603
09	STONE AND CLAY MINING	-123	538	620	396	145	250	250	153	335	287	160
10	CHEMICAL AND FERTILIZER MINING	-890	532	256	227	160	103	103	153	335	283	2072
11	NEW CONSTRUCTION	-890	1451	1648	762	162	1583	1040	1040	1120	1116	250
12	MAINTENANCE AND REPAIR	-246	1170	1695	797	160	994	915	1027	554	1202	138
13	FOOD AND KINDRED PRODUCTS	-89	1211	1102	188	188	443	144	163	598	137	2484
14	TOBACCO MANUFACTURERS	-46	120	132	189	143	144	144	24	54	56	138
15	FABRICS AND YARN	-67	128	257	114	24	19	163	6	13	31	1019
16	MISCELLANEOUS TEXTILES	-27	127	123	214	21	178	53	59	28	57	537
17	FABRICS AND YARN	-1	182	217	300	108	59	463	112	62	310	169
18	APPAREL	1	60	73	43	163	59	59	112	617	100	732
19	FABRICATED TEXTILES	-104	260	246	344	164	199	273	142	117	132	1036
20	LUMBER AND WOOD PRODUCTS	-134	216	305	275	234	199	273	273	102	137	913
21	WOOD CONTAINERS	-341	301	303	375	235	273	273	275	123	161	207
22	HOUSEHOLD FURNITURE	-653	914	3033	630	428	582	273	275	823	451	249
23	OTHER FURNITURE	-397	595	3063	407	182	315	469	923	743	166	309
24	PAPER AND ALLIED PRODUCTS	-741	558	1145	1385	1247	2811	2814	991	513	250	2543
25	PRINTING AND PUBLISHING	2	312	316	1387	1247	824	2814	961	563	3124	12367
26	CHEMICAL PRODUCTS	3	448	664	214	102	18	18	12	6	18	194
27	PLASTICS	-2	157	152	269	159	287	316	122	152	24	2220
28	DRUGS	2	208	132	266	390	273	222	116	153	254	809
29	PAINTS AND ALLIED PRODUCTS	-1	109	1	1	100	78	78	88	139	1485	598
30	RUBBER AND MISC PRODUCTS	0	2	3	6	6	0	47	29	13	308	1221
31	LEATHER	-45	224	225	72	111	45	78	28	13	308	192
32	FOOTWEAR	-77	242	256	175	111	81	36	68	345	44	352
33	GLASS PRODUCTS	-17	350	420	153	117	74	50	130	66	247	686
34	STONE AND CLAY PRODUCTS	-85	188	290	124	182	81	55	155	590	475	686
35	IRON AND STEEL	-102	184	801	660	205	68	309	107	588	59	298
36	NONFERROUS METALS	-21	44	444	578	445	57	309	114	74	475	382
37	METAL CONTAINERS	-12	111	230	228	188	719	39	39	38	154	559
38	FABRICATED METAL PRODUCTS	-12	113	192	121	797	665	103	74	35	1411	523
39	SCREW MACHINE PRODUCTS	-11	170	192	128	189	921	48	68	317	169	1258
40	OTHER FABRICATED METAL PRODUCTS	-11	174	192	280	179	143	34	183	185	208	258
41	ENGINES AND TURBINES	-1	32	377	367	182	205	205	85	75	298	1094
42	FARM MACHINERY	0	0	0	0	100	958	294	411	477	767	650
43	CONSTRUCTION MACHINERY	19	852	1237	332	209	213	213	608	257	1805	3720
44	MATERIAL HANDLING MACHINERY	-100	822	425	520	109	269	269	448	88	325	327
45	SPECIAL MACHINERY	-136	908	425	491	791	388	231	170	89	224	365
46	GENERAL MACHINERY	-48	1070	835	479	767	446	730	730	280	299	54
47	MISCELLANEOUS MACHINERY	-8	395	394	500	190	595	595	218	207	948	3048
48	SERVICE MACHINERY	-178	2463	2786	2891	3788	5478	5478	2048	1173	3370	26734
49	ELECTRICAL MACHINERY	-363	2665	3471	3054	5413	4148	4148	2371	1568	4406	26208
50	HOUSEHOLD APPLIANCES	-66	7440	3420	3094	5993	6705	6705	4855	4866	10071	54047
51	ELECTRICAL EQUIPMENT	-513	1208	1267	367	445	1278	1258	364	368	2010	5816
52	LIGHTING AND WIRING EQUIPMENT	-544	1093	1267	255	445	254	254	364	19	193	4784
53	COMMUNICATION EQUIPMENT	-172	1903	4135	180	331	475	475	338	58	73	756
54	RADIO AND TELEVISION	-21	304	415	800	391	387	387	108	56	60	1547
55	OTHER GOVERNMENT	-680	744	835	183	297	194	194	302	177	166	3190
56	FEDERAL GOVERNMENT	0	0	0	0	0	0	0	0	0	0	0
82	TOTAL CONSUMPTION	-7035	19373	22202	20160	19247	31651	33126	26276	13037	28413	206451

Table 7.4. Total Capital-Related Income Distribution Matrix for the United States, 1982 (millions of 1982 dollars)

#	Industry	UNDER $5000	5000–9999	10000–14999	15000–19999	20000–24999	25000–34999	35000–49999	50000–74999	75000–99999	OVER 100000	TOTAL
01	LIVESTOCK PRODUCTS	-3071	34	151	69	21	176	342	177	68	-2756	-2347
02	OTHER AGRICULTURAL PRODUCTS	-3890	43	192	887	22	218	435	114	87	-2768	-2277
03	FORESTRY AND FISHERY PRODUCTS	-266	37	135	26		213	52	14		-1528	2237
04	AGRICULTURAL SERVICES	-110	28	35	248	118	120	227	168	19	179	229
05	IRON & FERROALLOY MINING	-131	358	415	328	358	150	178	207	115	1034	379
06	NONFERROUS METAL MINING	-257	257	486	368	328	741	1178	843	404	3209	7663
07	COAL MINING	-89	586	677	450	167	306	302	223	118	1116	5694
08	CRUDE PETROLEUM AND GAS	-36	241	259	185	69	178	125	223	145	1523	3329
09	STONE AND CLAY MINING										2148	3137
10	CHEMICAL AND FERTILIZER MINING					69	73	306	911			1287
11	NEW CONSTRUCTION	-705	1750	1949	879	2006	656	1216	1851	1017	220	9005
12	MAINTENANCE AND REPAIR	-113	196	2115	2127	2215	675	114	125	81	220	9405
13	ORDNANCE	-113			212	135		20	13	13	174	741
14	FOOD AND KINDRED PRODUCTS	-204	1302	1351	2672	130	24	204	5	28	103	203
15	TOBACCO MANUFACTURERS	17	132	441	132	311	61	187	36	19	109	885
16	FABRICS AND YARN	17	631	592	435	10	206	62	22	108	38	975
17	MISCELLANEOUS TEXTILES	-65	248	282	319	205	197	501	184	101	210	3261
18	APPAREL	-81	369	471	161	28	186	617	253	108	257	12005
19	MISC FABRICATED TEXTILES	-1021	1098	1244	350	27	177	186	377	138	348	17003
20	WOOD CONTAINERS	-1524	1088	1244	24	163	2730	1093	1133	212	1395	6427
21	WOOD PRODUCTS	-317	667	756	519	108	470	664	229	129	680	2271
22	HOUSEHOLD FURNITURE	-56	1117	1213	1644	1657	1251	4002	1768	723	1120	3905
23	OTHER FURNITURE	-596	3223	3176	14421		1949		936		7152	21687
24	PAPER AND ALLIED PRODUCTS	261		146					31	37		21350
25	PAPER CONTAINERS AND BOXES	13	49	58	221	61	112	17	121	67	23	207
26	PRINTING AND PUBLISHING	3	54	164	63	39	209	347	188	181	278	600
27	CHEMICALS	-2	10	12	11	10	31	24	4	54	208	810
28	PLASTICS			3				9	98	30	1	64
29	DRUGS	-3	2	3	84	84	91	76	29	29	55	211
30	PAINTS AND ALLIED PRODUCTS	-3	2	17	83	112	107	48	18	13	52	200
31	PETROLEUM REFINING	-13	24	215	371	26	97	84	97	51	62	435
32	RUBBER AND MISC PRODUCTS	-11	28	255	130	9	185	191	189	100	88	869
33	LEATHER	-15	118	112	137	29	10	45	143	23	132	693
34	FOOTWEAR	-13	138	247	147	102	26	197	1512	28	17	197
35	GLASS PRODUCTS	-15	411	247	140	213	185	36	1622	43	112	376
36	STONE AND CLAY PRODUCTS	-2	269	311	99	145	91	72	109	86	139	742
37	IRON AND STEEL	1	94	105	69	146	191	129	14	58	297	1014
38	NONFERROUS METALS	-1			64	43	83	117	97	55	237	728
39	METAL CONTAINERS	-1	94		322	211	58	58	48	25	123	328
40	FABRICATED METAL PRODUCTS	-1	18	213	326	94	411	248	266	128	320	1368
41	SCREW MACHINE PRODUCTS	-2	213	213	385	54	104	104	1222	268	1045	384
42	OTHER FABRICATED METAL PRODUCTS	-2	347	398	887	140	335	157	147	278	1024	3854
43	ENGINES AND TURBINES	-1	3	84	39	107	85	552	552	88	354	1085
44	FARM MACHINERY	1	86	107	141	24	38	24	163	489	1169	2491
45	MATERIAL HANDLING MACHINERY	5	3	195	110	110	170	24	70	28	28	358
46	METAL WORKING MACHINERY	5	83	118	52	213	118	188	188	188	28	368
47	SPECIAL MACHINERY	2	91	116	268	877	447	748	748	310	158	5984
48	GENERAL MACHINERY	1	1141	1318	498	879	295	858	230	388	109	3121
49	MISCELLANEOUS MACHINERY	-51	398	1464	480	880	589	604	2307	107		
50	OFFICE MACHINERY	-1413	2964	3747	3837	4927	6295	7798	3637	2043	8016	40146
51	SERVICE MACHINERY	-1	2963	3350	3837	4967	6259	7090	3090	2043	8010	20136
52	ELECTRICAL MACHINERY	-37	2371	3432	3174	3043	2163	3461	5634	2681	5958	29985
53	HOUSEHOLD APPLIANCES	-16	752	802	161	6141	12757	7091	11407	5429	12063	59699
54	LIGHTING AND WIRING EQUIPMENT	-425	1278	1457	3119	549	357	1685	543	421	991	6569
55	COMMUNICATION EQUIPMENT	-2	201	234	94	515	857	598	585	330	420	6821
56	ELECTRONIC COMPONENTS	-52	400	345	194	158	186	146	146	94	104	1480
57	MISC ELECTRICAL EQUIPMENT	-548	929	1046	69	114	184	488	115	90	173	1427
58	MOTOR VEHICLES AND EQUIPMENT				245	409	307	1447	562	320	418	5135
80	SCRAP AND MISCELLANEOUS	-482	358	671	66	-540	412	2003	2930	2305	22917	31603
81	HOUSEHOLD CONSUMPTION	-12565	21915	25708	23286	21631	38325	43773	37466	19835	71456	290830
82	TOTAL	-12565	21915	25708	23286	21631	38325	43773	37466	19835	71456	290830

Wage-related Income

Estimation

Of all the income types, only pensions and annuities were assumed to be similar to the income distribution of wage and salaries. In the case of pensions, the rationale for the link to wages and salary income is best stated in terms of the definition used in the *SOI:* "Generally, pensions represented periodic income received after retirement and made in consideration of past services with an employer" (IRS 1984a, p. 95). Annuities are defined in the same source as income "in consideration of a specific premium." Some bias is introduced in our estimation, however, since annuities are often not obtained from employers. Thus, they are more likely to be based on total income as opposed to just the wage and salary portion. The *SOI* groups the two categories together, and data are unavailable for further refinement.[3] Also, the distribution of pensions and annuities among sectors is based on primary data from the *Statistics of Income for Coporations* (IRS 1984b).

Results

The combined wage/salary and pension/annuity distribution matrix is presented in table 7.5. Note that the table differs in format from that of table 5.5 in that the number of sectors has been expanded from forty-one to the eighty sectors of the IMPLAN classification.

The results are very similar to those of chapter 5 because pensions and annuities represent only about 3 percent of total income. Not only is the flows matrix relatively unaltered, therefore, but the coefficients matrix does not change at all.[4]

Total Personal Income Distribution

Tables 7.4 and 7.5 are combined (added) in table 7.6 to yield a matrix of the distribution of total personal income for the United States.[5] In addition, a coefficient version of the matrix is presented as table 7.7, where each element of table 7.6 is divided by its corresponding row sum. Our desired v_{kj} matrix is presented as table 7.8, which was computed by dividing each element of a given sector (reading across a row in the transposed matrix) by its corresponding 1982 total gross output.

The reader will note that the sum of the column and row sums or the intersection of row 82 and column 11 of table 7.6 equals the total reported gross income itemized by income type in chapter 4. One can readily see the relative prominence of each sector's contribution to personal income by reading down column 11, and one can see the economywide distribution of income by reading across row 82 in tables 7.6 and 7.7. One important, and not unexpected, result is also immediately evident. The economywide distribution of total personal income is much more even than that of dividend income reported in chapter 6. However, this improvement in the Gini coefficient for the economy is owing to the relative shift of proportions of non-dividend income from the upper income brackets *and* the lower income brackets[6] toward the middle and upper-middle income range (i.e., \$25,000–\$50,000). The major reason for the more even distribution is the influence of wage and salary income (and pensions and annuities), which is fairly evenly distributed in most sectors.

Gini coefficients for individual sectors are shown in table 7.9. The range of values extends from a low of .2352 in sector 72, lodging and personal services, to a high of .6390 in sector 2, other agriculture products.[7] In practically every case, the total income Gini is lower than the corresponding sector Gini for dividend income presented in Chapter 6. In

Table 7.5. Wage/Salary and Pension/Annuity Income Distribution Matrix for the United States, 1982 (millions of 1982 dollars)

		UNDER $5000	5000– 9999	10000– 14999	15000– 19999	20000– 24999	25000– 34999	35000– 49999	50000– 74999	75000– 99999	OVER 100000	TOTAL	
001	LIVESTOCK PRODUCTS	847	1476	1297	1113	921	1295	1049	483	169	319	9070	1
002	OTHER AGRICULTURAL PRODUCTS	1073	1809	1631	1167	1601	1601	812	612	217	404	11486	2
003	FORESTRY AND FISHERY PRODUCTS	86	167	147	123	198	231	106	98	34	27	1877	3
004	AGRICULTURAL, FORESTRY SERVICES	170	325	268	247	288	286	282	90	46	65	1847	4
005	IRON FERROALLOY MINING	16	20	17	14	10	145	138	300	18	120	3370	5
006	NONFERROUS METAL MINING	12	31	48	44	61	101	16	88	40	47	630	6
007	COAL MINING	122	313	482	516	571	1003	1041	508	478	147	24741	7
008	OIL AND GAS EXTRACTION	658	1713	2611	2780	3049	5003	5630	2948	425	796	25887	8
009	STONE AND CLAY MINING	125	305	410	197	197	297	606	246	67	217	589	9
010	CHEM. AND FERTILIZER MINING	35	58	105	125	126	126	41	11	4	6	546	10
011	NEW CONSTRUCTION	1662	4135	6270	6848	7545	12457	12794	4791	864	1623	60576	11
012	MAINTENANCE AND REPAIR	822	1758	2577	2684	3032	5721	5247	2355	697	660	24874	12
013	ORDNANCE	368	689	1031	1048	1053	1063	950	343	129	666	33385	13
014	FOOD AND KINDRED PRODUCTS	8027	2497	3483	3068	4037	7884	7025	2433	527	978	34368	14
015	TOBACCO MANUFACTURERS	236	107	195	495	246	211	293	187	44	129	3385	15
016	FABRICS MANUFACTURERS	277	610	1079	914	1186	2106	1350	294	94	145	8708	16
017	MISCELLANEOUS TEXTILES	317	235	358	313	355	589	537	230	91	176	2706	17
018	APPAREL	346	1213	1381	1014	1583	2810	1980	688	122	245	12008	18
019	MISC. FABRICATED TEXTILES	357	1430	1457	1262	1584	2453	2423	801	157	242	12577	19
020	LUMBER AND WOOD PRODUCTS	51	159	187	189	253	207	243	92	27	13	4168	20
021	HOUSEHOLD FURNITURE	359	289	485	492	520	969	809	522	193	744	3360	21
022	OTHER FURNITURE	321	1951	3591	4007	4220	7269	2683	193	193	361	13593	22
023	PAPER AND ALLIED PRODUCTS	3902	2517	3567	3997	5200	6251	5751	2262	655	1009	13543	23
024	PAPER CONTAINERS AND BOXES	622	1621	3052	2433	2647	3067	4208	1429	430	1001	24541	24
025	PRINTING AND PUBLISHING	3100	3566	4663	4503	5503	9330	5046	1628	475	1303	13090	25
026	PLASTICS PRODUCTS	1187	516	795	806	993	1193	2053	905	227	148	5845	26
027	DRUGS, PAINTS AND ALLIED PRODUCTS	333	1917	1761	1527	2173	4351	3788	1502	237	3327	8853	27
028	PETROLEUM REFINING	422	1007	1842	1815	1356	2351	3611	279	279	519	17559	28
029	RUBBER AND MISC PRODUCTS	106	302	475	467	535	536	948	32	69	105	14393	29
030	LEATHER	9	21	40	48	73	69	93	51	13	40	442	30
031	FOOTWEAR	46	275	401	541	423	422	207	197	52	72	1081	31
032	GLASS PRODUCTS	240	845	1015	1081	1223	1622	3865	965	353	805	10834	32
033	STONE AND CLAY PRODUCTS	394	722	1265	1002	1994	2431	2277	802	267	353	15834	33
034	IRON AND STEEL	287	1723	2563	1365	1475	2412	3312	2724	279	720	15834	34
035	NONFERROUS METALS	262	1023	563	1007	1653	2622	1623	1439	165	429	40452	35
036	METAL CONTAINERS	26	308	380	954	1044	1358	1225	685	142	289	5638	36
037	HEATING, PLUMBING PRODUCTS	209	258	870	428	1084	1030	1017	842	187	164	8938	37
038	SCREW MACHINE PRODUCTS	193	521	399	443	461	1215	1080	870	870	564	8335	38
039	OTHER FABRICATED METAL PRODUCTS	181	611	777	861	1002	1513	2047	561	561	348	18260	39
040	ENGINES AND TURBINES	174	221	1037	990	1063	1506	1785	170	131	211	17948	40
041	FARM MACHINERY	156	438	633	738	886	1896	1681	1735	250	259	6373	41
042	CONSTRUCTION MACHINERY	155	284	905	738	858	1769	1755	185	139	1139	18837	42
043	MATERIAL HANDLING MACHINERY	100	592	684	906	1409	2407	1602	1525	145	269	16837	43
044	METALWORKING MACHINERY	211	230	447	764	1678	1702	1702	1252	152	811	7585	44
045	SPECIAL MACHINERY	177	226	347	577	874	871	874	766	321	1430	3787	45
046	GENERAL MACHINERY	782	955	859	1092	1837	3728	3550	1483	395	1439	5736	46
047	OFFICE MACHINERY	327	557	1537	1937	3082	2921	2881	881	372	3564	29428	47
048	SERVICE MACHINERY	192	593	1355	3652	3962	5440	4824	2287	206	604	12281	48
049	ELECTRICAL APPARATUS	528	1003	1553	1795	2096	2185	2184	896	184	5749	29428	49
050	HOUSEHOLD APPLIANCES	363	446	703	707	950	1585	896	565	128	338	8678	50
051	ELECTRIC LIGHTING AND WIRING EQUIPMENT	153	638	645	687	797	795	1448	550	129	248	6598	51
052	RADIO AND TELEVISION	182	518	7580	7819	778	1542	1448	435	135	1278	6631	52
053	COMMUNICATION EQUIPMENT	578	1243	2422	2422	3526	8723	7046	3542	821	1407	68031	53
054	ELECTRONIC COMPONENTS	1578	1435	1840	1499	3520	3520	12490	5432	132	1237	51790	54
055	MISC. MANUFACTURING	8709	17559	22691	25678	26703	54703	57430	22769	1237	11688	250673	55
056	TRANSPORTATION AND WAREHOUSING	1768	14231	14751	25878	28780	54288	53750	22703	6234	12920	250671	56
057	COMMUNICATIONS	1986	2081	3890	5890	5028	3028	14432	227864	2606	2145	34080	57
058	RADIO, TV BROADCASTING	1582	2584	5543	5891	6492	15882	15082	25364	2314	1438	34797	58
059	ELECTRIC, GAS, WATER SERVICES	1549	2783	2545	2314	4534	13216	13391	18022	2002	4368	34368	59
060	WHOLESALE AND RETAIL TRADE	2495	14739	21846	14997	16418	33437	32091	13891	1607	1904	20335	60
061	FINANCE AND INSURANCE	578	1150	1840	1497	1641	3331	3091	998	302	302	21164	61
062	REAL ESTATE AND RENTAL	5874	11960	11560	14999	24694	26924	15460	15287	1237	1476	135712	62
063	HOTELS, PERSONAL SERVICES	2852	699	1121	12557	12557	32779	11590	15267	778	770	138712	63
064	BUSINESS SERVICES	2844	1215	1121	1132	137	282	276	117	60	330	52712	64
080	OTHER GOVERNMENT	57	57	57	57	57	57	57	57	57	57	801	80
081	SCRAP AND MISCELLANEOUS											286	81
082	HOUSEHOLD CONSUMPTION											82	82
	TOTAL	47116	109227	154307	162862	179901	350614	348837	150418	42480	79356	1625118	

Table 7.6. Total Income Distribution Matrix for the United States, 1982 (millions of 1982 dollars)

		UNDER $5000	5000–9999	10000–14999	15000–19999	20000–24999	25000–34999	35000–49999	50000–74999	75000–99999	OVER 100000	TOTAL
01	LIVESTOCK PRODUCTS	-2217	1510	1449	1282	1421	1472	1391	623	237	43	6723
02	AGRICULTURAL PRODUCTS	-2817	1914	1847	1630	1730	1761	1761	783	304	54	8510
03	FORESTRY AND FISHERY PRODUCTS	-225	358	271	266	195	349	203	127	48	9	1598
04	AGRICULTURAL SERVICES	1	503	163	112	945	497	204	145	45	11	1009
05	IRON AND FERROALLOY MINING	-19	930	1197	844	1650	1317	1375	788	129	91	7599
06	NONFERROUS METAL MINING	832	6759	2947	3169	3709	6648	6757	2850	189	153	3341
07	COAL MINING	178	1959	4197	167	3147	1628	1268	1628	829	3926	1884
08	OIL AND GAS EXTRACTION	1753	4970	7998	7393	7712	4125	13098	4516	982	2140	63713
09	STONE AND CLAY MINING	65	2034	2938	3037	110	5077	8288	3846	1075	1807	4592
10	CHEMICAL AND FERTILIZER MINING	178	4188	5470	4497	4240	8502	8288	3846	1545	1236	4293
11	NEW CONSTRUCTION	213	273	1700	1257	1102	4308	1638	1107	269	66	2907
12	MAINTENANCE AND REPAIR	267	2441	1308	1381	1582	2678	1538	733	279	279	1289
13	ORDNANCE	297	1209	1263	1316	1148	3009	2625	1488	127	345	1289
14	FOOD AND KINDRED PRODUCTS	375	1269	1088	1623	1195	2957	2627	872	188	105	1350
15	TOBACCO MANUFACTURERS	1207	1420	5480	4450	5213	3792	3030	651	295	84	4493
16	FABRICS AND YARN	2407	1177	4530	4405	4612	4886	2750	2995	617	188	3402
17	MISCELLANEOUS TEXTILES	257	1328	2705	2456	4922	4886	5131	3133	782	617	4303
18	APPAREL	5212	1948	3899	3091	2923	5768	6308	2463	881	1757	25851
19	MISC FABRICATED TEXTILES	-135	1488	2552	9609	1093	14053	10797	8088	168	158	27419
20	LUMBER AND WOOD PRODUCTS	-1229	1801	1385	1385	1089	4340	1339	1097	187	602	12758
21	WOOD CONTAINERS	-123	1403	3773	531	3786	5430	7787	3110	189	187	38649
22	HOUSEHOLD FURNITURE	-174	2421	3135	817	5572	11320	7788	3415	1272	8293	57453
23	OTHER FURNITURE	135	6225	3773	3541	211	217	1423	16	1072	2820	3893
24	PAPER AND ALLIED PRODUCTS	209	330	1305	457	1243	3985	3663	1907	107	175	4388
25	PAPER CONTAINERS AND BOXES	247	3350	1471	1457	12303	27985	3602	2150	2845	563	10981
26	PRINTING AND PUBLISHING	2907	1180	1726	1357	4255	2848	2327	1200	2910	567	16658
27	CHEMICALS	-67	1495	2877	3057	13490	26915	3685	888	1850	101	12658
28	PLASTICS	223	897	945	1015	25092	28481	6453	228	1504	5417	5270
29	DRUGS	210	2618	8935	9609	11552	6945	21261	7714	1261	1316	5738
30	PAINTS AND ALLIED PRODUCTS	287	6278	5997	757	11093	1093	1099	497	155	1099	4767
31	PETROLEUM REFINING	89	5597	4427	5224	15124	11127	1894	498	138	169	9589
32	RUBBER AND MISC PRODUCTS	174	1425	839	1025	5525	1161	2134	994	270	169	2745
33	LEATHER	175	1184	661	233	1026	1517	1885	276	215	2143	2189
34	GLASS PRODUCTS	197	3103	6441	8148	4449	1922	1922	1442	2617	1833	8221
35	STONE AND CLAY PRODUCTS	207	603	7633	878	3799	1248	1822	840	2150	656	5319
36	IRON AND STEEL	177	678	9168	568	5690	2498	2507	1021	846	456	10946
37	NONFERROUS METALS	178	2307	2471	1070	12552	2421	3944	1311	768	268	4095
38	METAL CONTAINERS	778	2330	3427	3405	1555	3923	3944	1002	393	268	4095
39	FABRICATED METAL PRODUCTS	196	578	3472	1018	1928	3915	2376	1688	1133	673	10448
40	OTHER FABRICATED METAL PRODUCTS	566	3822	2338	3395	1144	2913	9211	1003	2569	1031	5758
41	ENGINES AND TURBINES	538	1081	2401	2882	2819	5901	6050	6351	595	1162	20252
42	FARM MACHINERY	162	1532	1457	1834	807	2624	15806	2970	1137	266	7141
43	CONSTRUCTION MACHINERY	1693	5618	7761	739	938	1589	15889	5682	1134	3199	8968
44	MATERIAL HANDLING MACHINERY	1095	1299	8887	8747	3576	16830	14449	5676	1152	2600	8298
45	SPECIAL MACHINERY	1008	6841	3799	3576	9570	3435	18687	3578	1585	3109	35615
46	GENERAL MACHINERY	-1394	20924	25857	29500	28219	56830	56831	24953	11254	12788	27011
47	MISC NONELEC MACHINERY	-8726	20942	22086	28219	120671	157667	56831	26953	14311	127134	270716
48	MACHINERY	1723	3024	6640	18911	13745	15202	109000	36935	14679	13799	115666
49	ELECTRIC INDUSTRIAL EQUIPMENT	2631	2819	27259	8911	17997	25097	35664	23215	4659	135662	21889
50	HOUSEHOLD APPLIANCES	1500	2481	27259	12031	19797	34645	17065	1525	1012	21288	21889
51	ELECTRIC LIGHTING	192	1141	1556	15556	17797	3551	3278	1164	2503	4659	13802
52	RADIO AND TV	1028	1273	1405	1797	3576	18483	35435	2500	2503	1012	15647
53	COMMUNICATION EQUIPMENT	-1001	1299	6281	2278	1628	21463	30137	14310	2149	15254	35677
54	ELECTRONIC COMPONENTS	-1394	26842	10042	11048	28069	301371	301137	14314	9585	12788	26011
55	MISC ELECTRICAL MACHINERY	8726	6936	1242	1527	1629	30157	301657	24953	893	127795	270134
56	MOTOR VEHICLES	-8723	22616	2640	1540	1540	282	3279	24953	1593	1758	21738
57	AIRCRAFT AND PARTS	2854	991	671	1132	-540	282	203	4084	4084	73333	1286
58	OTHER TRANSPORTATION EQUIPMENT	4452	131358	180671	186148	201532	388612	392610	187884	62315	150812	1935949
59	SCIENTIFIC INSTRUMENTS		131141	180015		388939						

Table 7.7. Total Income Coefficient Matrix for the United States, 1982

	UNDER $5000	5000–9999	10000–14999	15000–19999	20000–24999	25000–34999	35000–49999	50000–74999	75000–99999	OVER 10000	TOTAL
01 LIVESTOCK PRODUCTS											
02 OTHER AGRICULTURAL PRODUCTS											
03 FORESTRY AGRICULTURAL PRODUCTS											
04 AGRICULTURAL SERVICES											
05 IRON & FERROALLOY MINING											
06 NONFERROUS METAL MINING											
07 COAL MINING											
08 CRUDE PETROLEUM & NATURAL GAS											
09 STONE AND CLAY MINING											
10 CHEMICAL AND FERTILIZER MINING											
11 NEW CONSTRUCTION											
12 MAINTENANCE AND REPAIR											
13 ORDNANCE											
14 FOOD AND KINDRED PRODUCTS											
15 TOBACCO MANUFACTURERS											
16 FABRICS AND YARNS											
17 MISCELLANEOUS TEXTILES											
18 APPAREL											
19 MISC FABRICATED TEXTILES											
20 HOUSEHOLD FURNITURE											
21 WOOD CONTAINERS											
22 OTHER FURNITURE											
23 PAPER AND ALLIED PRODUCTS											
24 PAPER CONTAINERS AND BOXES											
25 PRINTING AND PUBLISHING											
26 CHEMICALS											
27 PLASTICS											
28 DRUGS											
29 PAINTS AND ALLIED PRODUCTS											
30 PETROLEUM REFINING											
31 RUBBER AND MISC PRODUCTS											
32 LEATHER											
33 FOOTWEAR											
34 GLASS PRODUCTS											
35 STONE AND CLAY PRODUCTS											
36 IRON AND STEEL											
37 NONFERROUS METALS											
38 FABRICATED METALS											
39 SCREW MACHINE PRODUCTS											
40 OTHER FABRICATED METAL PRODUCTS											
41 ENGINES AND TURBINES											
42 FARM MACHINERY											
43 MATERIAL HANDLING MACHINERY											
44 METALWORKING MACHINERY											
45 SPECIAL MACHINERY											
46 GENERAL MACHINERY											
47 MISCELLANEOUS MACHINERY											
48 ELECTRIC MACHINERY											
49 ELECTRICAL EQUIPMENT											
50 HOUSEHOLD APPLIANCES											
51 LIGHTING AND WIRING EQUIPMENT											
52 COMMUNICATIONS EQUIPMENT											
53 ELECTRONIC COMPONENTS											
54 MISC ELECTRICAL EQUIPMENT											
55 MOTOR VEHICLES											
56 AIRCRAFT AND PARTS											
57 OTHER TRANSPORTATION EQUIPMENT											
58 SCIENTIFIC INSTRUMENTS											
59 OPTICAL AND PHOTO SUPPLIES											
60 MISCELLANEOUS MANUFACTURING											
61 TRANSPORTATION											
62 COMMUNICATION											
63 RADIO AND TELEVISION											
64 UTILITY SERVICES											
65 WHOLESALE AND RETAIL TRADE											
66 FINANCE AND INSURANCE											
67 REAL ESTATE											
68 BUSINESS SERVICES											
69 EATING AND DRINKING PLACES											
70 AUTO REPAIR AND SERVICES											
71 LODGING AND PERSONAL SERVICES											
72 AMUSEMENTS											
73 MEDICAL AND EDUCATIONAL SERVICES											
74 FEDERAL GOVERNMENT ENTERPRISES											
75 STATE AND LOCAL GOVERNMENT											
76 SCRAP AND MISCELLANEOUS											
77 HOUSEHOLD CONSUMPTION											
TOTAL											

Table 7.8. U.S. Income/Output Coefficient Matrix, 1982

		UNDER $5000	5000-9999	10000-14999	15000-19999	20000-24999	25000-34999	35000-49999	50000-74999	75000-99999	OVER 100000	TOTAL
01	LIVESTOCK PRODUCTS	-0.0313	0.0213	0.0204	0.0180	0.0133	0.0207	0.0196	0.0088	0.0033	0.0006	0.0946
02	OTHER AGRICULTURAL PRODUCTS	-0.0313	0.0213	0.0204	0.0180	0.0133	0.0207	0.0196	0.0088	0.0033	0.0006	0.0947
03	FORESTRY AND FISHERY PRODUCTS	-0.0313	0.0213	0.0204	0.0180	0.0133	0.0207	0.0196	0.0088	0.0033	0.0006	0.0946
04	AGRICULTURAL, FORESTRY SERVICES	-0.0313	0.0213	0.0204	0.0180	0.0133	0.0207	0.0196	0.0088	0.0049	0.0006	0.0946
05	IRON FERROALLOY MINING	-0.0003	0.0245	0.0326	0.0307	0.0256	0.0450	0.0478	0.0213	0.0069	0.0419	0.2759
06	NONFERROUS METAL MINING	-0.0003	0.0245	0.0197	0.0307	0.0256	0.0454	0.0453	0.0191	0.0056	0.0419	0.2235
07	COAL MINING	-0.0056	0.0131	0.0197	0.0212	0.0229	0.0466	0.0515	0.0191	0.0069	0.0263	0.2760
08	OIL AND GAS EXTRACTION	-0.0002	0.0195	0.0283	0.0307	0.0303	0.0555	0.0515	0.0177	0.0039	0.0084	0.2503
09	STONE AND CLAY MINING	-0.0062	0.0195	0.0283	0.0290	0.0303	0.0311	0.0617	0.0241	0.0047	0.0094	0.2503
10	CHEMICAL AND FERTILIZER MINING	-0.0069	0.0222	0.0317	0.0319	0.0343	0.0625	0.0509	0.0152	0.0037	0.0095	0.2940
11	NEW CONSTRUCTION	0.0007	0.0199	0.0208	0.0151	0.0168	0.0245	0.0264	0.0152	0.0034	0.0077	0.1552
12	MAINTENANCE AND REPAIR	0.0064	0.0300	0.0319	0.0143	0.0168	0.0263	0.0235	0.0152	0.0032	0.0071	0.1780
13	ORDNANCE	0.0061	0.0231	0.0316	0.0351	0.0353	0.0620	0.0511	0.0219	0.0058	0.0079	0.1751
14	FOOD AND KINDRED PRODUCTS	0.0094	0.0319	0.0422	0.0408	0.0401	0.0466	0.0472	0.0176	0.0047	0.0079	0.2658
15	TOBACCO MANUFACTURERS	0.0094	0.0314	0.0422	0.0408	0.0253	0.0498	0.0659	0.0295	0.0046	0.0097	0.3396
16	FABRICS AND YARNS	0.0038	0.0184	0.0256	0.0228	0.0253	0.0653	0.0432	0.0312	0.0093	0.0187	0.3396
17	MISCELLANEOUS TEXTILES	0.0038	0.0187	0.0333	0.0297	0.0234	0.0528	0.0615	0.0582	0.0235	0.0097	0.3396
18	APPAREL	0.0028	0.0254	0.0333	0.0297	0.0234	0.0528	0.0582	0.0235	0.0228	0.0228	0.2207
19	MISC FABRICATED TEXTILES	0.0028	0.0254	0.0333	0.0297	0.0176	0.0528	0.0387	0.0235	0.0228	0.0228	0.2735
20	LUMBER AND WOOD PRODUCTS	0.0028	0.0120	0.0176	0.0156	0.0188	0.0223	0.0387	0.0115	0.0073	0.0228	0.2735
21	WOOD CONTAINERS	0.0009	0.0124	0.0162	0.0121	0.0114	0.0244	0.0210	0.0082	0.0063	0.0412	0.1922
22	HOUSEHOLD FURNITURE	0.0026	0.0124	0.0162	0.0171	0.0144	0.0224	0.0210	0.0082	0.0021	0.0056	0.1144
23	OTHER FURNITURE	0.0080	0.0268	0.0382	0.0323	0.0359	0.0779	0.0710	0.0082	0.0070	0.0142	0.3561
24	PAPER AND ALLIED PRODUCTS	0.0069	0.0210	0.0281	0.0301	0.0342	0.0680	0.0641	0.0212	0.0044	0.0099	0.2941
25	PAPER CONTAINERS AND BOXES	0.0066	0.0191	0.0191	0.0301	0.0411	0.0677	0.0632	0.0223	0.0049	0.0099	0.2860
26	PRINTING AND PUBLISHING	0.0070	0.0224	0.0224	0.0411	0.0411	0.0910	0.0855	0.0391	0.0108	0.0099	0.2867
27	CHEMICAL PRODUCTS	0.0070	0.0224	0.0335	0.0335	0.0411	0.0910	0.0855	0.0391	0.0108	0.0132	0.3847
28	PLASTICS	0.0070	0.0224	0.0335	0.0335	0.0411	0.0910	0.0855	0.0391	0.0108	0.0132	0.3847
29	DRUGS AND ALLIED PRODUCTS	0.0070	0.0224	0.0335	0.0335	0.0418	0.0910	0.0866	0.0391	0.0108	0.0132	0.3847
30	PAINT AND ALLIED PRODUCTS	0.0072	0.0224	0.0316	0.0369	0.0418	0.0862	0.0866	0.0353	0.0088	0.0132	0.3847
31	PETROLEUM REFINING	0.0065	0.0208	0.0288	0.0337	0.0379	0.0769	0.0786	0.0332	0.0088	0.0026	0.3779
32	RUBBER AND MISC PRODUCTS	0.0065	0.0191	0.0288	0.0337	0.0379	0.0769	0.0786	0.0332	0.0085	0.0223	0.3453
33	LEATHER	0.0065	0.0191	0.0288	0.0337	0.0379	0.0769	0.0786	0.0332	0.0085	0.0223	0.3453
34	FOOTWEAR	0.0043	0.0191	0.0288	0.0337	0.0263	0.0518	0.0786	0.0332	0.0085	0.0223	0.3453
35	GLASS PRODUCTS	0.0063	0.0153	0.0218	0.0262	0.0374	0.0798	0.0898	0.0391	0.0100	0.0142	0.2373
36	STONE AND CLAY PRODUCTS	0.0063	0.0178	0.0275	0.0325	0.0374	0.0798	0.0931	0.0391	0.0195	0.0237	0.3577
37	IRON AND STEEL	0.0083	0.0265	0.0379	0.0377	0.0402	0.0809	0.0751	0.0290	0.0068	0.0133	0.3554
38	NONFERROUS METALS	0.0083	0.0265	0.0379	0.0377	0.0402	0.0809	0.0717	0.0332	0.0085	0.0223	0.3554
39	METAL CONTAINERS	0.0089	0.0309	0.0440	0.0407	0.0402	0.0798	0.0570	0.0388	0.0100	0.0172	0.3694
40	FABRICATED METAL PRODUCTS	0.0176	0.0178	0.0334	0.0325	0.0387	0.0931	0.0523	0.0388	0.0087	0.0072	0.3813
41	SCREW MACHINE PRODUCTS	0.0103	0.0275	0.0379	0.0377	0.0379	0.0998	0.0570	0.0178	0.0160	0.0207	0.2790
42	OTHER FABRICATED METAL PRODUCTS	0.0151	0.0073	0.0448	0.0377	0.0489	0.1091	0.0441	0.0385	0.0159	0.0123	0.2476
43	ENGINES AND TURBINES	0.0029	0.0073	0.0121	0.0180	0.0246	0.0506	0.0677	0.0147	0.0037	0.0035	0.2476
44	FARM MACHINERY	0.0349	0.0677	0.0595	0.0024	0.0134	0.0493	0.0288	0.0209	0.0116	0.0070	0.1474
45	CONSTRUCTION MACHINERY	0.0043	0.0153	0.0178	0.0262	0.0263	0.0519	0.0523	0.0332	0.0108	0.0132	0.2244
46	MATERIAL HANDLING MACHINERY	0.0063	0.0178	0.0275	0.0325	0.0374	0.0552	0.0522	0.0390	0.0100	0.0207	0.3307
47	METALWORKING MACHINERY	0.0103	0.0426	0.0523	0.0523	0.0601	0.1209	0.0999	0.0610	0.0293	0.0207	0.5368
48	GENERAL MACHINERY	0.0176	0.0188	0.0390	0.0405	0.0463	0.0857	0.0842	0.0394	0.0155	0.0188	0.3721
49	MISCELLANEOUS MACHINERY	0.0053	0.0108	0.0393	0.0080	-0.0003	0.0251	0.0310	0.0394	0.0104	0.0003	0.0346
50	OFFICE MACHINERY	0.0002	0.0002	0.0008	0.0000		0.0051	0.0010	0.0015	0.0011	0.0113	0.0156

Table 7.9. Total Income Distribution Gini Coefficients

Sector			Sector		
01	Livestock and its products	0.6388	41	Screw machine products	0.4342
02	Other agricultural products	0.6390	42	Other fabricated metals	0.4342
03	Forest and fish products	0.6383	43	Engines and turbines	0.4724
04	Agricultural and forestry and	0.6389	44	Farm machinery	0.4724
	fishery services		45	Construction and mining machines	0.4724
05	Iron and ferroalloy mining	0.4760	46	Materials handling machines	0.4724
06	Nonferrous metal mining	0.4760	47	Metal machines	0.4724
07	Coal mining	0.4760	48	Special machines	0.4724
08	Petroleum and natural gas	0.4907	49	General machines	0.4724
09	Stone and clay mining	0.4760	50	Miscellaneous machines	0.4724
10	Chemical and fertilizer mining	0.4761	51	Office machines	0.4871
11	New construction	0.3979	52	Service machines	0.4871
12	Maintenance and construction	0.3979	53	Electrical equipment	0.4908
13	Ordnance and accessories	0.4122	54	Household appliances	0.4908
14	Food and kindred	0.4190	55	Light and wire equipment	0.4908
15	Tobacco manufacturing	0.3926	56	Communications equipment	0.4908
16	Fabrics and yarn and thread	0.3703	57	Electronic accessories	0.4908
17	Miscellaneous textiles	0.3703	58	Miscellaneous electric	0.4908
18	Apparel	0.3614	59	Motor vehicle equipment	0.4584
19	Miscellaneous fabric textiles	0.3614	60	Aircraft and parts	0.5110
20	Lumber and wood	0.3586	61	Other transportation equipment	0.5110
21	Wood containers	0.3586	62	Science supplies	0.4222
22	Household furniture	0.3586	63	Optical and photo supplies	0.4222
23	Other furniture	0.3586	64	Miscellaneous manufacturing	0.4222
24	Paper and allied products	0.4151	65	Transportation	0.3847
25	Paper containers and boxes	0.4151	66	Communications	0.4886
26	Printing and publishing	0.4464	67	Radio and TV	0.4886
27	Chemical products	0.4689	68	Utility services	0.5429
28	Plastics	0.4689	69	Wholesale and retail trade	0.4247
29	Drugs	0.4689	70	Finance and insurance	0.6199
30	Paints and allied products	0.4689	71	Real estate and rental	0.6199
31	Petroleum refining	0.5772	72	Lodging and personal service	0.2352
32	Rubber and miscellaneous	0.3614	73	Business services	0.4960
33	Leather	0.3614	74	Eating and drinking places	0.2617
34	Footwear and other products	0.3614	75	Auto repair and service	0.4331
35	Glass	0.4245	76	Amusements	0.4261
36	Stone and clay products	0.4245	77	Health and educational services	0.4631
37	Iron and steel manufacturing	0.4183	78	Federal government	0.5029
38	Nonferrous metals	0.4183	79	Other government	0.5029
39	Metal containers	0.4342	80	Scrap	0.4349
40	Fabricated metal products	0.4342			

some cases the reduction is dramatic, as in the case of sector 31, petroleum refining, and sector 40, fabricated metal products. As would be expected, the results show the strong influence of the wage and salary distribution in each sector. The one major exception is the agriculture group, in which farm income and farm rental income predominate. In these sectors, the total Gini is higher than the dividend Gini because of the large number of households reporting farm-related losses.

Conclusions

This chapter has presented the methodology used to infer the distribution of some income types other than wage and dividend income from our primary data-based matrices and to tabulate the distribution of other income types from IRS census data. Although some of the empirical methodology is somewhat ad hoc, it is consistent with principles of national and regional income accounting (see, e.g., Kendrick 1972; Bulmer-Thomas 1982; Leontief 1986).

The accuracy of our results may be evaluated by indirect tests. Formal statistical tests are more powerful, but impossible to apply in evaluating potential bias in our estimates. First, while 9 percent of our final SAM had to be approximated by the use of secondary data, *we emphasize the fact that 91 percent of it is based on a refinement or direct use of primary data*. In addition, our results are consistent with a priori hypotheses relating to investment practices, capital/labor shares, and so forth. We emphasize that it would be inappropriate to draw conclusions about any sector or income class from a single coefficient, but that taken on a sector-by-sector basis, the model is a good depiction of the interindustry distribution of all types of personal income.

Improvements in the model are clearly possible. Obviously, more primary data would be helpful. Additional refinements, which we considered to be of low priority, would remove some small sources of bias as well. For example, for the sake of computational manageability, we used a mean annual salary for a given occupation across all sectors. This assumption is consistent with earnings that are normally distributed within and across each sector. Though, as we have noted, the earnings variance was small, the actual earnings distributions may be skewed. Future studies might, therefore, explore the impact of this assumption on the accuracy of our results.

III / APPLICATIONS OF THE MODEL

8 / Regionalization of the Model

Thus far, the empirical work on income distribution in this study has been performed at the national level. The reason for this emphasis is that income distribution data are more extensive for the United States as a whole than for any state or county area. The national results, however, provide a good reference point for analyzing natural resource policy impacts that are confined to small areas.

Empirical models at the small area level can be generated from a combination of the national results, regional control totals, and various "regionalization" procedures. This "top down" approach is used extensively in the field of input-output analysis for pragmatic reasons. It would be intolerably expensive to construct distributional models for every small area (e.g., every National Forest in the United States) from primary data. A more reasonable approach is to adapt an established model. This could, of course, be done by performing an in-depth collection of distributional data for one region and generalizing to others. Unfortunately, this is usually precluded because of its expense. The approach we have chosen is a conventional regionalization approach paralleling that applied to regional accounts and input-output tables.

The reader is reminded that we had to overcome gaps in data in constructing our national-level model. The problem was most often resolved by adapting related data. As we move down the scale to smaller units of analysis, the need for such adjustments increases. For example, in the absence of information on the sectoral distribution of dividends at the state or county level, we assume that the relative proportions are equivalent to those for the United States as a whole. Overall, the extent of our simplifying assumptions differs significantly among income types. Fortunately, the data pertaining to wage and salary income are usually specific to region, income class, and sector at all levels. This helps maintain the credibility of the model, since wages and salaries represent three-quarters of total personal income for the majority of regions.

The following sections contrast data availability at the national, state, and county levels, explain the construction of a regional income distribution matrix, and present results for the Monongahela National Forest.

Regional Data Requirements

Regionalization Methodologies

As noted earlier in this study, few areas of economics suffer from the lack of data that besets the analysis of income distribution. Chapters 5, 6, and 7 have illustrated the gaps in the data at the national level and the obstacles these present. Indeed, the compilation of the Social Accounting Matrix was much like fitting together a large puzzle composed of many pieces of varying shapes and sizes. Fortunately, the major component—wage and salary income—is based on a minor refinement of primary data at the national level, thus providing a solid foundation for the SAM. In addition, our extensive refinement of New York Stock Exchange data helped extend the primary data basis of our distribution matrix and provided a foundation for filling in the remaining unknown income components, mainly other types of capital-related income.

As difficult as the construction of a personal income distribution version of a SAM is for the United States as a whole, the obstacles increase as one attempts to construct such a matrix for geographic areas of decreasing size. The lack of data becomes especially acute as we approach areas the size of National Forests, for example.

In applying our empirical procedures at the subnational level, we invoked several standard "data reduction" techniques:

1. Scale-down of national data; this approach assumes that the underlying structure is the same for the region in question as for a larger region (or the nation) for which data exist. In our case, this means that income flows are reduced proportionally in terms of regional income and industry control totals. But, of course, the coefficients matrix (the "V" matrix) would be the same in both cases.

2. Use of data available for a previous year; this approach assumes that there are no significant structural shifts over the time periods in question. It is appropriate over short periods and is often invoked when there is a delay in data reporting or where a data series is terminated.

3. Use of data from a related variable; this approach is applicable when there is a strong similarity between income types or industry categories. For example, data available for one 4-digit SIC sector might be applied to other sectors within the same 2-digit grouping for which data are unavailable.[1]

Unfortunately, there is no precise guide as to which of the regionalization techniques to apply for specific types of data gaps. Our choices can therefore be characterized as ad hoc,[2] but the reader should bear in mind that they are based on the following criteria: (1) our intent to promote the highest degree of accuracy possible, and (2) the need to avoid unnecessary computational complexity in order to yield an operational model.

Data Availability

The extent of regional data on income distribution is illustrated in table 8.1. The table provides a comparison of the availability of data for each of fourteen income types at the national, state, and county levels. Two types of data are pertinent. The columns labeled "Distribution" refer to the existence of a matrix containing income/industry flows. The columns headed "Control" refer to the availability of totals for income or industry groups and for separate income class or industry categories as indicated.[3] Even in cases where an income-flows matrix exists, control totals are needed, because the basic data matrix is not

Table 8.1. Income Distribution Data Availability for Regions of Different Size

Income Type	National		State		County	
	Distribution	Control	Distribution	Control	Distribution	Control
Wage and salary	Manpower matrix	Income/industry[a]	Manpower matrix	Income/industry[a]	—	Income[b]/industry
Pension and annuity	—	Income/industry	—	—[c]	—	—[c]
Dividend	Dividend matrix	Income/industry[a]	—	Income	—	Income[d]
Interest	—	Income/industry	—	Income	—	Income[d]
Business and professional	—	Income/industry	—	Income agg.[e]	—	Income agg.[e]
Partnership	—	Income class	—	Income agg.[e]	—	Income agg.[e]
Small corporation	—	Income class	—	—[c]	—	—[c]
Sale of property	—	Income class	—	Income agg.[e]	—	Income agg.[e]
Estate	N.A.[f]	Income class	N.A.[f]	—[g]	N.A.[f]	—[g]
Rental	N.A.[f]	Income class	N.A.[f]	Income	N.A.[f]	Income[d]
Sale of assets	N.A.[f]	Income class	N.A.[f]	Income agg.[e]	N.A.[f]	Income agg.[e]
Farm	N.A.[f]	Income class	N.A.[h]	Income	N.A.[h]	Income
Farm rental	N.A.[f]	Income class	N.A.[h]	—[g]	N.A.[h]	—[g]
Royalty	N.A.[f]	Income class	N.A.[h]	Income	N.A.[h]	Income[d]

[a]Not applicable for cases where the income distribution is known.
[b]Income control totals are derived from occupational control totals.
[c]Not reported separately.
[d]Not published, but provided by the U.S. Bureau of Economic Analysis via special tabulation.
[e]Part of an aggregate reported as "Non-Farm Proprietary Income."
[f]Not applicable for cases where income stems only from household financial activities.
[g]Typically less than 0.5% of total income; subsumed under other categories.
[h]Not applicable for cases where income stems only from a single sectoral group (agricultural or mining).

87

available in the desired units (i.e., occupational requirements must be transformed into wage income and stock ownership must be transformed into dividends). Also, some income types, such as those pertaining to household financial activities, are derived from only a single sector, so a matrix would not be applicable.

At the national level, two distributional submatrices are directly derived from the matrices listed in the first column of table 8.1 according to the methodologies presented in chapters 5 and 6. The estimation of other types of income proceeded with the application of these two basic matrices to other income types as discussed in chapter 7. In other words, we have already invoked one of our "data reduction" techniques at the national level.

The decrease in data availability when one moves to the state level should be readily apparent from table 8.1. There, only one distributional matrix exists, that for manpower requirements. Hence, the wage and salary portion of the matrix will vary by state. The more dramatic shift, however, pertains to control totals. With the exception of wage income, control totals may not be available for the distribution of other income types from each sector or to each income class for individual states.[4] In that case, both the row and column weights for most income types in state total income distribution matrices will be based on national weights.

On the other hand, data availability at the state and county levels are very similar. For example, the only significant difference in West Virginia is the availability of a state occupation/industry (manpower requirements) matrix that is not available at the county level. Our discussion refers to our experience with the state of West Virginia, but our conclusions apply to most other states as well.

The Monongahela National Forest Income Distribution Matrix

We shall illustrate our regionalization methodology by applying it to the Monongahela National Forest (MNF),[5] comprised of parts of ten counties in eastern West Virginia (the counties are Barbour, Grant, Greenbrier, Nicholas, Pendelton, Pocahontas, Preston, Randolph, Tucker, and Webster). The total area of the MNF, which is a mix of private, state, and federal lands, is 1,647,000 acres (U.S. Forest Service 1985). The total population of the overall ten-county (trading) area in 1983 was 200,670.

Recall that national personal income level data are disaggregated according to fourteen income types (see table 4.2). Ideally, we would like to have similar control totals at the small area level.

As noted in the previous section, income data by source, sector of origin, and household income class become more sparse as the area of analysis decreases in size. To compensate for the lack of data at the forest area level, several simplifying assumptions must be invoked. For instance, pension and annuity income is based on the ratio of pension and annuity income to adjusted gross income in West Virginia in 1981. Similarly, small business corporation income in the MNF is based on its share of 1981 West Virginia adjusted gross income. Using this methodology, pension and annuity income comprised approximately $26.3 million in the MNF in 1982, and small business corporation income comprised $3 million (see table 8.2).

Although data pertaining to the county level income from dividends, interest, and rents and royalties are not published in *Local Area Personal Income* (U.S. Bureau of Economic Analysis 1984), these data were obtained through special tabulations initiated by the Bureau at the request of the authors (U.S. BEA, pers. com., 1984). Four other income

Table 8.2. Sources of Personal Adjusted Gross Income in
the MNF, 1982
(millions of dollars)

Source	Amount	Percentage of Total AGI
Salaries/wages	749.0	74.9
Interest	156.0	15.6
Dividends	21.6	2.2
Business/professional	31.1	3.1
Sale of capital assets	10.7	1.1
Sale of property	−.3	[a]
Partnership	3.1	0.3
Farm	−12.4	−1.2
Farm rental	[b]	—
Pensions/annuities	26.3	2.6
Small business	−3.0	−0.3
Rent	7.6	0.8
Royalties	10.6	1.1
Estate	[c]	—
Total[d]	1,000.3	100.0

Sources: Internal Revenue Service 1984a; U.S. Bureau of Economic Analysis 1984b.

[a]Less than 0.05%

[b]Unavailable

[c]Largely subsumed under other income categories.

[d]Totals may not add, owing to rounding error.

types, business and professional income, income from the sale of capital assets, income from the sale of property, and partnership income are again derived by using the proportions of each income share realized in West Virginia in 1981. An overall control total for the four income types is reported as nonfarm proprietor's income by the Bureau of Economic Analysis.

Since data are not available for estate income and farm rental income, these income types are excluded from the total adjusted gross income calculations. The exclusion of these income components is not a significant omission in the derivation of total adjusted gross income because the greatest share of estate income is subsumed under income derived from capital ownership, and only contributed .2 percent of total AGI in West Virginia in 1981. Farm rental income comprised only .1 percent of total AGI in 1982 nationally, and cannot be computed indirectly from the 1981 income account data for West Virginia. Two major income types—wage and salary income and farm income—are directly obtained from published data and require no special tabulation or derivation (U.S. Bureau of Economic Analysis 1984b).

Construction of the MNF Matrix

Wage and salary income is allocated across income classes in the same proportions as for the state as a whole (IRS 1984a). All other capital-related income is allocated according to the income class residuals derived by taking the difference between total income and wage and salary income for each income class. An exception is made for farm income and royalty income, which are distributed among the ten income classes according to the product of the ratio of farm and royalty income per income class nationally and the number of tax returns per income class in West Virginia in 1981.

Sector allocations of specific income types are derived using some straightforward procedures. First, wage and salary income is allocated to the region by scaling the West Virginia occupation/industry matrix to the MNF control totals available from the Bureau of the Census (1984b). Sectoral weights are then derived by multiplying estimated 1982 MNF gross outputs by value-added coefficients for the MNF in 1977 derived from IMPLAN. Second, dividend income is allocated across sectors according to sector-specific estimated 1982 MNF gross outputs multiplied by the U.S. dividend-output coefficients. Finally, business and professional, partnership, small business corporation, property income, and interest income are all allocated in the same manner as dividend income.

Presentation of the Results

The total personal income distribution matrix for the Monongahela National Forest is presented in table 8.3. Coal mining accounts for 39 percent of total personal income in this forest area. The utilities and trade sectors follow, each accounting for approximately 10 percent of total AGI. Contributing least to total AGI are the construction and mining machinery, special industrial machinery, and miscellaneous manufacturing sectors, collectively accounting for only .03 percent of total AGI.

Households in the $20,000–$50,000 income class receive about 39 percent of the total AGI in the region. The wealthiest households, those with incomes over $75,000, account for 9 percent of the region's AGI, while those households in the lower income class, under $10,000, captured 14 percent of the region's AGI. Those households with incomes of less than $5,000 experienced net income losses in 1983 in the four agriculture-based sectors. These same households also experienced net income losses in the household financial activities sector, which includes the income generated from the sale of capital assets and rental income.

Income distribution coefficients derived from table 8.3 are given in table 8.4, and reveal the relative prominence of each sector's contribution to AGI across all income classes.[6] For example, the households in the Under $5,000 income class received about 7 percent of the total income generated by the personal services and eating and drinking places sectors. Of the total income generated by the coal-mining sector, 22 percent accrued to the $25,000–$50,000 income classes. About 15 percent of the coal-mining income went to households in the two lowest income classes and 9 percent went to the two highest income classes.

Another way of reading table 8.4 is to interpret each cell entry as the income received for every dollar of income generated by each sector. The agricultural and radio/television sectors generated $.234 of income in the $5,000–$9,999 income class for every dollar of income generated by these sectors. This represents the highest relative payment of income for all sectors and income classes. Conversely, the lowest payment to any income class by any sector for each dollar of income generated comes from the chemical products, plastics, and drugs sectors. Only $.009 of income was paid to the Under $5,000 income class for every dollar of income generated by this sector.

Table 8.3. Total Personal Income Distribution Matrix for the Monongahela National Forest, West Virginia (millions of 1982 dollars)

	UNDER $5000	5000–9999	10000–14999	15000–19999	20000–24999	25000–34999	35000–49999	50000–74999	75000–99999	OVER 100000	TOTAL
001 LIVESTOCK PRODUCTS	-3.083	7.826	6.957	7.781	5.317	4.485	1.753	1.161	0.769	0.532	33.492
002 AGRICULTURAL PRODUCTS	-0.466	1.939	0.773	1.028	0.598	0.582	0.234	0.288	0.191	0.132	4.390
003 FORESTRY AND FISHERY PRODUCTS	-1.766	1.939	1.729	1.928	1.408	1.425	0.530	0.322	0.164	0.152	8.300
004 AGRICULTURAL SERVICES	-7.616	51.365	66.388	73.551	54.788	60.898	25.480	16.832	6.754	27.005	389.685
005 COAL MINING	0.037	5.130	1.380	0.203	0.787	1.898	1.530	0.822	0.022	0.053	8.298
006 OIL AND GAS EXTRACTION	0.159	0.257	1.087	1.519	1.239	1.256	0.505	0.353	0.145	0.563	8.102
007 STONE AND CLAY MINING	0.571	1.027	1.803	1.945	1.861	1.987	0.821	0.403	0.154	0.215	10.107
008 NEW CONSTRUCTION	0.070	0.582	0.567	0.607	0.540	0.677	0.265	0.442	0.148	0.058	3.627
009 MAINTENANCE AND REPAIR	0.049	1.387	0.633	0.847	0.575	0.679	0.232	0.130	0.054	0.057	6.772
010 FOOD AND KINDRED PRODUCTS	0.081	0.045	0.591	0.717	0.625	0.689	0.079	0.029	0.013	0.011	3.409
011 FABRICS AND YARN	0.841	1.407	0.587	0.244	0.063	0.617	0.079	0.034	0.010	0.057	3.536
012 APPAREL	-1.407	2.387	2.015	3.017	3.401	3.617	2.234	1.607	0.230	0.547	19.125
013 MISC FABRICATED TEXTILES	-2.387	1.407	0.591	0.717	0.625	0.079	0.306	0.603	0.310	0.243	19.125
014 LUMBER AND WOOD PRODUCTS	-5.631	0.019	0.015	0.017	0.016	0.013	0.034	0.001	0.001	0.001	0.069
015 WOOD CONTAINERS	0.019	0.019	0.145	0.365	0.228	0.369	0.306	0.627	0.002	0.005	1.956
016 HOUSEHOLD FURNITURE	0.064	0.240	0.523	0.289	0.349	0.674	0.298	0.224	0.118	0.042	1.393
017 OTHER FURNITURE	0.246	0.470	0.723	0.589	0.369	0.658	0.287	0.174	0.097	0.137	3.703
018 PAPER AND ALLIED PRODUCTS	0.093	0.429	0.631	0.451	0.369	0.489	0.213	0.714	0.073	0.236	3.657
019 PRINTING AND PUBLISHING	0.093	0.229	0.194	0.154	0.314	0.416	0.078	0.081	0.099	0.106	2.720
020 CHEMICAL PRODUCTS	0.025	0.162	0.427	0.358	0.349	0.349	0.078	0.034	0.034	0.143	1.091
021 PLASTICS	0.042	0.162	0.223	0.258	0.314	0.349	0.133	0.052	0.023	0.030	1.001
022 DRUGS	0.035	0.330	0.595	0.684	0.534	0.593	0.226	0.106	0.019	0.051	1.724
023 PETROLEUM REFINING	0.162	0.423	0.346	0.379	0.395	0.752	0.283	0.130	0.038	0.033	4.417
024 RUBBER AND MISC PRODUCTS	0.330	0.211	0.314	0.528	0.548	0.438	0.109	0.078	0.026	0.050	3.766
025 LEATHER	0.043	0.130	0.436	0.090	0.593	0.615	0.248	0.119	0.017	0.030	2.101
026 FOOTWEAR	0.130	0.051	0.427	0.654	0.578	0.104	0.261	0.117	0.027	0.030	2.955
027 STONE AND CLAY PRODUCTS	0.053	0.308	0.459	0.090	0.425	0.820	0.302	0.274	0.053	0.009	2.501
028 IRON AND STEEL	0.033	0.301	0.309	0.308	0.678	0.957	0.278	0.218	0.116	0.005	3.113
029 NONFERROUS METALS	0.013	0.068	0.269	0.569	0.525	0.717	0.278	0.238	0.108	0.061	3.707
030 FABRICATED METAL PRODUCTS	0.771	0.020	0.309	0.507	0.095	0.107	0.043	0.042	0.005	0.053	3.217
031 SCREW MACHINE PRODUCTS	0.010	0.045	0.069	0.156	0.125	0.123	0.048	0.066	0.017	0.061	0.245
032 OTHER FABRICATED METAL PRODUCTS	0.025	0.078	0.079	0.158	0.156	0.193	0.054	0.046	0.028	0.053	0.031
033 ENGINES AND TURBINES	0.062	0.053	0.099	0.187	0.205	0.130	0.080	0.046	0.047	0.646	0.551
034 CONSTRUCTION MACHINERY	0.003	0.078	0.062	0.013	0.015	0.193	0.054	0.125	0.001	0.079	0.953
035 METAL WORKING MACHINERY	0.119	0.424	0.013	0.015	0.782	0.017	0.293	1.003	0.047	0.055	0.646
036 SPECIAL MACHINERY	0.013	0.003	0.002	0.015	0.015	0.017	0.006	0.002	0.001	0.001	0.079
037 MISCELLANEOUS MACHINERY	0.053	0.330	0.618	0.372	0.771	0.868	1.460	0.835	0.546	0.544	3.853
038 COMMUNICATION EQUIPMENT	0.091	0.897	1.618	2.372	2.025	2.868	1.243	0.797	0.038	0.353	0.081
039 ELECTRONIC ACCESSORIES	0.002	1.054	1.918	16.139	13.556	19.239	8.243	8.997	2.628	2.794	0.027
040 SCIENCE SUPPLIES	0.099	3.892	2.538	18.465	16.556	19.780	8.585	2.172	1.347	1.677	31.404
041 TRANSPORTATION EQUIPMENT	0.002	1.193	1.235	3.264	3.965	1.967	2.079	2.515	0.445	5.030	102.269
042 OPTICAL AND PHOTO SUPPLIES	0.761	1.580	7.617	7.793	9.191	11.959	1.079	6.913	0.521	0.602	103.448
043 MISCELLANEOUS MANUFACTURING	0.264	5.121	4.797	4.872	4.175	3.959	0.915	0.703	0.437	0.637	65.040
044 TRANSPORTATION	0.025	2.934	2.451	2.274	1.439	1.630	1.915	0.468	0.362	0.032	28.555
045 COMMUNICATION	1.054	0.227	2.221	1.459	1.623	1.623	0.185	0.098	0.313	0.362	13.008
046 RADIO AND TELEVISION	3.892	0.199	0.599	0.351	0.375	0.475	0.351	0.158	0.032	0.035	1.973
047 UTILITY SERVICES	1.288	0.037	0.359	0.376	0.346	0.301	3.229	2.344	0.096	1.035	2.418
048 WHOLESALE AND RETAIL TRADE	1.847	0.318	0.573	3.208	0.713	0.835	0.443	0.268	0.158	1.778	39.730
049 FINANCE AND INSURANCE	0.231	0.957	0.091	0.638	0.265	0.301	0.257	0.097	0.160	0.178	4.215
050 REAL ESTATE AND RENTAL	0.923	0.336	0.207	0.119	0.129	0.129	0.143	0.031	0.058	0.064	1.520
051 LODGING AND PERSONAL SERVICES	0.037	1.026	0.091	0.972	0.440	2.117	0.788	1.826	0.775	0.018	1.675
052 BUSINESS SERVICES	-0.223	122.907	154.801	177.705	147.040	169.738	73.021	51.118	26.900	55.775	18.300
061 HOUSEHOLD CONSUMPTION	-17.320	122.907	154.801	177.705	147.040	169.738	73.021	51.118	26.900	55.775	1000.326

91

Table 8.4. Total Personal Income Coefficient Matrix for the Monongahela National Forest, West Virginia, 1982

	UNDER $5000	5000–9999	10000–14999	15000–19999	20000–24999	25000–34999	35000–49999	50000–74999	75000–99999	OVER 100000	TOTAL
01 LIVESTOCK PRODUCTS	-0.092	0.234	0.208	0.232	0.159	0.134	0.052	0.035	0.023	0.016	1.000
02 OTHER AGRICULTURAL PRODUCTS	-0.092	0.234	0.208	0.232	0.159	0.134	0.052	0.035	0.023	0.016	1.000
03 FORESTRY AND FISHERY PRODUCTS	-0.092	0.234	0.208	0.232	0.159	0.134	0.052	0.035	0.023	0.016	1.000
04 AGRICULTURAL SERVICES	-0.092	0.234	0.208	0.232	0.159	0.134	0.052	0.035	0.023	0.016	1.000
05 COAL MINING	-0.009	0.132	0.144	0.187	0.175	0.155	0.081	0.043	0.017	0.069	1.000
06 OIL AND GAS EXTRACTION	-0.027	0.097	0.170	0.187	0.141	0.155	0.065	0.045	0.018	0.041	1.000
07 STONE AND CLAY MINING	-0.019	0.106	0.155	0.186	0.180	0.193	0.080	0.039	0.015	0.069	1.000
08 NEW CONSTRUCTION	-0.026	0.136	0.169	0.204	0.135	0.166	0.068	0.092	0.039	0.021	1.000
09 MAINTENANCE AND REPAIR	-0.025	0.116	0.159	0.201	0.194	0.193	0.066	0.028	0.009	0.016	1.000
10 FOOD AND KINDRED PRODUCTS	-0.019	0.136	0.159	0.203	0.188	0.195	0.092	0.032	0.012	0.014	1.000
11 FABRICS AND YARN	-0.023	0.116	0.162	0.186	0.178	0.189	0.068	0.032	0.012	0.013	1.000
12 APPAREL	-0.033	0.125	0.162	0.186	0.178	0.189	0.070	0.032	0.012	0.013	1.000
13 MISC FABRICATED TEXTILES	-0.033	0.125	0.162	0.162	0.164	0.180	0.070	0.032	0.012	0.013	1.000
14 LUMBER AND WOOD PRODUCTS	-0.033	0.122	0.170	0.157	0.154	0.149	0.078	0.060	0.022	0.030	1.000
15 WOOD CONTAINERS	-0.027	0.143	0.120	0.167	0.099	0.149	0.078	0.063	0.027	0.045	1.000
16 HOUSEHOLD FURNITURE	-0.009	0.097	0.155	0.167	0.131	0.202	0.077	0.081	0.034	0.065	1.000
17 OTHER FURNITURE	-0.012	0.113	0.158	0.179	0.182	0.202	0.084	0.036	0.013	0.065	1.000
18 PAPER AND ALLIED PRODUCTS	-0.025	0.113	0.147	0.179	0.182	0.209	0.084	0.036	0.013	0.143	1.000
19 PRINTING AND PUBLISHING	-0.025	0.100	0.147	0.181	0.188	0.208	0.084	0.036	0.013	0.018	1.000
20 CHEMICALS	-0.025	0.102	0.147	0.179	0.186	0.208	0.084	0.037	0.014	0.017	1.000
21 PLASTICS	-0.025	0.102	0.124	0.176	0.186	0.208	0.084	0.038	0.014	0.016	1.000
22 PETROLEUM REFINING	-0.019	0.083	0.124	0.176	0.163	0.223	0.086	0.031	0.019	0.017	1.000
23 RUBBER AND MISC PRODUCTS	-0.019	0.083	0.124	0.176	0.163	0.223	0.086	0.031	0.019	0.019	1.000
24 LEATHER	-0.019	0.083	0.124	0.166	0.163	0.223	0.086	0.074	0.029	0.019	1.000
25 FOOTWEAR	-0.017	0.082	0.122	0.181	0.165	0.202	0.084	0.069	0.038	0.064	1.000
26 STONE AND CLAY PRODUCTS	-0.026	0.076	0.110	0.183	0.187	0.186	0.088	0.093	0.038	0.084	1.000
27 IRON AND STEEL	-0.024	0.066	0.154	0.174	0.177	0.203	0.076	0.033	0.012	0.014	1.000
28 NONFERROUS METALS	-0.010	0.093	0.136	0.174	0.136	0.195	0.110	0.041	0.030	0.017	1.000
29 FABRICATED METAL PRODUCTS	-0.030	0.113	0.117	0.178	0.160	0.208	0.081	0.063	0.025	0.033	1.000
30 SCREW MACHINE PRODUCTS	-0.055	0.066	0.139	0.151	0.141	0.183	0.093	0.100	0.062	0.082	1.000
31 OTHER FABRICATED METAL PRODUCTS	-0.065	0.180	0.117	0.148	0.150	0.139	0.058	0.032	0.018	0.077	1.000
32 ENGINES AND TURBINES	-0.024	0.098	0.171	0.175	0.128	0.125	0.057	0.043	0.024	0.021	1.000
33 CONSTRUCTION MACHINERY	-0.071	0.186	0.148	0.148	0.178	0.204	0.094	0.050	0.016	0.046	1.000
34 METAL WORKING MACHINERY	-0.019	0.101	0.149	0.156	0.138	0.155	0.094	0.059	0.040	0.016	1.000
35 SPECIAL MACHINERY	-0.037	0.125	0.154	0.162	0.174	0.198	0.081	0.059	0.041	0.042	1.000
36 MISCELLANEOUS MACHINERY	-0.023	0.080	0.136	0.151	0.149	0.198	0.094	0.064	0.038	0.042	1.000
37 COMMUNICATION EQUIPMENT	-0.039	0.112	0.135	0.162	0.165	0.192	0.084	0.045	0.027	0.027	1.000
38 ELECTRONIC ACCESSORIES	-0.012	0.167	0.155	0.162	0.057	0.116	0.043	0.105	0.042	0.150	1.000
39 SCIENCE TRANSPORTATION EQUIPMENT	-0.017	0.123	0.155	0.178	0.147	0.170	0.073	0.055	0.027	0.056	1.000

Conclusions

This chapter has presented a detailed explanation of how the methodology developed in previous chapters can be used to generate multisectoral income distribution matrices at the regional level. Extensions of the methodology are required to compensate for the lack of data for states and small areas. For the most part, we invoked a "top down" approach that makes use of relatively more extensive national data and applies them to the regional level on the assumption that the underlying distributional structure of the nation and the region are similar. This is a reasonable assumption in cases where scale and vintage of production techniques, labor productivity, and land and capital ownership patterns in a given region are representative of the nation as a whole. To illustrate our regionalization methodologies, we constructed a multisectoral income distribution matrix for the Monongahela National Forest. The MNF matrix will be used in a case study application in the following chapter.

Still, the regionalization methodology we have presented is incomplete. An important, but difficult, extension would involve adjusting the income distribution matrix to account for income flows across regions. Not all income generated within a given region is retained and spent there. In the case of wages and salaries, a greater proportion of the income generated and spent will remain for those who work and live in a given region than for those who work in the region but live elsewhere. Similarly, a subset of the resident population may work elsewhere. Any dollars flowing into the region in this way are likely to be independent of a policy stimulus affecting the region alone. Overall, the ideal wage and salary income distribution impact matrix will capture the effect of income generated and retained in the region. This is best accomplished by adjusting the matrix to allow for outflows with the aid of data on commuters, available from the U.S. Bureau of Economic Analysis (1984b) at the state and county level. A similar adjustment is desirable for dividend and other types of capital income, though in this case it would be seriously inhibited by the confidentiality of data on asset ownership in general and the sensitivity of the absentee owner issue.

9 / Policy Analysis at the Regional Level
Distributional Impacts of Coal Surface-Mining

This chapter illustrates several important aspects of our model by applying it to the estimation of the distributional impacts of a possible increase in coal surface-mining in the Monongahela National Forest. Both positive and normative analyses are performed. That is, we investigate the distribution of gains and losses in order to predict public response to a policy change and to assess the "fairness" of the outcome.

While the Monongahela National Forest (MNF) is a major recreational area for the Middle Atlantic States, it also is a major potential mining and logging site.[1] A transition from the former role to one that places a greater emphasis on extractive industries would involve both gains and losses to the MNF-area economy. Gains would stem from both direct and higher order increases in employment, income, and output associated with, say, surface mining. Losses would stem from negative externalities, such as aesthetic blight, water pollution, increased flooding, and property damage. It is likely that gains and losses would have very different distributions across income groups and, hence, important policy implications.

The empirical basis for the case study is the IMPLAN I-O table for the MNF and a modified version of the income distribution matrix for the MNF constructed in chapter 8. The distributional matrices derived in this study thus far are based on income payments transmitted through the market. In this chapter, we construct a supplemental vector of the distribution of possible nonmarket damages associated with coal surface-mining.

Background

As noted in chapter 8, the Monongahela National Forest (MNF) is located in eastern West Virginia and consists of all or part of Barbour, Grant, Greenbrier, Nicholas, Pendleton, Pocahontas, Preston, Randolph, Tucker, and Webster Counties (see figure 9.1). The total area of the forest is 1,647,000 acres, of which 852,000 acres, or 52 percent, is National Forest land (U.S. Forest Service 1985a).

Among the resources found in the MNF, coal is the most abundant of the fossil fuels. Approximately 150 million tons of coal in the MNF fall under U.S. surface ownership rights. In 1982 production in the ten-county area totaled 6,156,000 and 12,078,000 tons of surface- and deep-mined coal, respectively, or approximately 25 percent of the state's surface coal production and 12 percent of its underground coal production.

The Forest Service owns the coal outright in 62 percent of the MNF proper. On 38

Figure 9.1. Monongahela National Forest Region

percent of the land, the Forest Service has only limited control of mining activity, since the government owns the surface rights but private interests own the mineral rights. On other acreage within the ten-county area not classified as forest land, the Forest Service has no control over mining activity, since ownership of surface and mineral rights is private. However, there is currently a national moratorium on coal leasing of federal lands, as well as a prohibition on strip-mining of eastern National Forest lands according to PL 95-87. The strip-mining in the MNF economy is currently taking place only where private surface ownership prevails. Opening up portions of the National Forest to strip-mining would therefore necessitate a major policy change.

Interest in public land management planning is clearly evident within the MNF. Following the circulation of a draft Forest Plan and Environmental Impact Statement distributed in 1984 for public review, the Forest Service initially received over 2,400 comments, and then received letters from 17,000 individuals or groups (including many nonresidents) in just a five-month period. The Forest Service identified several areas of concern, but the dominant theme overall was the preservation of natural conditions, dispersed recreational opportunities, and habitat preservation for wildlife. Preference for the natural state of the forest over commodity and employment opportunities was often expressed. Furthermore, the public indicated objections to the leasing of coal in the forest. The revised plan for the MNF, approved in mid-1986, specifies federal coal leasing only on a case-by-case basis, and with provisions for public involvement (U.S. Forest Service 1985c; U.S. Forest Service, pers. com., January 1987).

The Empirical Model

The empirical income distribution model has two components: an input-output table and a multisector income distribution matrix for the Monongahela National Forest economy. Two significant modifications were needed to adapt the model to the case study.

The Basic Model

The I-O table for the MNF economy follows the standard IMPLAN format.[2] At the two-digit BEA level, the table (not shown) contains fifty-nine sectors, which had a combined total gross output of $2.9 billion in 1982. Coal mining is the major sector, comprising about 28 percent of the region's intermediate output. In contrast, the forestry sector contributes only about 1 percent to the region's intermediate production. However, its major forward linkage, the lumber and wood processing sector, is the third largest contributor, with about 7 percent of the region's intermediate output.

The MNF personal income distribution matrix is presented in table 9.1. The table is actually a variant of the "*V* matrix" defined in chapter 2. The denominator for each cell in the table is the total income of the associated sector (as opposed to total gross output), thus standardizing each column of coefficients. For the region as a whole, the most egalitarian sectors are machinery, equipment, and transportation. The least egalitarian are chemicals, mining, and business services. The lumber, wood, and furniture sectors are at the more egalitarian end of the spectrum.

Modifications of the Model

The two-digit IMPLAN I-O table for the Monongahela National Forest contains only a single sector representing coal mining. Because the production and income distribution structures of underground and surface mining differ significantly, we deemed it necessary to modify the table. The existing coal row and column were each divided into distinct underground and surface components from data in a survey-based table for West Virginia developed by Miernyk et al. (1970) and updated by Loviscek et al. (1979). Additionally, the modified I-O table was updated to 1982 by using statewide sectoral growth rates for the period 1977–82.

Likewise, the coal column of the MNF income distribution matrix was divided into two distinct columns. The disaggregation was based on survey data used to compile a 1975 West Virginia I-O table by Loviscek et al. (1979). As would be expected, these data showed a much higher wage and salary share for more labor-intensive deep mining than for surface mining. These labor and capital shares were used as control totals for the distribution of wage and salary income (based on occupational distinctions between the two types of mining) and capital-related income (based on the national distribution from chapter 7 without further relative distinctions between the two types of mining because of lack of data). The results, in income coefficient terms are presented in table 9.2. One further adjustment was made for the surface-mining coefficients used in the simulations. Royalties are omitted from the matrix because the simulation involves mining on federal lands. Any royalties or lease payments to the federal government flow out of the region and are not a part of personal income distribution, which is the focus of this study.

The most significant refinement was the development of a damage vector to account for the effects of negative externalities associated with surface mining. Together, the income-distribution matrix and damage-distribution vector yield a net distributional impact matrix. Strip-mining results in five types of damage: (1) aesthetic damages incurred by

Table 9.1. Total Personal Income Distribution Coefficient Matrix, Monongahela National Forest, West Virginia, 1982

		UNDER $5000	5000–9999	10000–14999	15000–19999	20000–24999	25000–34999	35000–49999	50000–74999	75000–99999	OVER 100000	TOTAL
001	LIVESTOCK PRODUCTS	0.092	0.234	0.208	0.232	0.159	0.134	0.052	0.035	0.023	0.016	1.000
002	OTHER AGRICULTURAL PRODUCTS	0.092	0.234	0.208	0.232	0.159	0.134	0.052	0.035	0.023	0.016	1.000
003	FORESTRY AND FISHERY PRODUCTS	0.092	0.234	0.208	0.232	0.159	0.134	0.052	0.035	0.023	0.016	1.000
004	AGRICULTURAL SERVICES	0.092	0.234	0.208	0.232	0.159	0.134	0.052	0.035	0.023	0.016	1.000
005	COAL MINING	0.019	0.132	0.144	0.187	0.141	0.155	0.081	0.043	0.018	0.069	1.000
006	OIL AND GAS EXTRACTION	0.027	0.097	0.170	0.179	0.175	0.197	0.065	0.064	0.018	0.041	1.000
007	STONE AND CLAY MINING	0.019	0.132	0.155	0.141	0.181	0.195	0.080	0.039	0.015	0.021	1.000
008	NEW CONSTRUCTION	0.019	0.106	0.155	0.186	0.180	0.193	0.068	0.039	0.039	0.016	1.000
009	MAINTENANCE AND REPAIR	0.025	0.136	0.169	0.161	0.184	0.166	0.070	0.092	0.011	0.017	1.000
010	FOOD AND KINDRED PRODUCTS	0.019	0.106	0.159	0.203	0.188	0.195	0.066	0.028	0.009	0.014	1.000
011	FABRICS AND YARN	0.022	0.116	0.159	0.203	0.188	0.195	0.066	0.012	0.009	0.014	1.000
012	APPAREL	0.023	0.116	0.162	0.186	0.178	0.189	0.070	0.032	0.012	0.013	1.000
013	MISC FABRICATED TEXTILES	0.033	0.125	0.162	0.186	0.178	0.189	0.070	0.032	0.012	0.013	1.000
014	LUMBER AND WOOD PRODUCTS	0.033	0.125	0.162	0.162	0.173	0.189	0.070	0.050	0.012	0.013	1.000
015	WOOD CONTAINERS	0.027	0.122	0.155	0.167	0.164	0.180	0.073	0.063	0.032	0.030	1.000
016	HOUSEHOLD FURNITURE	0.009	0.143	0.170	0.157	0.099	0.180	0.078	0.063	0.022	0.040	1.000
017	OTHER FURNITURE	0.009	0.097	0.122	0.154	0.131	0.149	0.078	0.081	0.027	0.065	1.000
018	PAPER AND ALLIED PRODUCTS	0.112	0.113	0.155	0.179	0.182	0.202	0.077	0.063	0.034	0.065	1.000
019	PRINTING AND PUBLISHING	0.025	0.112	0.158	0.181	0.184	0.202	0.075	0.036	0.013	0.018	1.000
020	CHEMICAL PRODUCTS	0.025	0.102	0.147	0.179	0.188	0.209	0.084	0.037	0.013	0.017	1.000
021	PLASTICS	0.025	0.102	0.147	0.186	0.186	0.208	0.084	0.038	0.014	0.016	1.000
022	DRUGS	0.019	0.083	0.124	0.163	0.163	0.208	0.084	0.038	0.014	0.017	1.000
023	PETROLEUM REFINING	0.019	0.083	0.124	0.163	0.163	0.223	0.086	0.074	0.031	0.019	1.000
024	RUBBER AND MISC PRODUCTS	0.019	0.082	0.124	0.176	0.176	0.223	0.086	0.074	0.031	0.019	1.000
025	LEATHER	0.019	0.082	0.122	0.166	0.163	0.202	0.084	0.069	0.029	0.064	1.000
026	STONE AND CLAY PRODUCTS	0.017	0.076	0.156	0.161	0.145	0.188	0.088	0.033	0.038	0.044	1.000
027	IRON AND STEEL	0.026	0.110	0.156	0.183	0.177	0.203	0.076	0.033	0.012	0.017	1.000
028	NONFERROUS METALS	0.024	0.066	0.194	0.174	0.197	0.195	0.077	0.047	0.020	0.033	1.000
029	FABRICATED METAL PRODUCTS	0.019	0.063	0.117	0.148	0.136	0.211	0.110	0.061	0.030	0.027	1.000
030	SCREW MACHINE PRODUCTS	0.010	0.113	0.136	0.178	0.141	0.208	0.083	0.088	0.025	0.082	1.000
031	OTHER FABRICATED METAL PRODUCTS	0.038	0.113	0.117	0.151	0.147	0.191	0.093	0.100	0.062	0.027	1.000
032	ENGINES AND TURBINES	0.020	0.055	0.169	0.175	0.128	0.139	0.058	0.032	0.018	0.077	1.000
033	CONSTRUCTION MACHINERY	0.065	0.080	0.171	0.148	0.130	0.125	0.057	0.043	0.024	0.046	1.000
034	SPECIAL MACHINERY	0.071	0.186	0.152	0.175	0.128	0.254	0.096	0.050	0.016	0.016	1.000
035	MISCELLANEOUS MACHINERY	0.019	0.132	0.148	0.162	0.139	0.204	0.094	0.059	0.040	0.042	1.000
036	ELECTRIC MACHINERY	0.037	0.125	0.154	0.162	0.149	0.198	0.081	0.064	0.044	0.044	1.000
037	COMMUNICATION EQUIPMENT	0.023	0.080	0.136	0.151	0.174	0.192	0.084	0.045	0.024	0.042	1.000
038	ELECTRONIC ACCESSORIES	-0.039	0.112	0.135	0.162	0.165	0.116	0.043	0.100	0.038	0.027	1.000
039	TRANSPORTATION EQUIPMENT	0.012	0.167	0.175	0.162	0.057	0.192	0.084	0.045	0.024	0.027	1.000
040	HOUSEHOLD CONSUMPTION	0.017	0.123	0.155	0.178	0.147	0.170	0.073	0.055	0.027	0.056	1.000

Table 9.2. Income Distribution Coefficient Vectors for Coal Mining

	Under $5,000	5,000– 9,999	10,000– 14,999	15,000– 19,999	20,000– 24,999	25,000– 34,999	35,000– 49,999	50,000– 74,999	75,000– 100,000	Over 100,000	Total
Deep mining	.021	.125	.167	.190	.156	.169	.070	.040	.015	.047	1.000
Surface mining	.023	.116	.162	.189	.169	.181	.075	.037	.014	.034	1.000

Table 9.3. Damages Associated with Surface-mined Coal
(in 1982 dollars per household)

Income Class	Aesthetic	Water Treatment	Recreation	Land and Buildings	Flood	Total
0–5,000	40.988	.458	.428	0	0	41.874
5,000–9,999	45.296	.458	.428	3.915	2.565	52.662
10,000–14,999	49.604	.458	.428	5.043	3.304	58.837
15,000–19,999	53.913	.458	.428	5.662	3.710	64.171
20,000–24,999	58.221	.458	.428	5.857	3.838	68.802
25,000–34,999	64.683	.458	.428	6.052	3.965	75.586
35,000–49,999	75.454	.458	.428	6.730	4.409	87.479
50,000–74,999	92.688	.458	.428	44.374	29.073	167.021
75,000–99,999	114.229	.458	.428	55.840	36.584	207.239
100,000 +	146.542	.458	.428	244.062	159.901	551.391

residents, (2) water treatment costs incurred by municipalities, (3) recreation-based damages, (4) flood damages owing to increased runoff, and (5) damage to land and buildings from earth moving.

Damage estimates per household, by type and income class, are presented on a million tons of coal basis in table 9.3.[3] Aesthetic damages dominate in the case of low- and middle-income groups, but property income damages are comparable to aesthetic damages for the upper-income groups. Column 6 of the table is a summation of damages for each income class. Total damages per household per million tons of strip-mined coal range from a low of $41.9 per million tons for the lowest income class to a high of $551.4 per million tons for the highest income class. Since 6,156,000 tons of coal were strip-mined in the region in 1982, if the damage function is linear, total damages would amount to $25.2 million.

Note also that relevant damage information consists of a vector (column 6 of table 9.3) rather than a matrix. The overall net distributional impact, however, is still expressed in matrix form because gains differ in magnitude across sectors, resulting in several income change size classes (see chapter 3).[4]

Simulation

Basic Results

We simulated the distributional impact of a doubling of surface mining in the MNF through a doubling of the final demand for surface-mined coal in the MNF I-O table, and calculated both normative and positive measures. A $221 million increase in the final demand for

Table 9.4. Analysis of Income Distribution Impacts of Surface Mining in the MNF

Case	Income Level (millions of 1982 dollars)	Normative Index (Gini coefficient)	Positive Index (percent gainers)
1. Baseline	1,000.3	.4197	
2. Damage Simulation			
a. Damage Vector	25.2	.1542	
b. Increased Surface Mining	76.1	.4149	
c. Increased Surface − Damage (2*b* −	50.9	.5441	
d. 2*a*)	1,051.2	.4257	
Baseline + Net Increase (1 + 2*c*)			.4273
3. Damage Simulation (Lower Bound)			
a. Damage Vector	12.6	.1542	
b. Increased Surface Mining	76.1	.4149	
c. Increased Surface − Damage (3*b* −	63.5	.4661	
d. 3*a*)	1,063.8	.4225	
Baseline + Net Increase (1 + 3*c*)			.5467
4. Damage Simulation (Upper Bound)			
a. Damage Vector	37.8	.1542	
b. Increased Surface Mining	76.1	.4149	
c. Increased Surface − Damage (4*b* −	38.3	.6715	
d. 4*a*)	1,038.8	.4289	
Baseline + Net Increase (1 + 4*c*)			.3550

surface-mined coal leads to a $273 million increase in *aggregate* regional gross output and a $76.1 million increase in total regional income. This gain in income is significantly greater than the $25.2 million damage total.

The results of our first simulation pertaining to income distribution are presented in rows 2*a* to 2*d* of table 9.4. The three columns of the table correspond to the summation of the distributional impact vector and the normative and positive analyses respectively. Note that the *distribution* of the gross gains and gross losses differs significantly. The total direct and indirect impact Gini for the surface-mining sector is .4149 (as compared to its direct Gini of .6002 calculated from table 9.1). The damage vector Gini is .1542, meaning that damages are spread much more evenly than income gains. This also means that they are highly regressive. The net income change Gini of .5441 is thus significantly greater than the gross change Gini of .4149. The overall effect on the Gini coefficient for the entire regional economy is an increase from .4197 to .4257, or a 1.4 percent increase in inequality. Overall then, an increase in surface-mining activity will have a slightly adverse effect on the existing skewness of income distribution in the MNF economy.

Somewhat surprisingly in light of the relative size of gains and losses, the community impact index is .4273. This means that a slight majority of the households in the MNF economy suffer net losses as a result of the proposed policy. A dissection of the index according to income class reveals the reason for the apparent paradox of strongly positive aggregate net benefits to the region coupled with a majority of residents incurring net losses. Recall that environmental damages were rather evenly distributed, meaning that they represent a higher proportion of the income of lower-income residents than of upper-income residents. On the other hand, gains are skewed more favorably toward upper-income residents. Thus, net losses of a rather small magnitude are prevalent among the many lower-income and, to a lesser extent, middle-income group members, while large net gains are experienced by the vast majority of the much less well-represented upper-income groups.[5]

We should point out, however, that there is a great deal of uncertainty regarding estimates of environmental damage in general, and in particular in our case study, since we have adapted data from another region. For example, the data developed by Randall et al. (1978) may very well represent an underestimate of regional damages since the aesthetic damages are based on willingness to pay (not compensation for damages incurred) and in-region hunting and fishing recreation losses are not estimated, nor are damages to recreators originating outside the region. On the other hand, environmental damages associated with the simulation could be interpreted as being much lower than those cited above (see Rose et al. 1984). To examine the implications for our results of a misspecification of environmental losses, we simulated the effects of both a 50 percent decrease and a 50 percent increase in our initial estimates. The results are presented in rows 3a to 3d and 4a to 4d of table 9.4. Note that the damage vector Gini remains the same as in our original simulation, since the level of damages changes but the relative proportions across income classes do not. For the lower bound case, the decrease in the size of damages relative to the size of the income gains (which remain unchanged) causes the distribution of net impacts to become less skewed than before. The bottom-line result indicates that the Gini coefficient in the MNF would change more slightly than in the base case, from .4197 to .4225. On the other hand, there is a significant change in the community impact index, which is .5467, meaning that a majority of the households in the MNF would receive net gains. The upper bound case, presented in rows 4a to 4d, results in a higher Gini coefficient (.4289) and a smaller community impact index value (.3550) than the baseline. The reason the two indexes move in the opposite direction is again that environmental damages are estimated to fall disproportionately on lower income groups.

The Influence of Institutional Considerations

Thus far we have made two very tenuous assumptions about the distribution of benefits from strip-mining: (1) that all property-related income is retained and respent within the MNF economy; and (2) that all employment is distributed incrementally across the work force—that is, additional manpower is obtained via overtime pay, as opposed to hiring new workers. There are two reasons for invoking these assumptions, which are typical of research in this field. First, lack of data did not enable us to distinguish between income generated and income retained within the region. Also, the straightforward application of I-O models (see equation 3 of chapter 2) calls for income changes going to existing income groups, without a change in the number of households in each group and without an actual upward or downward shift in income status (i.e., average and marginal income increments are assumed to be equal).

We shall now proceed to alter these two crucial assumptions and modify our empirical model and computations accordingly. We begin by noting the broad ramifications of the adjustments. The immediate leakage of capital income (flowing to "absentee" property owners) lowers the overall benefits of strip-mining. On the other hand, the hiring of unemployed workers does not reduce the total wage benefits, but does concentrate them in the hands of the newly employed. Both of these factors will reduce the number of households that receive net gains from strip-mining, and thus the simulation in the previous section is expected to be an upper boundary for the community impact index.[6]

In the absence of the necessary data to pinpoint the extent of property income leakage and new hiring vs. overtime pay for existing workers, we examine a range of alternatives for the 0, 50, and 100 percent levels. The combination of assumptions leads to nine cases, five of which (labeled *a* through *e* in the schematic below) we shall examine in detail.

New Workers (percent)	Property Income Retention (percent)		
	0	50	100
100	*a*		*d*
50		*c*	
0	*b*		*e*

The results will be bounded by cases *a* and *e*. Under assumptions of equal likelihood, case c will be the most meaningful. The effects of alternative assumptions can be readily evaluated by interpolation of the results of our five cases.

Underlying our sensitivity analysis, however, are the following additional conditions and assumptions:

1. There is a sufficient skilled, but unemployed, work force to fill all additional jobs. (For our simulation year, 1982, unemployment in the ten-county area was 11.0 percent, and unemployment among coal miners even higher.)

2. There will be no significant in-migration of population as a result of the policy. (In-migration poses problems in comparing Gini coefficients and community indices).

3. Any property income leakages are considered to be proportional across sectors and income groups. (Obviously, some bias is introduced, because local ownership is likely to be inversely correlated with the size of business enterprise, which, in turn, is positively correlated with income class of owner.)

The computations for the sensitivity analysis proceed as follows. The property income leakage is simply a scalar multiplication of the property income distribution matrix. The wage income adjustment amounts to shifting households out of the two lowest income brackets as they become employed. Any overtime work by the existing workforce is determined by a straightforward application of the wage/salary and pension/annuity matrix.

The results are displayed in table 9.5. The values of the community impact index indicate that the majority of MNF residents will not benefit from the policy in any of the five cases. Still, the results are quite sensitive in magnitude to institutional considerations.[7] Under case *a,* only a small minority of MNF residents would benefit from the policy to increase mining. This is not surprising, since this case concentrates all additional wage and

Table 9.5. Sensitivity Analysis of Income Distribution Impacts

Case	Positive Index (community impact index)	Normative Index (Gini coefficient)
a	.0714	.3846
b	.3981	.4258
c	.3475	.3844
d	.1501	.3845
e	.4273	.4257

salary income in the hands of the newly employed, with no capital-related income retained by residents.

It appears that the results relating to "positive" economic impacts are more sensitive to hiring practices than to capital retention. For example, case d is a smaller departure from case a than is case b in terms of the community impact index. However, the importance of both these factors, typically neglected in impact studies, is clearly demonstrated here.

The values of the Gini coefficient indicate positive improvement in three of the five cases and negligible worsening in the others. Overall, the relative changes are much smaller in the case of the Gini coefficients than in the community impact index. For the former, none of the improvements over baseline are much more than 10 percent, and in cases b and e they are less than a negative .2 percent. Such relatively small changes, however, are not unusual in income distribution studies (see, e.g., Rose et al. 1981 and 1982). In a multisector context, this result can be explained as a relatively low standard deviation among Gini coefficients for individual sectors. For the case in point, the direct Gini coefficient for surface mining of .6 is not much above the baseline average for the MNF economy. Moreover, the total (direct, indirect, and induced) Gini coefficient for that sector is only about .49, or about 17 percent above the average.

Like the positive impacts, the normative impacts appear to be more sensitive to the employment practices in the region than to the retention of capital income within the region. The changes in Ginis in table 9.5 are negligible for variations in capital income retention because capital income is a rather small proportion of total income gains in this case (about 15 percent of the total) and because property income is relatively more evenly distributed in the MNF than in other regions or the United States as a whole.

Of all the scenarios modeled, c is perhaps the most indicative of the policy effects on income distribution. With respect to employment to meet the increased demand for coal, it is not likely that all job opportunities would accrue to workers already employed. From 1978 to 1984, for example, the average number of days actually worked by coal miners ranged from 55 to 60 percent of the available work days in any given year. It would be unreasonable to assume that none of the employment opportunities would accrue to the ranks of the unemployed, particularly in light of stated union policy.[8] Extending the analysis to all sectors of the economy within the MNF, unemployment is so high that one would expect at least some of the added job opportunities to go to idle workers.

Similarly, with respect to capital income retention within the MNF, it appears that because of the rural nature of the region, coupled with its narrowly defined boundaries, little of the capital income generated would accrue to the MNF resident population. The ownership of income-generating capital would not be expected to be concentrated in the hands of a rural population, particularly one whose poverty levels are significantly higher than the nation's.[9] On the other hand, it would be unreasonable to assume that all capital income would leave the region under any development scenario. Again, scenario c best represents a reasonable middle ground.

The concern over the distribution of income gains has important implications for long-term growth in resource regions. Previous experience is, however, serious cause for concern, as summarized by a federal government study:

> Where a society depends primarily on the extraction of natural resources for its income and employment—as did the people of Appalachia—it is extremely important that a high proportion of wealth created by extraction be reinvested locally in other activities. The relatively low production of native capital did not produce such a reinvestment in large

sections of the region. Much of the wealth produced by coal and timber was seldom seen locally. It went downstream with the great hardwood logs; it rode out on rails with the coal cars; it was mailed between distant cities as royalty checks to nonresident operators who had bought rights to the land for 50 cents or a dollar an acre. (U.S. Geological Survey 1968, 4)

Conclusion

In this chapter we have illustrated the usefulness of our model for analyzing both the positive and normative implications of natural-resource policy decisions at the regional level. The case study should be typical of such applications. It indicates that an income distribution matrix regionalized from our basic matrix for the United States, supplemented by a conventional input-output table and data on any negative externalities that may arise, can yield valuable insights into distributional outcomes.

The analyses also show why multisectoral income distribution models should not be applied in a mechanical fashion. That is, the ordinary regional I-O model does not account well for income leakages and variations in average and marginal income coefficients. We illustrate how sensitive the results are to these factors, especially with reference to the community impact index.

Given the implications of our results and the current inadequacy of data, there is clearly a need for further study of the structural and institutional aspects of natural-resource policy. In the meantime, sensitivity analyses, the disaggregation of income distribution by type of income, and sound judgment can be combined in a pragmatic way by policy-makers to address some important distributional issues.

10/ Policy Analysis at the National Level
*Distributional Impacts of Oil and Gas
Tax Reform Proposals*

The previous chapter focused on how a policy to encourage natural resource development in an individual National Forest changed the income distribution in the surrounding region. In this chapter, we address a very different type of case. We examine the distributional impacts nationwide of a set of 1985–86 federal income tax proposals concerning the oil and gas industries. The goals of the reform are to improve the tax system by making it more efficient and equitable. As noted in chapter 1, however, there are numerous ways that income distribution can be affected via the natural resource sectors. With respect to their impact on natural resources, the tax reforms are more indirect than the policy presented in the previous chapter, since they operate through a system of fiscal incentives rather than by direct regulation. Also in contrast, the focus of this chapter will be on the normative, rather than positive, implications of the policy.

Specifically, the reforms to be examined are: (1) the elimination of the percentage depletion allowances (PDA) on oil and gas production, and (2) the elimination of expensing of intangible drilling costs (IDC). These deductions have often been viewed as tax shelters for the well-to-do (see Galper and Zimmerman 1977; Piet 1984). Eliminating them is intended to close tax "loopholes" and make the system more equitable. However, existing analyses of this policy have been superficial, since they only consider its direct impact, and only a portion of its direct impact at that. They typically neglect the loss of jobs and income in the oil and gas industry owing to the ensuing higher operating costs, as well as the multiplier effects arising from reduced indirect and induced input requirements. It is possible that once all of the general equilibrium effects are taken into account, the full incidence of the tax reforms may turn out to be inequitable. This is the hypothesis we test below.

The following section examines the fiscal incentives and disincentives in the oil and gas industries. Therefore, we present a discussion of alternative versions of the current tax reforms. The direct effects of these reforms are determined from major studies by the Treasury Department, Congressional Budget Office, and Office of Management and Budget. Finally, we apply our model to the estimation of the total effects of the reforms.

Fiscal Incentives in the Oil and Gas Industries

Investments in the oil and gas industries have long been considered excellent tax shelters because of several important "tax breaks" available to partnerships and small corporations in these industries. One prime example is the percentage depletion allowance for independent producers, which is 15 percent of the *gross* income from the property. It can be applied even after the recovery of all acquisition and development expenses. A second example is the expensing of intangible drilling costs, which includes labor, fuels, repairs, and site preparation. It permits a quick write-off for expenditures that apply to the life of the well.

There are two alternative views of this preferential taxation. One focuses on the strategic and economic importance of the oil and gas industries, which provide valuable products with few good substitutes. Proponents of this view express concern about the adequacy of domestic reserves and the claim that the social cost of oil should include both scarcity and security premiums (see Hogan 1979). This provides a rationale for subsidizing the discovery of new reserves in the United States and their production. Moreover, given the uncertainty of exploratory drilling, there is a risk premium, which is used to justify a higher rate of return in the industry. Overall the relatively higher rate of return is seen as evidence of the orderly functioning of markets in the short run, and the subsidies are viewed as necessary to overcome imperfections associated with externalities and myopia as to long-run supply considerations.

An opposing view emphasizes the concentration of large firms in the oil and gas industries and the resultant wielding of market power. The profits reaped by the oil industry in the aftermath of the Arab oil embargo of 1973–74 and the OPEC price escalations of the late 1970s and early 1980s are considered pure windfalls at the expense of the consumer. Preferential tax provisions are viewed as further benefiting the well-to-do in general. Holders of this viewpoint characterize the market as working poorly and the current tax system as exacerbating the situation.

Various studies have been able to shed light on some of these issues, though not to resolve them completely. For example, Chapman (1983) and others have found that the oil industry has been characterized by greater than average profits since the embargo, but significantly greater profits in only two years. Galper and Zimmerman (1977) found that the benefits of preferential taxation in oil and gas were skewed more toward higher income groups than any other sector. Overall, however, studies of the distributional implications of these fiscal incentives are rare, and none to date have been done in a general equilibrium context.

Tax Reform Proposals

Several alternative tax reform plans have been proposed, including the U.S. Department of the Treasury, Kemp-Kasten (H.R. 6165, S. 2948), and Bradley-Gephardt (S. 1421, H.R. 3271) plans, and a proposal favored by the Reagan administration.[1] Each of these plans would affect the oil and gas industry somewhat differently. The purpose of this section is to discuss how these proposals differ with respect to the percentage depletion allowance, expensing of intangible drilling costs, and the windfall profits tax on domestically produced crude oil.

As noted above, the current tax code allows nonintegrated producers of oil and natural gas a tax deduction for depletion of the oil and/or gas reservoir and current year expensing of specific drilling costs even if the well has not produced any oil or gas. A windfall profits tax is also applied to domestic crude oil.

The Treasury Department proposal would repeal all three provisions in the tax code. However, the percentage depletion allowance would be replaced by an annual deduction equal to current unrecovered costs multiplied by the percentage of reserves depleted that year. This percentage would be defined by oil or natural gas sold that year relative to known reserves at the beginning of the year. The Treasury Department refers to this method as cost depletion. Expensing of intangible drilling costs would be replaced by a set of depreciation rules similar to those proposed for other industries with multiperiod production. The general thrust of the cost capitalization rules is to allow firms a deduction for costs of production incurred at the time the product is sold. Current rules allow some development costs to be deducted during the year they are incurred: in many cases this occurs before the well begins producing. Dry holes would be fully expensed during the year the site is abandoned as a nonproducing well. Inflation indexation would be allowed for both the depletion of reserves and costs of development.

The Bradley-Gephardt and Kemp-Kasten proposals would both follow the Treasury Department plan in repealing the percentage depletion allowance and intangible drilling cost deductions and replacing them with asset depreciation. Neither proposal would allow inflation indexing of costs; both would retain the windfall profits tax. An alternative plan favored by the Reagan administration would repeal the depletion allowance but retain the intangible drilling cost deduction. However, oil and gas producers would be subject to a minimum tax. This proposal also retains the windfall profits tax.

The Treasury Department has offered several arguments in favor of these revisions of the tax code. Primarily, the arguments are that many of the current rules pertaining to the oil and gas industries result in inefficient resource allocation and that they are inequitable. The Treasury claims that the percentage depletion allowance is a production subsidy, since the deduction can be claimed even after all development costs have been recovered, which tends to reduce post-tax costs. Thus, the current tax code encourages more production of oil and natural gas than is economically justifiable on the basis of the costs of development. Also, through the provision for deduction of intangible drilling costs it biases exploration in favor of drilling as opposed to other methods such as seismic surveys or satellite surveys.

The current tax code is viewed as inequitable, since most of the benefits accrue to upper income bracket taxpayers. The U.S. Treasury study (1984, pp. 231–33) concludes that 90,000 taxpayers with adjusted gross incomes over $75,000 garner half the benefits from the percentage depletion allowances, averaging about $6,400 each; while half of the intangible drilling cost benefits go to just 31,000 taxpayers with adjusted gross incomes greater than $100,000, averaging about $28,000 per taxpayer. Note that if these data are accurate and equity is our main concern, elimination of current year expensing of intangible drilling costs would perhaps be a higher priority than eliminating the percentage depletion allowance. However, this does not account for any other direct or indirect economic effects resulting from tax reform specifically directed at the oil and gas industries.

Opponents of the proposals argue that a significant reduction in domestic crude output is likely to result. Repeal of the windfall profits tax is intended to offset such output effects, but the effect of such repeal is likely to be curtailed by the recent decline in crude oil prices, and the prospect that they are likely to remain at or below $20 per barrel until the end of the decade. Moreover, proponents of the current tax code argue that current tax treatment is similar to tax treatment of investment in other industries under Accelerated Cost Recovery. Finally, such tax treatment may be necessary if the industry is inherently more risky than other types of industrial enterprise. Small firms may not be able to attract investor funds without relatively favorable tax treatment (Congressional Budget Office 1985).

Direct Effects of Tax Reform on the Oil and Gas Industries

Examination of the distributional impacts of eliminating the percentage depletion allowance (PDA) and expensing of intangible drilling costs (IDC) involves two steps. First, an analysis of the direct impacts of tax reform on tax liabilities across income groups and the resulting reduction in income is undertaken in this section. The Treasury study has provided one estimate, but it is not sufficiently disaggregated to be useful. Estimates of the resulting output reductions in oil and gas are also required.

Second, the output reductions in the oil and gas industries are used to "drive" our I-O income distribution model in the following section. Gini coefficients of income distribution are computed and analyzed for the pre-reform case, direct impacts, and total incidence scenarios. In addition, the model is capable of calculating the distribution of total effects across sectors and occupational categories, and can provide some insight into regional implications.

The Treasury study estimates of the distribution of benefits serves as the basis of our estimates for all income groups. First, assuming that exactly half the benefits from IDC expensing flow to income earners in the $100,000 or greater income bracket, and that each member of this bracket averages $28,000 in tax preferences, their loss of benefits is $868 million for the first effective year of the reforms.[2] The remaining $868 million flows to the other income groups. Recall that the Treasury estimates of the PDA give half the benefits to income earners above $75,000. We have incorporated this information in distributing the tax, and the benefits of the PDA are thus slightly less skewed than those of the IDC.

In the absence of direct data to distribute the total tax benefits of the PDA and IDC to the lower income investors, we used an indirect method involving two steps. First, we made use of data provided by Galper and Zimmerman (1977), who have estimated the share of unincorporated business losses by marginal tax rates for oil and gas extraction. We justify the use of these data as a proxy for the distribution of tax write-offs for the PDA and IDC on the basis of the statement by Galper and Zimmerman that "restricting the[ir] analysis to investors with gross losses may come closer to identifying the set of tax-motivated investors" (p. 390). Second, data associating adjusted gross income brackets with marginal tax rates from a study of Thompson and Hicks (1983) enable us to distribute tax benefits (whether positive or negative, as in the context of reforms evaluated here) among investors according to their incomes.

Before presenting the results, we should point out that one of the basic assumptions of tax reform analysis is that there is an "actual" level of income from any activity, such as oil and gas investment, and that the "net" income, following deductions, is simply a "paper" amount. Elimination of tax preferences would otherwise appear to *raise* income, because there would be less to deduct. But the Treasury estimates cited above in effect refer to a lowering of tax deductions, thereby increasing the income subject to tax, and hence tax liability, and thus *lowering* the "actual" *after-tax* income.

Our initial distribution of direct tax reform impacts only represents the change in tax liability. A further adjustment is required to compute the post-reform after-tax income reduction. The computation is simplified if we think of the situation directly as one in which a taxpayer can no longer shelter, say, $1,000 of income. The after-tax reduction is the portion of the $1,000 that is taxed away. The actual post-reform income reduction from the oil and gas sector is thus simply the change in tax liability times the marginal tax rate.[3]

The post-reform reduction in income is shown in column 2 of table 10.1. Column 1 of the table shows the level of net (after-tax) pre-reform income from the oil and gas sector, and

Table 10.1. Direct Income Reductions from Oil and Gas Tax Reforms, 1987 (in millions of 1982 dollars)

Income Bracket	Pre-Reform Income from Oil and Gas	Reduction in Income Owing to Tax Reform	Percentage Change
0–4,999	1,071	35.6	3.32
5,000–9,999	2,422	28.2	1.16
10,000–14,999	3,507	4.4	0.13
15,000–19,999	3,687	18.3	0.50
20,000–24,999	3,913	31.8	0.81
25,000–34,999	7,468	88.5	1.19
35,000–49,999	7,441	219.7	2.95
50,000–74,999	2,998	103.3	3.44
75,000–99,000	825	350.9	42.53
100,000+	3,463	751.4	21.70
Total	36,795	1,632.1	4.44
Gini	.4576	.8482	N.A.

column 3 shows the percentage reduction from this baseline. As we would expect from a proposal intended to promote vertical equity, the direct burden of the tax reform is highly progressive, ranging from less than 1 percent of all income received from the petroleum sector by some of the lowest brackets to 42.53 and 21.70 percent by the two highest brackets. The Gini coefficient of .8482 for the direct reduction[4] causes the post-tax Gini coefficient[5] for the petroleum sector to fall from a pre-reform .4576 to a post-reform .4396, a 3.93 percent improvement.

Two estimates of the impact of the Treasury Department proposal on oil and gas production are available from the American Petroleum Institute. One set of estimates is based on an industry survey it conducted (see American Petroleum Institute 1985a) and another set is based on forecasts (see American Petroleum Institute 1985b). Both sources ultimately derive their volumetric estimates of the production decrease by combining their information with data from *Annual Energy Outlook, 1984* (Energy Information Administration 1985).

The API survey asked for percentage estimates of the effect of the Treasury proposal on industry levels of drilling and production of petroleum and natural gas for 1986, 1990, and 1995. The companies participating regularly prepare such forecasts; moreover, the range of estimates is likely to contain the true impact of the proposals, since the responses are from several different corporations. The questionnaire asked for estimates under two regimes: (1) the original Treasury proposal, and (2) the original proposal minus repeal of the windfall profits tax and reductions in corporate tax rates. Since the survey took place before the recent decline in oil prices, the second set of estimates is likely to understate the effects of the Treasury (or similar) proposal if enacted now. Also, windfall profits are now a moot point. Accordingly, we make use of the responses under the first regime, presented in table 10.2. They show that the average estimated percentage decrease in drilling activity is initially quite large, with some lag before reduced drilling activity begins to have a significant effect on production. Actually, the forecasts prepared by the API compare favorably with the estimates presented in table 10.2. For example, the forecasted reduction for 1995 is a range of 1,105 to 1,702 TBD, while the API projection based on the survey is 1,518 TBD. Overall, we interpret these studies as suggesting there will be a 10 percent annual reduction

Table 10.2. Direct Impact of Oil and Gas Tax Reforms
(percentage change)

Year	Drilling Oil and Gas	Production Crude Oil	Natural Gas
1986	−17.0	−2.5	−2.8
1990	−17.0	−5.4	−6.8
1995	−13.8	−8.4	−10.2

Source: American Petroleum Institute 1985a.

in the output of the oil and gas industry for the remainder of this decade. We perform our analysis on this basis for the year 1987.

Second-order Effects

One of the major themes of this book has been the importance of second-order, or general equilibrium, impacts of natural resource policy. We have illustrated this theme in previous chapters by pointing to the complexities and subtleties beyond the obvious direct, or partial equilibrium, aspects of these policies. In the context of the economics of taxation, the terminology is different, but the basic insight is the same—the direct "imposition" of a tax (or tax reform) is likely to differ considerably from its ultimate "incidence." This has been acknowledged for years in the public finance literature (see, e.g., Musgrave 1959; Harberger 1962), but the difficulty has been in finding an operational methodology by which to perform the analysis. More recently, input-output (see, e.g., Golladay and Haveman 1977) and computable general equilibrium models based on I-O data (see, e.g., Ballard et al. 1985) have proven successful in this effort. Our model is specifically geared to evaluating the distributional aspects of tax incidence.

In the context of this chapter, we wish to examine the extent to which general equilibrium effects override the initial progressivity of tax reforms on the oil and gas industries. The issue is whether a policy designed, at least in part, to improve the distribution of income might in fact worsen it. A priori, one would expect that the indirect and induced effects would be more normally distributed than the imposition of a set of reforms intended to eliminate tax shelters, usually utilized by those in upper income brackets. If the linkage between the oil and gas sector and its direct and indirect suppliers is such as to cause a relatively greater reduction in employment in less-skilled occupations and a relatively greater reduction in capital-related income among low- and middle-income groups, the direct egalitarian effects could be more than offset.

Basic Computations

The simulation of the distributional impacts of the tax reforms is a straightforward application of our model. First, a change in final demand for oil and gas extraction is multiplied by the closed Leontief inverse of the U.S. input-output table (U.S. Forest Service 1986) to determine the gross output reductions in each sector of the economy.[6] The ten sectors affected most are shown in table 10.3. Overall, there is a strong similarity between the results for those sectors affected directly and those affected by the totality of multiplier effects. Only two sectors that are not among the top ten in the direct requirements column appear in the total requirements column, and the rank order between the top sectors is

Table 10.3. Sectors Most Affected by Oil and Gas Industry Tax Reforms

Sector[a]	Direct Requirements[b]	Total Requirements[b]
Real estate	.087	.244
Maintenance	.054	.093
Utilities	.016	.081
Business services	.015	.081
Finance	.008	.091
Petroleum refining	.008	.065
Trade	.008	.160
Restaurants	.007	[c]
Mining machinery	.005	[c]
Transportation	.005	.059
Food and kindred products	[d]	.083
Other services	[d]	.099

[a]Does not include "own-use" of oil and gas by the petroleum sector.
[b]Reduction per dollar decreases in final demand for petroleum sector.
[c]Among the top 10 sectors in terms of direct impacts only.
[d]Among the top 10 sectors in terms of total impacts only.

reasonably close. Still, some sectors, such as maintenance and mining machinery, are stimulated primarily by the oil and gas industries themselves, while others, such as business services, are linked to oil and gas even more through various rounds of indirect suppliers, and still others, such as food and kindred products or trade, are stimulated primarily by the induced effects of income payments and subsequent consumer purchases. Thus several sectors that would not appear to be significantly affected by the oil and gas tax reforms will, in fact, have a major influence on the overall change in income distribution.

Second, a vector of sectoral gross output changes is multiplied by our multisector income distribution matrix, which is adjusted to reflect post-tax levels. The matrix also contains a modified oil and gas sector column to reflect the tax reforms themselves. This yields a vector of total after-tax income changes differentiated by income group. The results pertain to the first potential effective year of the reforms, though we have used a 1982 I-O table. This is possible because computations were performed with the coefficients of the table, which represent the structure of the economy, and adjusted final demand, which accounts for different output levels for 1987. The structural coefficients of an I-O model are impervious to scale. As typically is the case because of lack of data, we have applied a table specified for one year to another. Errors in the results arise to the extent that changes in production technology or input substitution are not reflected by the set of fixed coefficients. It is highly likely that substitution effects will arise from the shift of resources out of oil and gas into other sectors, or that other fuels will be substituted for oil and gas. However, while likely significant in the long run, these are beyond the scope of this study. First, substitution possibilities are limited in the first year of the reforms. Second, a set of powerful predictive models would be required to evaluate these and future substitutions in an I-O context (e.g., elasticities of substitution of fuels on a sector-by-sector basis, labor and capital market models).

Results

The results of our income distribution analysis are displayed in table 10.4 in terms of individual income bracket effects and the Gini coefficient. Column 1 of the table is the

Table 10.4. Total Impact of Oil and Gas Tax Reforms on the U.S. Economy, 1987 (in billions of 1982 dollars)

Income Bracket	Pre-Reform Income Economywide	Reduction in Income Owing to Tax Reform	Percentage Change
0–4,999	42	.274	0.65
5,000–9,999	162	.884	0.55
10,000–14,999	214	1.253	0.59
15,000–19,999	217	1.318	0.61
20,000–24,999	231	1.443	0.63
25,000–34,999	437	2.787	0.64
35,000–49,999	433	2.796	0.65
50,000–74,999	198	1.344	0.68
75,000–99,000	62	.386	0.62
100,000+	133	1.151	0.87
Total	2,129	13,636	0.64
Gini	.4493	.4804	N.A.

baseline income distribution of the U.S. economy (all sectors) projected to 1987. Column 2 contains the distribution of the direct and indirect income reductions associated with the decrease in oil and gas output, and column 3 contains the percentage change.

The entries in the income reduction column represent the combination of three effects: (1) the direct income reduction as a result of the tax reforms for those who receive payments from the oil and gas sector (see again table 10.1), (2) the direct income reductions within the oil and gas sector stemming from the 10% decline in production in that sector, and (3) the indirect and induced multiplier effects of the output reduction. Together they total $13.636 billion ($1.632, $3.543, and $8.461 billion respectively). This means that the overall outcome is dominated by the first- and second-order output effects of the reform. The distribution of these income reductions is similar to the baseline (post-tax) income distribution of the economy as a whole (.4513 vs. .4493 respectively). Sectors with some of the most uneven distributions, such as real estate, bear a high proportion of the effects of the petroleum sector output reductions, but these are the exceptions rather than the rule. The Gini coefficient of the combination of impacts is .4804, meaning that the total income reductions are only modestly skewed toward high-income groups (note the percentage reductions in column 3 of table 10.4).

It is not surprising then that the overall Gini coefficient for the economy is reduced only slightly from .4493 to .4491, or .04 percent. Thus, the general equilibrium effects of the oil and gas sector tax reforms are "income distribution neutral." Or, in terms of our initial hypothesis, they do not have the opposite of the intended effect (i.e., adversely affect low-income groups in a disproportionate way). At the same time, we should reiterate that the second-order effects nullified most of the intended equalization.

While the impact of the reforms on the size distribution of personal income in the United States as a whole does not raise any concern, the spatial distribution of the impacts may be troublesome. A 10 percent reduction in petroleum sector output is likely to be concentrated in the Texas-Oklahoma, Central Gulf Coast, and Appalachian regions. The economies of these areas have already been hit hard by the sharp decline in oil prices, and further loss of income, either absolute or relative, exacerbates the situation.

Conclusion

We have endeavored to show how our model can provide considerable improvement in the estimates of the equity impacts of changing the tax code. Few studies of the current tax reform proposals, or any previous tax reform, evaluate impacts outside the industry directly affected. In our example, there are broader distributional implications of job losses in the oil and gas industries and of cutbacks in the purchase of drilling and operating supplies resulting from tax reform. Moreover, there are income "multiplier" effects relating to the reduction in indirect and induced input requirements. Thus, the full "incidence" of the reforms can only be examined in a general equilibrium framework. If government policy-makers intend to promote equity, the incidence of their proposals, as measured by direct and indirect effects on the size distribution of personal income, should be evaluated to ensure that the proposals do not have an effect opposite to that intended.

11/ Conclusion

Summary

This study has endeavored to advance the state of the art of modeling income distribution in both theoretical and empirical directions. In relation to natural resource policy in particular and economic policy in general, income distribution impacts have received little attention. This neglect is not attributable to a lack of importance of the subject matter, but rather to obstacles and controversies associated with its evaluation. The authors believe they have contributed to the diminution of some of these problems by building an empirical model, based largely on primary data, that can be used for positive as well as the more typical normative analysis of distributional impacts.

At the same time, our analyses of the setting in which natural-resource development takes place and our illustrative uses of the model should heighten awareness of distributional issues. Areas in which natural resources are typically located are characterized by disproportionate numbers of poor and other low-income groups, who in many cases have not shared in the rewards of resource development. They and various other interest groups have effectively staked a property rights claim to natural resources held in the public domain by virtue of recent legislation requiring citizen participation in natural resource policy-making. No longer can the analyst or the policy-maker be satisfied that the mere evaluation of aggregate net benefits of a proposal will be sufficient basis on which to make a decision.

There were several good reasons to choose an input-output framework for this purpose. Since much of this nation's natural resources are in the public domain, officials of agencies such as the U.S. Forest Service and the U.S. Bureau of Land Management are concerned with the ramifications of their actions among the population at large. Thus, it is necessary to look beyond the evaluation of policies on the basis of the more narrow criteria used by individual firms and interest groups directly involved and to consider those indirectly affected as well. The general equilibrium nature of I-O makes it well suited to this task. The multisector base of the I-O model also renders it effective in analyzing structural change. This is important because the major impetus to a change in income distribution in the relatively small, rural economies that characterize natural resource areas is the enhancement of a sector or addition of a new one—that is, a structural economic shift.

Overall, this study includes:

1. Establishment of a basis for using I-O analysis for the study of the distributional impacts of natural resource policy; this was done on both theoretical and empirical levels by showing the prominent effects of structural and institutional variables in the distributional outcome.

2. Development of positive economic indicators of income distribution to be used for predictive purposes; these measures may also facilitate public participation in policy making.

3. Construction of the first multisector dividend distribution matrix based on primary data; this was based on the refinement of data obtained from a New York Stock Exchange survey.

4. Construction of the most comprehensive multisector model of income distribution to date; this model includes all fourteen major types of personal income and is based on primary data for over 90 percent of the income.

5. Formulation of procedures to regionalize income distribution to the small area level.

6. Application of the model to important policy issues; the applications indicate how the model could be used to evaluate precisely the direct and second-order gains and losses from natural resource policy.

Applicability of the Model

The modeling system we have developed should be of substantial use to policy-makers in addressing important issues relating to natural resources. The assessment of who gains and who loses from proposed policies can be made from two perspectives. One is the conventional, although controversial, normative economic analysis of the "fairness" of the distribution of income changes. The other, developed expressly in this study, deals with a positive economic analysis of income changes—the ability to use distributional information for predictive purposes. The conventional cost-benefit analysis approach assumes people will support a policy for which the net benefits are positive as a whole for the region in question. This imputes an unwarranted degree of altruism to residents in many cases, since it is possible for regional net benefits to be positive while the majority of the affected population individually suffer a net loss. Our positive approach yields a matrix of probabilities of how each person will be affected on an individual basis. It also provides insight into how a person will react to such information, either in active opposition or support, or with apathy.

There are mounting pressures on public land management agencies for mutually exclusive uses of their lands. The models we have developed give these agencies the ability to assess an important dimension of alternatives, such as mining and logging initiatives, in comparison to the status quo. This capability will aid these decision-makers in evaluating the full opportunity costs of their actions.

Another kind of encroachment on natural resource areas arises more subtly. As population grows and spreads out, more developments border forests, rangelands, and wilderness areas. Given the interdependence of economic trading areas, growth such as this will have its repercussions on the residents of these natural resource areas. Distributional changes that accompany urbanization may be as prevalent as those brought about by resource-management policies, but can be modeled in a similar fashion.

Important contemporary issues pertaining to public lands, such as acid rain, endangered species, water depletion, infrastructure development, and the maintenance of wilderness areas all have distributional implications. The modeling capability presented in this book can help agencies such as the U.S. Forest Service and the Bureau of Land

Management evaluate public attitudes about these issues by resource region residents and nonresidents alike.

Finally, we note the many issues outside the field of natural resources that can be addressed by the model: (1) the direct analysis of income distribution trends in the United States or any of its subregions, and (2) more general current issues, such as tax reform, public assistance, and deindustrialization, all of which have important distributional elements. In many of these cases, the fixed coefficient assumption of our distributional matrices may be overly restrictive, but the reader is reminded that several methods have been developed to incorporate changing coefficients into an I-O framework.

Future Research

Given limitations of time and resources, this study was not able to develop as complete a model as envisaged at its outset. Moreover, as the research progressed, additional worthwhile aspects of the subject were revealed. It is hoped that future research will address these concerns.

First, our empirical models deal mainly with the before-tax/transfer distribution of income. In addition to local government fiscal impacts of natural resource development, large sums may flow to the federal government from leases. Federal laws call for a portion of this money to be returned to the host regions, and it is likely that the impacts of this reinvestment will not be uniform across income groups. Our conceptual framework can serve as the basis for a *net* analysis, but some empirical work still needs to be done on the income profile of public expenditure recipients.

Another incomplete area pertains to the distribution of damages. Chapter 9 illustrates how important estimates of this portion of income change can be. Additional work is needed on the distribution of direct damages associated with mining, logging, and recreation in forest areas and their links to indirect damages stemming from economic activity in general.

A crucial gap in modeling income distribution, and in regional impact analysis in general, is the distinction between income generated and income retained. The matrices developed represent only the former income category. In a largely self-contained area, this results in no loss of accuracy, but many natural-resource regions are small and prone to large inflows and outflows of income to commuting workers or absentee property owners. These income flows are not pertinent when the impacted population is defined as residents of the host region, and some empirical adjustments are needed. In chapter 8 we note how published data on commuters can be used to adjust regional matrices, but comparable data on the residence of owners of firms or vacation homes do not appear to exist.

Overall, the greatest obstacle to future research is a lack of data, especially at the regional level. An extensive search was needed to uncover the New York Stock Exchange data used to derive our dividend matrices. Searches for data on other income types were unsuccessful. At the same time, it should be noted that practically all of the data needed to construct a comprehensive multisector income distribution model, including the distinction between income generated and income retained, are in the possession of the U.S. Internal Revenue Service. Efforts should be made to provide access to these data while upholding confidentiality requirements.

Our work has sought to illustrate the usefulness of modeling the income distributional impacts of natural resource policy. It is hoped that this study will provide an impetus to further conceptual breakthroughs, more extensive data collection, and a broader set of applications with regard to distributional analysis.

Notes

1 / Important Dimensions of Natural Resource Policy

1. For example, Gianessi and Peskin (1980) have estimated the distribution of net environmental policy benefits, LeVeen and Goldman (1978) have examined the distribution of irrigation water subsidies, and Ervin et al. (1984) have analyzed the bias in cross-compliance between soil conservation and farm commodity programs.

2. Public lands administered by the Forest Service and Bureau of Land Management are strongly resource-based. For example, roughly 10 percent of the nation's known oil and gas reserves occur on public lands and the Outer Continental Shelf, half of the nation's coal reserves are on federal lands, and 60 percent of the nation's nuclear minerals and almost all of the known oil shale deposits in the United States occur on federally owned lands (U.S. Department of Interior 1981). Public lands contain an abundance of the principal sources of molybdenum, phosphate, and potash. An extensive amount of renewable resources such as timber and rangeland is found on federal holdings. All of these potential development alternatives compete with recreational, wilderness preservation, and wildlife refuge uses of these lands.

3. The Forest Service had established participation as official policy as early as 1970, and by 1972 had initiated its "Inform and Involve" program (see Duerr 1975).

4. Downing applies this model to the implementation of the Clean Air Act of 1970. Other authors have used this general framework, with more detail in terms of number of agents and less emphasis on constrained self-interest, to analyze a wide range of topics including land-use planning in Louisville, Kentucky (Garkovich 1982); potential support/opposition in the Northwest to changes in logging policy (Stevens 1984); and interaction among participants in selected Forest Service and Bureau of Land Management study areas in the western United States (Culhane 1981).

5. Elo and Beale (1984) discuss differences in the concepts "rural" and "nonmetropolitan," both of which are used by federal agencies in data collection and tabulation, though neither concept is entirely satisfactory in practice. The concept we have in mind parallels that of Elo and Beale—areas with low population density.

6. The situation is, of course, exacerbated by the high degree of absentee ownership of public land leases or private mineral rights in regions such as this.

2 / Input-Output Analysis of Income Distribution Impacts

1. The credit for the first application of input-output analysis to the study of income distribution belongs to Alfred Conrad (1955), who worked with the Harvard Economic Research Project in the early 1950s. Although Conrad makes reference to an I-O framework, his model aggregates production to a single sector and involves a cumbersome solution algorithm. Miyazawa's work on income distribution, which is the most detailed and complete of the contributions, first appeared in Japanese journals in the 1960s (see Miyazawa 1968).

2. The ability theory category also encompasses the closely related screening, filtering, and signaling theories (Arrow 1973, Stiglitz

1975, and Spence 1974 respectively), in which education imperfectly identifies ability.

3. Sahota (1978) suggests that the Cambridge theory of functional income distribution (represented in the list of references by Meade 1964) is related to the inheritance theory. We suggest, however, that it is more properly included in the "complete" theories discussed later in this chapter.

4. Life cycle here refers simply to the composition of earnings in terms of age and not to the broader microeconomic-based theory of the consumption function by Modigliano and Ando (1960).

5. The marginal productivity theory has often been criticized as being overly simplistic. Bronfenbrenner (1971) points out that the theory by itself is incomplete and really just represents a "microdistribution" explanation of the pricing of productive inputs. It needs to be extended to the "macrodistribution" problem of "adding-up" the relative shares of functional income payments. Only two major macrodistribution theories are discussed here. The reader is referred to Bronfenbrenner for an exposition of others.

6. We say "basic" because there have been numerous extensions of the static, linear model to include dynamic and nonlinear elements, as well as reactions to price change (see Leontief 1970; Sandberg 1973; Hudson and Jorgenson 1974).

7. There is some dispute over the characterization of the institutionalist school, though most experts would suggest that its principles encompass the work of J. S. Mill, T. Veblen, R. T. Ely, J. R. Commons, and W. C. Mitchell. The key principle is that institutions other than the marketplace dominate, and that these institutions and their implications are highly variable from case to case. Bronfenbrenner (1971) quotes Mill's summary of distribution as "a matter of human institutions only," and suggests that several "institutional" theories have followed Mill in considering income distribution to be highly variable according to the institutional context. In this study we emphasize these aspects of institutionalism without feeling compelled to add all of the other trappings of the school expressed by its members or attributed to it by its critics.

8. The term "structure" is often used in a different manner in industrial organization, in which it refers to the "market environment" (competitive, oligopolistic, or monopolistic). In our usage this would be an "institutional" consideration. Obviously, the existence of monopoly profits has an effect on income distribution.

9. By production alternatives we refer to entire processes (e.g., in steel making this includes direct oxygen, electric arc, or open hearth furnaces). Substitution is often a matter of the rate of adoption of a technological innovation. This is well within the grasp of several I-O extensions such as the generalized I-O model that includes a choice of techniques (see Chenery and Clark 1959), and the "best-practice" dynamic I-O model (see Miernyk 1968).

10. Institutional and structural differences may be as important on the consumption side as the production side. That is, the consumption basket will differ among income groups such that initial changes in distribution have feedback effects through differential spending patterns (see Miyazawa 1976; Golladay and Haveman 1977; Henry and Martin 1984).

11. We have chosen these two extremes for pedagogical reasons only. Empirical investigation would probably find marginal adjustments operative in both cases, though the adjustments in the consumption pattern of the newly employed would be much greater. Similarly, both income payments groups would also be likely to receive "marginal" payments—i.e., overtime pay for the continuously employed would be greater than regular pay on an hourly basis (and by different proportions in different occupations, hence income classes). This is one way to introduce nonlinearities, or at least piece-wise nonlinearities, into an I-O framework.

12. The convention of using an apportioning factor, ρ_j, keeps the empirical work of this study manageable. That is, it enables us to limit the specifications to the two extremes (the wage distribution associated with all overtime vs. all new jobs), and then to easily calculate any combination of the two by the expression $Y_k = \rho_j w_{kj} X_j + (1 - \rho_j) w_{kj} X_j$.

13. For purpose of simplification we abstract from the income and consumption of the unemployed (rich and poor). They are implicitly included in the "status quo" group.

3 / A Positive Economic Approach to Distributional Analysis

1. An excellent example of the early literature on this topic, which focused on feasibility and efficiency considerations in planned economies, is contained in Lange and Taylor (1964).

These and related concerns are applicable to the public sector of mixed economies as well and have been evaluated by Tullock (1970), Niskanen (1971), and many others.

2. Of course, other group characteristics, such as age, education, ethnicity, and political orientation may also be of interest to policy-makers. Although this chapter emphasizes redistribution across groups, minor alterations in the methodology can accommodate redistribution within groups.

3. Three studies of attitudes toward rural development (Maurer and Napier 1981; Krannich 1981; Fliegal et al. 1981) suggest that the first and second arguments are found in the individual's utility function. The extensive literature on the positive economics of redistribution (see Rodgers 1974 for a summary) would suggest that affected residents will view changes in regional income distribution as an important aspect of Forest Service policies. An empirical study by Ladewig and McCann (1980) lends support to the hypothesis that equity does affect rural residents' attitudes about their community.

4. So as to avoid confusion when we refer to distributional considerations, we shall drop our references to equity in the remainder of this chapter. This should not be construed as a lack of support for it as a worthy personal or public objective. Altruistic motivations can still be illustrated in our analysis, by the "net aggregate gain" variable, as when an individual who stands to lose from a public project votes for it because it offers a positive net benefit to the community.

5. We interpret Culhane and Friesema's (1981) reference to professional merits as going beyond efficiency goals, i.e., to include quality standards of the forestry profession with regard to fire safety, growing practices, etc.

6. Rational self-interest may be consistent with other motivations for political activity. Other behavioral hypotheses would include "minimax regret" (Ferejohn and Fiorina 1974 and 1975). Although the remainder of this section assumes some expected cost-benefit calculus on the part of affected citizens, other behavioral assumptions could be incorporated in the calculation of the community impact index and the political articulation index.

7. This observation was made by Downs (1957) and is the basis of the "voting paradox." Our concern here is not with the internal consistency of various decision-making processes nor with ensuring that all affected residents participate. Rather, it is with efficiency gains in a real world context.

8. We choose to utilize the convention of assigning income classes according to pre-impact status to maintain a point of reference for evaluating the policy in question.

9. Note that the income multiplier effect in the mining sector of our hypothetical example is 2. A total of $20 million of income is generated throughout the economy directly and indirectly as a result of a $10 million increase in income from mining but the $10 million in indirect gains is spread over four sectors. Therefore, our assumption of the equivalence of marginal and average distributions in the nonmining sectors is plausible if existing employees work the small amount of overtime hours needed for these support sectors to increase their production. Also, the overall increase in returns to labor is assumed to be matched by proportionally higher returns to capital.

10. In this example, these other two matrices are each simply vectors (elements distinguished by income class) since they are applied to such aggregate measures as community net gain and equity.

11. The symbol $\otimes$ represents Kroenecker (inner product) multiplication of matrices or vectors.

12. We use a single weighting matrix and, for the purpose of simplification, do not distinguish between attitudes toward community net benefits and equity in order to simplify the example. In reality the improvement in equity, through the 3.3 percent reduction in unemployment and the net positive community gain, may offset some of the impetus to oppose the policy by those who stand to sustain net individual income losses.

4 / A Social Accounting Matrix of Income Distribution

1. We have referred to Miyazawa's as the most general multisector income distribution formulation. However, an even more general multisector model framework has recently been developed by Batey (1985) along the lines of what has come to be known as "extended" I-O models, in which "sectoral" distributions are based on economic-demographic variables (e.g., distinguishing between the consumption patterns of local residents and immigrants, or of employed and unemployed residents. The focus of the extended I-O model is on the disaggregation of the payments and final de-

mand components rather than the explicit modeling of institutions. Thus, the model presented in this book is an example of an extended model but also a type of SAM by its inclusion of institutional features (e.g., distinguishing between the employment practices in union vs. nonunion settings). The reader is again referred to the theoretical presentation in chapter 2.

2. This study analyzes the size distribution of Adjusted Gross Income, rather than the more oft used Personal Income (PI) for two major reasons. First, on the conceptual level, the AGI definition is considered by the authors to be a superior measure of "net income" since it excludes most moving expenses, employee business expenses, etc. Second, for the case of distributional analyses, the U.S. Internal Revenue (IRS) data base is considered superior to the U.S. Bureau of the Census data base on personal income. Overall, AGI is on average about 3 percent lower than PI, with only a modest variation in this proportion across income groups.

3. Throughout this book, we will use the terms *primary data* and *survey-based* data interchangeably, and in contrast to *non-survey data*. Primary data thus refer to data collected directly from individual income units, as opposed to being adapted for one context (e.g., a region) from individual or aggregate data in another context (e.g., the United States as a whole). In many cases, the primary data sets we used were compiled by others and in some cases were even published in aggregated form. Thus, we do not make the distinction between another definition of *primary data* as being compiled by the author of a work, as opposed to *secondary data* as being the use of data compiled by others. The emphasis here is on the soundness of the data rather than on those who collected it.

4. Note that the construction of the model is fully automated so that it can be replicated by the U.S. Forest Service or other users and updated as new data become available. Computer programs are also available to apply the distributional impact methodology to the analysis of policy issues, as will be done in chapters 9 and 10.

5 / The Wage and Salary Income Distribution Matrix

1. Applying confidence interval estimation to published data on mean wage and salary incomes for the United States (U.S. Bureau of the Census 1982d), the error incurred from

using mean income levels appears to be negligible. The standard errors associated with mean incomes are typically less than 5 percent. The greatest deviation is found in farming occupations—$83 or 12 percent of their mean monthly wage and salary levels.

2. As to other aspects of the overall consistency among data sources, the Bureau of the Census data validate employment statistics only once, in that any one laborer may only be counted once, according to the occupation worked most. Conversely, the Bureau of Labor Statistics data allow for labor services to be counted more than once if employment is held in more than one occupation. Similarly, workers on unpaid absences from work are included under Census surveys.

3. Still another point of divergence is occupation classification according to place of residence (BOC) versus place of employment (BLS). Published data available from BLS reconcile these differences. Additionally, BOC data are derived from household survey data, while BLS nonagricultural data are compiled from business surveys. Since business survey data are thought to be more reliable, BOC data may therefore be deficient. However, because it excludes certain occupation categories, BLS utilizes BOC data to tabulate total employment. Among the groups excluded are private household occupations, the self-employed, agricultural workers, and unpaid family workers.

4. Certain occupational categories are narrowly defined, while other categories are much more widely encompassing. For example, the category "Lawyers and judges" includes only those two occupations. On the other hand, the category "Artists, entertainers, and athletes" includes authors, technical writers, designers, musicians and composers, actors and directors, painters, sculptors, photographers, dancers, editors, announcers, and athletes.

6 / The Dividend Income Distribution Matrix

1. Easterbrook (1984) has pointed out that one would not expect to witness a strong correlation between a firm's short-run profits and dividend payouts. The first function of dividends is to keep firms in the capital market. Any increase in dividends would be expected to lag considerably behind any increase in profits. Other arguments have been advanced as to the proper interpretation of dividend increases through time. For example, failing

firms may disinvest or liquidate via dividends, signaling a deteriorating business climate.

2. Theory and empirical verification have established that price-dividend ratios vary across income classes because of the relatively lower risk aversion and greater marginal tax bracket of upper income earners. However, much of the variation in the dividend return may be caused by differential investment across sectors. Even if there is some remaining variation in percentage dividend levels across income groups within sectors, changes in these levels may be uniform.

3. Again we emphasize that advances in I-O analysis allow for nonlinearities or readily allow for changes in coefficients (see Rose 1984).

4. The work was done under strict safeguards to maintain the confidentiality of individual returns. The cost of the effort was such as to make it prohibitively expensive in today's era of tight research funding.

5. The "P-D" ratios ranged from .030 for the $5,000–$10,000 bracket to .021 for the $500,000 and over bracket, as based on stock market data and individual portfolio holdings. The decline in the ratio as income increased was not, however, monotonic.

6. An example of a "non-similarity" was: "For filers with incomes of less than $25,000 the percentages invested in the telephone and communication industry ranged from 5.0 to 10.5; for incomes of $200,000 and above, the percentages ranged from 0.6 to 3.6" (Blume, Crockett, and Friend 1974, p. 31).

7. We refer to the "potential" number of sectors because the survey results yielded several three-digit sectors without any shareowners being represented. This is because of the sample size (1,537 individuals, but only 511 useable observations) or problems in classification. Two ensuing sectoral aggregations were utilized to rectify the problem, the first being a 45-sector classification scheme (basically two-digit SIC for all but the service sector) for the transfer of data and a subsequent 24-sector classification to meet statistical significance requirements. For similar reasons we also later aggregated the ten income classes to seven. Still, a small number of zero entries or entries based on a statistically insignificant sample remained, and were filled in by interpolation.

8. There are two alternative weighting methods for multiholding portfolios. The first makes use of data on the percentage of the total value of outstanding stock by sector. A sector captur-

ing 3 percent of the total outstanding stock value would receive a percentage of the total dollar holdings in each portfolio equal to 3 percent divided by the total outstanding percentage of the several stocks held in the portfolio. A second method combines the percentage of total outstanding stock values of each sector, as in the first method, with the frequency of stockholdings of each sector as determined by the NYSE data. This is done by multiplying the frequency matrix of step 1 by a diagonalized matrix of sectoral percentages of total outstanding stock values. Each cell entry within this matrix is divided by the summation of weights across all sectors for each respective portfolio size class. The results of the alternative weighting methods were not significantly different. Part of the reason is the relatively undiversified nature of stock portfolios (also noted by Blume et al. 1974). In fact, only 29 percent of the stockholders surveyed by the NYSE owned securities in more than one sector of the economy.

9. Note that sectors such as finance/insurance/real estate, in which key cells were based on an interpolation of the data, are not included in the above examples. The thirty interpolated entries represent 18.6 percent of the 161 cells in the dividend matrix.

10. Estimates of the degree of underreporting range from 2 percent (Blume et al. 1974) to 10 percent (Holland 1962). Another form of "underreporting" stems from the optional treatment of small corporation profits as "income from partnerships." In the absence of any more recent data on dividend omissions, we have decided to go with the IRS totals. In any case, the focus of this chapter is on relative, rather than absolute, levels.

11. Note that the elements of table 6.5 are y_{kj}/Y_j. They can readily be transformed into the V matrix of equation 3 of chapter 2 by multiplying each element by Y_j/X_j. The form in table 6.5 is used to facilitate our analysis of relative proportions.

12. Note that this relatively higher representation does not hold for each income class in each sector. For example, the proportion of people in the 0 to $15,000 income class holding shares in transportation companies is considerably higher than the representation of this income class in the total population, but that the situation reverses for the next three income classes. Thus, the Lorenz curves for the transportation sector "cross," and there is inherent ambiguity in comparing their corresponding Gini coefficients.

7 / The Total Income Distribution Matrix

1. Overall then, the economywide rental payments will exceed personal rental receipts by an amount equal to rental payments between businesses (a large amount, but not relevant to our accounting) and from businesses to households (a relatively very small amount).

2. The disaggregation was accomplished by assuming each subsector of a given aggregate in our previous 23-sector classification had the same income payment structure. Total flows were then apportioned between members of the subgroup according to estimated 1982 gross output weights.

3. There is a possibly significant source of bias even for pensions in that we have linked them to the current salary levels of our income/occupations analysis rather than a historical average of salaries or job tenure.

4. Strictly speaking, the result is based on a simplifying assumption that all workers receive some pensions and annuities. This is obviously not the case for farm workers and several other occupational categories, however.

5. We emphasize that this is before-tax/transfer income and thus omits tax refunds, alimony, unemployment compensation, etc., which tend to be more evenly distributed.

6. Note that some of the negative incomes in the lower income categories probably result from accounting definitions of favorable tax treatment of capital or rental transactions, i.e., they are "paper" losses.

7. Unique distributions were calculated at the 41-sector level and then "disaggregated" to the 80-sector level. This amounted to maintaining relative proportions among brackets for each of the subsectors of the 41-sector classification. This translated into identical Gini coefficients (not always to the fourth decimal place because of rounding) for several subsectors, as in the case of agriculture.

8 / Regionalization of the Model

1. Note also that imbalances generated by the application of any of the three techniques are removed by the application of a biproportional adjustment technique known as the RAS method (see, e.g., Bacharah 1972).

2. Our methods are, however, very similar to those used in gross state product accounting (see, e.g., Kendrick and Jaycox 1965; Weber 1979) as well as in regional input-output analysis (see, e.g., Morrison and Smith 1974; Round 1983).

3. For example, the entry "Income" means that only the total level of income in 1982 is known for the income type in question. "Income Class" means that its income distribution is known. "Income/Industry" (the term class is omitted for lack of space) means that the income distribution is known, and that the flow emanating from each sector is known. Please note, however, that these are just the row and column sums and not the entire matrix required.

4. The income class distribution is available at the state level from the IRS by special tabulation. Also, several state taxation departments, such as California's, have a publication similar to the IRS's *Statistics of Income*.

5. Note that forest area economies extend beyond National Forest boundaries. In general, they may not conform to any jurisdictional boundaries, but for the sake of practicality we have chosen to use county demarcations.

6. The reader will note that the coefficients are identical for several sectors. This occurs primarily because basic data are available only for a 41-sector disaggregation instead of the 80-sector sectoral breakdown shown in table 8.4.

9 / Policy Analysis at the Regional Level: Distributional Impacts of Coal Surface-Mining

1. Almost half the nation's population resides within three hundred miles of the MNF boundaries. Increasing use of the forest by recreationists is being accompanied by renewed interest in the extraction of the extensive mineral resources found within the MNF.

2. The table does not conform to strict MNF boundaries, but rather to a slightly larger ten-county area. This is because of data limitations, but may not be a shortcoming, since the ten counties probably more closely conform to a meaningful trading area than does the MNF itself.

3. The estimates were adapted from a study of southeastern Kentucky by Randall et al. (1978). Major adjustments were made for differences in population and economic activity between the two regions. Randall offered estimates of the present value of damages for each of several regulatory alternatives. Aesthetic damages were computed for different stages of reclamation over an eight-year period. Our analysis assumes reclamation takes place at a somewhat more rapid pace (backfilling within 60 days and a total five-year reclamation peri-

od), given the more stringent requirements of the Surface Mining Act and the higher likelihood of strict enforcement in a national forest. For our estimates, the present value of aesthetic damages was therefore computed using mean monthly willingness to pay (adjusted by the income elasticity of the bid) for strip-mined land prior to reclamation, converted to an annual figure and discounted at 8 percent per year. Additionally, damages are assumed to decline linearly over time, on the basis of bid estimates in Randall et al. For the Monongahela National Forest, the bid vector was then multiplied by the number of households in each income class (the latter figure was computed from percentages of households in each income class for West Virginia). Data on total surface-mined acreage in Randall's study area and on coal tonnage produced per acre are used to convert the vector to dollars per ton.

Some limitations of the data adjustments for aesthetic damages are obvious. Three that seem rather important are: (1) aesthetic damages are the same in both regions, (2) proximity to the mine site does not affect damages incurred by a household, and (3) the income elasticity of the bid is the same for households in each income class.

Present value estimates for other damage categories are computed using the regional damages reported for the Kentucky statute and then adjusted for the relative proportions between the present value of damages reported for the Kentucky and federal statutes. Again, we utilize a shorter time horizon than the one employed by Randall and his associates. For lack of a better assumption, water treatment and recreation-based damages are distributed equally per household among the ten income classes. Damages to land and buildings and flooding damage are distributed according to the income class proportions of capital-related income for West Virginia. Note that the lowest income bracket received a negative amount of such income during 1982. Since it is impossible to incur negative property damage, the corresponding values were set equal to zero for those earning under $5,000 (see table 9.2).

Our estimates and those of Randall et al. are not directly comparable. Our adjustments have the effect of increasing damages in some instances (e.g., greater population) and lowering the damages in others (more stringent reclamation requirements) Our midpoint estimate yields a present value of damages equal to 2.5

percent of regional income, whereas Randall's estimates are slightly less than 1.0 percent of regional income.

4. In most cases the distribution of damages differs among individuals in the same income class because of: (1) differences in utility functions and property location, and (2) sector-specific damages (e.g., black lung disease and other occupational hazards). In the first instance a normal distribution of damages can readily be represented by the mean if the analysis is performed in income, as opposed to utility, terms.

5. Note that for expository purposes we include only the residents of the 10-county MNF economy in the base of our distributional indexes. Given the fact that a national forest is in the public domain, the negative impacts on actual and potential visitors could legitimately be taken into account as well. At the same time, those that benefit from increased coal extraction (e.g., electric utility customers who reap a cost savings from a relatively low-priced fuel) could also be counted. Such an analysis, specifically, as well as the delineation of the appropriate population, in general, is beyond the scope of this study.

6. There is a similar, but much smaller, source of bias with respect to the owners of coal companies. At issue is whether the increased production will be shared proportionally by the existing firms in the region, will be concentrated in the hands of one firm, or some combination in between. The outcome, in our case study depends less on institutional features than on the distribution of coal-mining wage income, so we have not given it separate attention. The straight application of our model again calls for the distribution of the capital-related income among all owners of mining companies (note that it does not call for distributing these returns throughout an economywide income bracket). To the extent that this capital income is not shared, our positive index will be biased upward and the Gini coefficient downward. The effect will be small because only a small proportion of MNF-area residents receive capital income from mining.

7. Qualitatively, the results have been more sensitive to the accuracy of the environmental damage estimates, since they make a difference in whether the majority gains or loses from an increase in strip mining. However, it should be emphasized that this is merely an idiosyncratic result of the case analyzed. If we were to scrutinize the lower-bound case of the previous

section further, we would find that institutional considerations would tip the scales from a majority of gainers to a majority of losers.

8. We do note, however, that a significant number of workers involved in surface coal mining are not unionized.

9. Many surface-mining operations within the ten-county boundary of the MNF economy, but outside the MNF itself, are smaller, locally owned firms. The opening up of the forest to mining could, however, attract large firms. The volatility of mineral earnings from year to year, particularly within the coal industry, precludes many of the independent mining firms from taking advantage of the public money markets for the sale of debt or equity securities (Wilson 1976). These firms must often then rely on private investors for their venture capital needs. Lindley (1976) asserts that most of this venture capital is obtained from wealthy individuals or groups of wealthy individuals living in metropolitan centers. This has profound implications for the modeling of income generation within a rural area, since metropolitan centers are apt to be some distance away.

10 / Policy Analysis at the National Level: Distributional Impacts of Oil and Gas Tax Reform Proposals

1. At the time of this writing (May 1986), the House had passed a bill on tax reform. The Senate Finance Committee had reported a tax reform bill out of committee, which President Reagan had stated he would support. However, the bill was debated and voted upon by the full Senate, and differences between the House and Senate bills resolved in a conference committee. Given the fluid nature of tax reform, we chose to concentrate on the original proposals rather than attempt to guess what the final form might be. More recently, a final tax reform bill was passed, which called for significant reductions in the IDC, with minimal change in the PDA. However, since the major direct effect of these modifications is on the level of output

reductions, there is only a minimal effect on *relative* income reductions across income brackets. Hence, there is likely to be little change in the equity implications of our results.

2. In fact, the total benefits to the upper income group are probably larger than $868 million, since the Treasury study indicates that they receive more than half the benefits. We are assuming they garner exactly half, which produces a less skewed distribution of the tax benefits. Moreover, the Treasury study gives no clue as to whether the $28,000 per taxpayer is itself the mean of a normal probability distribution within this income group. It most likely is not, but without more information, we are forced to assume this figure will give us a reasonable estimate of total benefits to the upper income group.

3. The analysis assumes that the highest marginal tax rate for a given income group applies to the change in tax liability. This assumption is reasonable since the change in tax liability is marginal income.

4. The high Gini is "progressive" in this case because it pertains to an income *reduction*.

5. Note that the income payments listed in column 1 of table 10.1 represent net (after federal tax) income, which we consider the best context in which to evaluate tax reform. These were obtained by multiplying gross oil and gas sector income projected to 1987 by a set of average tax rates (IRS 1984a). Recall from chapter 7 that the pre-tax Gini coefficient for the oil and gas sector is .4907. We assumed no change in this distribution for our base case projection.

6. There is one preliminary step to account for the oil and gas sector's own use of its output. The projected 10 percent reduction in gross output in the oil and gas sector amounts to an 8.54 percent change in final demand for that sector, after dividing it by the diagonal element (equal to 1.171) of the closed Leontief inverse of the U.S. I-O table for 1982.

References

Adelman, I., and C. Morris. 1973. *Economic Growth and Social Equity in Developing Countries.* Stanford, Calif.: Stanford University Press.

Adelman, I., and S. Robinson. 1978. *Income Distribution Policy in Developing Countries.* Stanford, Calif.: Stanford University Press.

Ahluwalia, S., and H. Chenery. 1974. "A Model of Distribution and Growth." In *Redistribution with Growth,* edited by H. Chenery, M. Ahluwalia, C. Bell, J. Duloy, and R. Jolly. London: Oxford University Press.

Alward, G., H. C. Davis, K. Despotakis, and E. Lofting. 1985. "Regional Non-Survey Input-Output Analysis with IMPLAN." Paper presented at the Southern Regional Science Association Conference, Washington, D.C.

American Petroleum Institute. 1985a. "Impact of the Treasury Department's Proposal 'Tax Reform for Fairness, Simplicity, and Economic Growth' on Domestic Drilling and Petroleum Production Activities." Washington, D.C.

———. 1985b. "An Estimate of the Treasury Department Tax Proposal on Oil and Gas Production." Washington, D. C.

Appalachian Land Ownership Task Force. 1983. *Who Owns Appalachia: Land Ownership and Its Impacts.* Lexington: University of Kentucky Press.

Arrow, K. J. 1972. "Models of Job Discrimination." In *Discrimination in Economic Life,* edited by A. Pascal. Lexington, Mass.: D. C. Heath.

———. 1973. "Higher Education as a Filter." *Journal of Public Economics* 2(July): 193–216.

Atkinson, A. 1970. "On the Measurement of Inequality." *Journal of Economic Theory* 2(September): 244–63.

———. 1975. *The Economics of Inequality.* London: Oxford University Press.

———, ed. 1976. *The Personal Distribution of Income.* London: Allen & Unwin.

Bacharach, M. 1972. *Biproportional Matrices and Input-Output Change.* Cambridge: Cambridge University Press.

Ballard, C., D. Fullerton, J. Shoven, and J. Whalley. 1985. *A General Equilibrium Model for Tax Policy Evaluation.* Chicago: University of Chicago Press.

Batey, P. W. J. 1985. Input-Output Models for Regional Demographic-Economic Analysis: Some Structural Comparisons." *Environment and Planning A* 17(January): 73–99.

Batey, P. W. J., and M. Madden. 1983. "The Modeling of Demographic-Economic Change within the Context of Regional Decline: Analytical Procedures and Empirical Results." *Socio-Economic Planning Sciences* 17(January): 73–99.

Bell, C., P. Hazell, and R. Slade. 1982. *Project Evaluation in Regional Perspective.* Baltimore: Johns Hopkins University Press.

Blau, P. M., and O. D. Duncan. 1964. *The American Occupational Structure.* New York: Wiley.

Blume, M., J. Crockett, and I. Friend. 1974. "Stockownership in the U.S.: Characteristics and Trends." *Survey of Current Business.* 54(November): 16–40.

Boskin, M. J., M. S. Robinson, T. O'Reilly, and P. Kumar. 1985. "New Estimates for the Value of Federal Mineral Rights and Land." *American Economic Review* 75(December): 923–36.

125

Bronfenbrenner, M. 1971. *Income Distribution Theory.* Chicago: Aldine.

———. 1977. "Ten Issues in Distribution Theory." In *Modern Economic Thought,* edited by S. Weintraub. Philadelphia: University of Pennsylvania Press.

Bulmer-Thomas, V. 1982. *Input-Output Analysis in Developing Countries.* New York: John Wiley & Sons.

Burch, W. 1976. "Who Participates—A Sociological Interpretation of Natural Resource Decisions." *Natural Resources Journal* 16(January): 41–53.

Burns, C. S. 1981. "Impact of Land Withdrawals on Mining." *Mining Congress Journal* 67(January): 26–29.

Carter, A. 1970. *Structural Change in the American Economy.* Cambridge, Mass.: Harvard University Press.

Chao, H. 1982. "Resource Exhaustion, Economic Growth, and Income Distribution." *Journal of Policy Modeling* 4(June): 191–209.

Chapman, D. 1983. *Energy Resources and Energy Corporations.* Ithaca, N.Y.: Cornell University Press.

Chenery, H., and P. Clark. 1959. *Interindustry Economics.* New York: John Wiley & Sons.

Clark, J. B. 1899. *The Distribution of Wealth.* New York: Macmillan.

Clawson, M. 1975. *Forests for Whom and For What?* Baltimore: Johns Hopkins University Press.

———. 1983. *The Federal Lands Revisited.* Washington, D.C.: Resources for the Future.

———. 1984. "Ownership Patterns of Natural Resources in Rural America: Implications for Distribution of Wealth and Income." Rural Development, Poverty, and Natural Resources Workshop Paper Series, part 4. Washington, D.C.: Resources for the Future.

Coleman, J. S. 1966. *Equity of Educational Opportunity.* Washington, D.C.: Department of Health, Education and Welfare.

Congressional Budget Office. 1985. *Reducing the Deficit: Spending and Revenue Options.* Washington, D.C.: GPO.

Conrad, A. 1955. "The Multiplier Effect of Redistributive Public Budgets." *Review of Economics and Statistics* 37(May): 160–73.

Council of Economic Advisors. 1985. *Economic Report of the President, Annual Report.* Washington, D.C.: GPO.

Cowell, F. 1977. *Measuring Inequality.* New York: John Wiley & Sons.

Crockett, J., and I. Friend. 1963. "Characteristics of Stock Ownership." In *Proceedings of the Business and Economic Statistics Section of the American Statistical Association.* Washington, D.C.: American Statistical Association.

Crow, P. 1986. "Higher Taxes Threaten Industry in Second Half of 99th Congress." *Oil and Gas Journal,* 84(January 27): 41–46.

Culhane, P. 1981. *Public Lands Politics.* Baltimore: Johns Hopkins University Press.

Culhane, P., and H. Friesema. 1979. "Land-Use Planning for Public Lands." *National Resources Journal* 19(April): 339–56.

———. 1981. "Public participation in RPA/NFMA." In *A Citizen's Guide to the Forest and Range Renewable, Resource Planning Act,* edited by W. Shands. Washington, D.C.: U.S. Forest Service.

Dana, S., and S. Fairfax. 1979. *Forest and Range Policy: Its Development in the U.S.* New York: McGraw-Hill.

Danziger, S., R. Haveman, and R. Plotnick. 1981. "How Income Transfer Programs Affect Work, Savings, and Income Distribution." *Journal of Economic Literature* 8(September): 975–1028.

Danziger, S., and M. K. Taussig. 1979. "The Income Unit and the Anatomy of Income Distribution." *Review of Income and Wealth* 25(December): 365–75.

Deavers, K., and D. Brown. 1983. "Sociodemographic and Economic Changes in Rural America." Rural Development, Poverty, and Natural Resources Workshop Paper Series. Washington, D.C.: Resources for the Future.

Denison, E. F. 1954. "Income Types and the Size Distribution." *American Economic Review* 44(May): 254–69.

Despotakis, K. 1985. "Economic Impact Analysis: From Input-Output to Social Accounting Matrices." Technical Note EEA-85-TN-02. Berkeley, Calif.: Engineering Economic Associates.

Downing, P. 1981. "A Political Economy Model of Implementing Pollution Laws." *Journal of Environmental Economics and Management* 8(September): 255–71.

Downs, A. 1957. *An Economic Theory of Democracy.* New York: Harper & Row.

Duerr, W. 1975. "American Forest Resource Management." In *Forest Resource Management,* edited by W. Duerr. Corvallis: Oregon State University Press.

Duchin, F., and D. Szyld. 1985. "A Dynamic Input-Output Model with Assured Positive Output." *Metroeconomica* 37 (October): 269–82.

Easterbrook, F. H. 1984. "Two Agency Cost Explanations of Dividends." *American Economic Review* 74(September): 650–59.

Elo, I. T., and C. L. Beale. 1984. "Natural Resources and Rural Poverty." Rural Development, Poverty, and Natural Resources Workshop Paper Series. Washington, D.C.: Resources for the Future.

Energy Information Administration. 1985. *Annual Energy Outlook, 1984.* Washington, D.C.

Ervin, D., W. Heffernan, and G. Green. 1984. "Cross-Compliance for Erosion Control." *American Journal of Agricultural Economics* 66(August): 273–78.

Federal Trade Commission. 1983. *1982 Quarterly Financial Reports for Manufacturing, Mining and Trade Corporations.* Washington, D.C.: GPO.

Ferejohn J., and M. P. Fiorina. 1974. "The Paradox of Not Voting: A Decision Theory Analysis." *American Political Science Review* 68(June): 525–36.

———. 1975. "Closeness Counts Only in Horseshoes and Dancing." *American Political Science Review* 69(September): 920–25.

Ferguson, C. E. 1969. *The Neo-Classical Theory of Production and Distribution.* Cambridge: Cambridge University Press.

Flick, W., P. Trenchi III, and J. Bowers. 1980. "Regional Analysis of Forest Industries: Input-Output Methods." *Forest Science* 26(December): 548–60.

Fliegal, F., A. Sofranko, and N. Glasgow. 1981. "Population Growth in Rural Areas and Sentiments of the New Migrants toward Further Growth." *Rural Sociology* 46(Fall): 411–29.

Freeman, R. 1980. "An Empirical Analysis of the Fixed Coefficients and Manpower Requirements Models." *Journal of Human Resources* 15, no. 2(Winter): 176–99.

Friedman, M. 1953. "Choice, Change, and the Personal Distribution of Income." *Journal of Political Economy* 61(August): 277–90.

Galper, H., and D. Zimmerman. 1977. "Preferential Taxation and Portfolio Choice: Some Empirical Evidence." *National Tax Journal* 30(December): 387–97.

Garkovich, L. 1982. "Land Use Planning as a Response to Rapid Population Growth and Community Change." *Rural Sociology* 47(Spring): 47–67.

Garnaut, R., and A. C. Ross. 1975. "Uncertainty, Risk Aversion and the Taxing of Natural Resource Projects." *Economic Journal* 85(June): 272–87.

Gianessi, L. P., H. M. Peskin, and E. Wolff. 1979. "Distributional Effects of Uniform Air Pollution Policy in the United States." *Quarterly Journal of Economics* 93(May): 281–301.

Gianessi, L. P., and H. M. Peskin. 1980. "The Distribution of the Costs of Federal Water Pollution Control Policy." *Land Economics* 56(February): 85–102.

Gibrat, R. 1931. *Les Inégalités économiques.* Paris: Recueil Sirey.

Gilmore, J. S. 1976. "Boom Towns May Hinder Energy Resource Development." *Science* 191(February): 535–40.

Golladay, F., and R. Haveman. 1977. *The Economic Impact of Tax-Transfer Policy.* New York: Academic Press.

Gordon, R. L. 1981. *An Economic Analysis of World Energy Problems.* Cambridge, Mass.: MIT Press.

Hagenstein, P. R. 1984. "The Federal Lands Today—Uses and Limits." In *Rethinking the Federal Lands,* edited by S. Brubaker. Washington, D.C.: Resources for the Future.

Harberger, A. 1962. "The Incidence of the Corporate Income Tax." *Journal of Political Economy* 70(June): 215–40.

Hazilla, M., and R. Kopp. 1984. "An Introduction to Numerical General Equilibrium Models Used for Applied Welfare Analysis." Discussion Paper QE85-05. Washington, D.C.: Resources for the Future.

Henry, M., and T. Martin. 1984. "Estimating Income Distribution Effects on Regional Input-Output Multipliers." *Regional Science Perspectives* 14(no. 2): 33–45.

Herfindahl, O., and A. Kneese. 1974. *Economic Theory of Natural Resources.* Columbus, Ohio: Merrill Publishing Co.

Hewings, G., and M. Romanos. 1981. "Simulating Less Developed Regional Economies under Conditions of Limited Information." *Geographical Analysis* 13(October): 373–90.

Hogan, W. 1980. "Import Management and Oil Emergencies." In *Energy and Security,* edited by D. Deese and J. Nye. Cambridge, Mass.: Ballinger.

Holland, D. 1962. *Dividends under the Income Tax.* Princeton, N.J.: Princeton University Press.

Houthakker, H., and L. Taylor. 1970. *Consumer Demand in the United States: Analysis and Projections.* Cambridge, Mass.: Harvard University Press.

Hudson, E., and D. Jorgenson. 1974. "U.S. Energy Policy and Economic Growth." *Bell Journal of Economics* 5(Autumn): 461–514.

Hunt, J. M. 1961. *Intelligence and Experience.* New York: Ronald Press.

Internal Revenue Service. 1984a. *Statistics of Income: Individual Income Tax Returns.* Washington, D.C.: Department of the Treasury. [*SOI*]

————. 1984b. *Statistics of Income: Corporation Income Tax Returns.* Washington, D.C.: Department of the Treasury.

Investment Company Institute. 1983. *Mutual Fund Factbook.* New York.

Irland, L., and J. Vincent. 1974. "Citizen Participant in Decision Making: A Challenge for the Public Land Manager." *Journal of Range Management* 27(May): 182–85.

Isserman, A., and J. Merrifield. 1987. "Quasi-Experimental Control Group Methods for Regional Analysis." *Economic Geography.* Forthcoming.

Jaszi, G. 1955. "The Statistical Foundations of the Gross National Product." *Review of Economics and Statistics* 38(May): 205–14.

————. 1986. "An Economic Accountant's Audit." *American Economic Review* 76(May): 411–17.

Juster, F. T., and K. Land, eds. 1981. *Social Accounting Systems: Essays on the State of the Art.* New York: Academic Press.

Kakwani, N., and N. Podder. 1976. "Efficient Estimation of Lorenz Curves and Associated Inequality Measures from Grouped Observations." *Econometrica* 44(January): 137–48.

Kaldor, N. 1956. "Alternative Theories of Distribution." *Review of Economic Studies* 23(1955–56): 83–100.

Kendrick, J. W. 1972. *Economic Accounts and Their Uses.* New York: McGraw-Hill.

Kendrick, J. W., and C. M. Jaycox. 1965. "The Concept and Estimation of Gross State Product." *Southern Economic Journal* 32(October): 153–68.

Krannich, R. 1981. "Socioeconomic Impacts of Powerplant Developments on Nonmetropolitan Communities: An Analysis of Perceptions and Hypothesized Impact Determinants in the Eastern United States." *Rural Sociology* 46(Spring): 128–42.

Krutilla, J., A. Fisher, and R. Rice. 1977. *Economic and Fiscal Impact of Coal Development.* Baltimore: Johns Hopkins University Press.

Krutilla, J., A. Fisher, W. Hyde, and V. K. Smith. 1983. "Public Versus Private Ownership: The Federal Lands Case." *Journal of Policy Analysis and Management* 2(Summer): 548–58.

Kuznets, S. 1953. *Shares of Upper Income Groups in Income and Savings.* New York: National Bureau of Economic Research.

————. 1955. "Economic Growth and Income Inequality." *American Economic Review* 45(March): 1–28.

————. 1976. "Demographic Aspects of the Size Distribution Income." *Economic Development and Cultural Change* 25(October): 1–94.

Ladewig, H., and G. McCann. 1980. "Community Satisfaction: Theory and Measurement." *Rural Sociology* 45(Spring): 110–31.

Lambert, H. 1973. "The Spotlight Has Shifted to Land Use Planning and the Forester's Place in It." *Forest Industry* 100:28–29.

Lange, O., and F. Taylor. 1964. *On the Economic Theory of Socialism.* New York: McGraw-Hill.

LeMaster, D. 1976. "The Resources Planning Act as Amended by the National Forest Management Act." *Journal of Forestry* 74(December): 798, 836–40.

Leontief, W. 1970. "The Dynamic Inverse." In *Contributions to Input-Output Analysis,* edited by A. P. Carter and A. Brody. Amsterdam: North-Holland.

————. 1986. *Input-Output Economics.* 2d ed. New York: Oxford University Press.

Leontief, W., and F. Duchin. 1986. *The Future Impact of Automation on Workers.* New York: Oxford University Press.

LeVeen, P., and G. Goldman. 1978. "Reclamation Policy and the Water Subsidy: An Analysis of the

Distributional Consequences of Emerging Policy Choices." *American Journal of Agricultural Economics* 60(December): 929–34.

Levinson, H. 1954. "Collective Bargaining and Income Distribution." *American Economic Review* 44(May): 308–16.

Lindley, A. H., R. Shorr, F. Crerie, and F. Stewart. 1976. "Mineral Financing." In *Economics of the Mineral Industries,* edited by W. A. Vogely. 3d ed. New York: American Institute of Mining, Metallurgical, and Petroleum Engineers.

Loehman, E., and V. N. De. 1982. "Application of Stochastic Choice Modeling to Policy Analysis of Public Goods: A Case Study of Air Quality Improvements." *Review of Economics and Statistics* 64(August): 474–80.

Loviscek, A., R. Holliday, L. Robinson, and M. Wolford. 1979. *The 1975 West Virginian Input-Output Study.* Morgantown: Regional Research Institute, West Virginia University.

Lydall, H. 1959. "The Long Term Trends in the Size Distribution of Income." *Journal of the Royal Statistical Society* 122(part 1): 1–37.

———. 1976. "Theories of the Distribution of Earnings." In *The Personal Distribution of Income,* edited by A. Atkinson (see above).

Maurer, R., and T. Napier. 1981. "Rural Residents' Perspectives of Industrial Development." *Rural Sociology* 46(Spring): 100–111.

Meade, J. 1964. *Efficiency, Equality, and the Ownership of Property.* London: Allen & Unwin.

Medoff, J. 1975. "The General Equilibrium Effects of Governmental Expenditures on the Family Distribution of Income." Ph.D. diss., Harvard University.

Miernyk, W. 1968. "Long-Range Forecasting with a Regional Input-Output Model." *Western Economic Journal* 6(June): 165–76.

———. 1982. *Regional Analysis and Regional Policy.* Cambridge: OGH Publishers.

Miernyk, W., E. Bonner, J. Chapman, and K. Shellhammer. 1967. *Impact of the Space Program on a Local Economy: An Input-Output Analysis.* Morgantown: West Virginia University Library.

Miernyk, W., K. Shellhammer, D. Brown, T. Coccari, C. Gallagher, and W. Winema. 1970. *Simulating Regional Economic Development.* Lexington, Mass.: Heath Lexington.

Mincer J. 1976. "Progress in Human Capital Analyses of the Distribution of Earnings." In *The Personal Distribution of Income,* edited by A. Atkinson (see above).

Miyazawa, K. 1968. "Input-Output Analysis and Interrelational Income Multiplier as a Matrix." *Hitotsubashi Journal of Economics* 18(February): 39–58.

———. 1976. *Input-Output Analysis and the Structure of Income Distribution.* Berlin: Springer-Verlag.

Modigliano, F., and A. Ando. 1960. "The 'Permanent Income' and the 'Life Cycle' Hypothesis of Saving Behavior: Comparisons and Tests." In *Proceedings of the Conference on Consumption and Savings.* Philadelphia: University of Pennsylvania, 1960.

Morrison, W. I., and P. Smith. 1974. "Nonsurvey Input-Output Techniques at the Small Area Level: An Evaluation." *Journal of Regional Science* 14(April): 1–14.

Musgrave, R. 1959. *The Theory of Public Finance.* New York: McGraw-Hill.

Nelson, E. 1977. "The Measurement and Trend of Inequality: Comment." *American Economic Review* 67(June): 497–501.

New York Stock Exchange. 1982. *New York Stock Exchange Fact Book.* New York: NYSE.

———. 1984a. "1983 Major Planning Study." Computer print-out. New York: NYSE.

———. 1984b. *Shareownership, 1983.* New York: NYSE.

Niskanen, W. 1971. *Bureaucracy and Representative Government.* New York: Aldine-Atherton.

Nowak, P., R. Rickson, C. Ramsay, and W. Goudy. 1982. "Community Conflicts and Models of Political Participation." *Rural Sociology* 47(Summer): 333–48.

Office of Federal Statistical Policy and Standards. 1980. *Standard Occupational Classification Manual.* Washington, D.C.: GPO.

Olson, M. 1965. *The Logic of Collective Action.* Cambridge, Mass.: Harvard University Press.

Oosterhaven, J. 1983. "Evaluating Land Reclamation Plans for Northern Friesland." *Papers of the Regional Science Association* 52: 125–37.

Orcutt, G., S. Caldwell, R. Wertheimer, and S. Franklin. 1976. *Policy Exploration Through Microanalytic Simulation.* Washington, D.C.: Urban Institute.

Pareto, V. 1897. *Cours d'economie politique.* Lausanne: Rouge.

Paukert, F., J. Skolka, and J. Maton. 1976. "Redistribution of Income Patterns, Consumption, and

Employment," In *Advances in I-O Analysis,* edited by K. Polenske and J. Skolka. Cambridge, Mass.: Ballinger.

Peskin, H. M., P. Portney, and A. Kneese, eds. 1981. *Environmental Regulation and the U.S. Economy.* Baltimore: Johns Hopkins University Press.

Piet, P. 1984. "Partnership Returns for 1981 Reflect Tax Shelter Activity." In *Statistics of Income: Background Material,* prepared for the Brookings Conference on Data Needs for Effective Tax Policy. Washington, D.C.: Internal Revenue Service.

Polenske, K. 1980. *The U.S. Multiregional Input-Output Accounts and Model.* Lexington, Mass.: Lexington Books.

Portney, P. R., and R. B. Haas, eds. 1982. *Current Issues in Natural Resource Policy.* Washington, D.C.: Resources for the Future.

Pyatt, G. 1976. "On the Interpretation and Disaggregation of Gini Coefficients." *Economic Journal* 86(June): 243–55.

Pyatt, G., and A. Roe. 1977. *Social Accounting for Development Planning.* Cambridge: Cambridge University Press.

Pyatt, G., and J. I. Round. 1979. "Accounting and Fixed Price Multipliers in a Social Accounting Matrix." *Economic Journal* 79(December): 850–73.

Randall, A., O. Grunewald, A. Pagoulatos, R. Ausness, and S. Johnson. 1978. *Estimating Environmental Damages from Surface Mining of Coal in Appalachia.* Final Report to U.S. EPA. Lexington: University of Kentucky.

Rees, J. 1985. *Natural Resources: Allocation, Economics and Policy.* London: Methuen.

Reder, M. W. 1976. "A Partial Survey of the Theory of Income Size Distribution." In *Six Papers on the Size Distribution of Wealth and Income,* edited by L. Soltow. New York: National Bureau of Economic Research.

Reynolds, M., and E. Smolensky. 1978. *Public Expenditures, and the Distribution of Income.* New York: Academic Press.

Rodgers, J. 1974. "Explaining Income Redistribution." In *Redistribution through Public Choice,* edited by H. Hochman and G. Peterson. New York: Columbia University Press.

Rose, A. 1977. *The Economic Impact of Geothermal Energy Development.* Riverside, Calif.: Dry Lands Research Institute, University of California.

———. 1983. "Modeling the Macroeconomic Impacts of Air Pollution Abatement." *Journal of Regional Science* 23(November): 441–59.

———. 1984. "Technological Change and Input-Output Analysis: An Appraisal." *Socio-Economic Planning Sciences* 18(no. 5): 305–18.

Rose, A., S. Edmunds, and E. Lofting. 1978. "The Economics of Geothermal Energy at the Regional Level." *Journal of Energy and Development* 5(Autumn): 126–52.

Rose, A., D. Isenberg, D. Kolk, J. Duffy, A. Soofi, and D. Hurd. 1981. *Natural and Human Resource Implications of Industrial Development.* Riverside, Calif.: Dry Lands Research Institute, University of California.

Rose, A., B. Nakayama, and B. K. Stevens. 1982. "Modern Energy Region Development and Income Distribution." *Journal of Environmental Economics and Management* 9(June): 149–64.

Rose, A., B. K. Stevens, G. Davis, C. Y. Chen, and P. Speaker. 1985. "Procedures for Estimating Income Distribution Effects." Final report to the U.S. Forest Service. Morgantown: Department of Mineral Resource Economics, West Virginia University.

Round, J. I. 1983. "Nonsurvey Techniques: A Critical Review of the Theory and the Evidence." *International Regional Science Review* 8(December): 189–212.

Ruggles, R., and N. Ruggles. 1970. *The Design of Economic Accounts.* New York: Columbia University Press.

Russell, C. 1979. "Applications of Public Choice Theory: An Introduction." In *Collective Decision-Making: Applications From Public Choice Theory,* edited by C. Russell. Baltimore: Johns Hopkins University Press.

Sahota, G. 1978. "Theories of Personal Income Distribution: A Survey." *Journal of Economic Literature* 16(March): 1–55.

Sandberg, I. 1973. "A Non-Linear Input-Output Model of a Multisectoral Economy." *Econometrica* 41(November): 1167–82.

Scarf, H., and J. Shoven. 1984. *Applied General Equilibrium Analysis.* New York: Cambridge University Press.

Schultz, T. W. 1960. "Capital Formation by Education." *Journal of Political Economy* 68(December): 571–83.

———. 1961. "Investment in Human Capital." *American Economic Review* 51(March): 1–17.

Smith, J. D., ed. 1980. *Modeling the Distribution and Intergenerational Transmission of Wealth.* Chicago: University of Chicago Press.

Speaker, P. 1985. "Normative Measures of Income Distribution." In "Proceedings for Estimating Income Distribution Effects," edited by A. Rose, B. K. Stevens, G. Davis, C. Y. Chen, and P. Speaker (see above).

Spence, A. M. 1973. "Price Quality and Quantity Interdependencies." Center for Research in Economic Growth Memorandum no. 161. Stanford, Calif.: Stanford University Press.

———. 1974. *Market Signaling.* Cambridge, Mass.: Harvard University Press.

Standard and Poor's Corporation. 1984. *Standard and Poor's Industry Surveys.* New York: Standard and Poor's Corporation.

Starrett, D. 1976. "Social Limitations, Imperfect Information and Distribution of Income." *Quarterly Journal of Economics* 90(May): 261–84.

Stevens, B. H. 1980. *Input-Output Forecasting and Policy Simulation for the South Florida Region.* Amherst, Mass.: Regional Science Research Institute.

Stevens, B. H., and A. Rose. 1985. "Regional Input-Output Methods for Tourism Impact Analysis." In *Economic Impacts of Recreation and Tourism,* edited by D. Propst. Ashville, N.C.: U.S. Forest Service.

Stevens, J. 1984. "Development and Management of Forest Resources for Rural Development in the Pacific Northwest." Rural Development, Poverty, and Natural Resources Working Paper Series. Washington, D.C.: Resources for the Future.

Stigler, G. 1970. "Director's Law of Public Income Redistribution." *Journal of Law and Economics* 13(April): 1–10.

Stiglitz, J. E. 1969. "Distribution of Income and Wealth Among Individuals." *Econometrica* 37(July): 382–97.

Stiglitz, J. E. 1975. "The Theory of 'Screening', Education and the Distribution of Income." *American Economic Review* 65(June): 283–300.

Stone, R. 1961. *Input-Output and National Accounts.* Paris: OECD.

Taubman, P. 1976. "Personal Characteristics and the Distribution of Earnings." In Atkinson 1976.

Tawney, R. H. 1931. *Equality.* London: Allen & Unwin.

Thurow, L. 1975. *Generating Inequality: Mechanics of Distribution in the U.S. Economy.* New York: Basic Books.

Thompson, R., and C. Hicks. 1983. "Average and Marginal Tax Rates, 1981: Individual Tax Returns." *Statistics of Income Bulletin* 3(Fall): 41–50.

Tiebout, C. 1969. "An Empirical Regional Input-Output Projection Model: The State of Washington 1980." *Review of Economics and Statistics* 51.

Treyz, G., G. Duguay, C. Chen, and R. Williams. 1981. "A Family Income Distribution Model for Regional Policy Analysis." *Journal of Policy Modeling* 3(February): 77–92.

Tullock, G. 1970. *Private Wants, Public Means.* New York: Basic Books.

U.S. Bureau of Economic Analysis. 1979. *Survey of Current Business.* Washington, D.C.: GPO.

———. 1984a. "Detailed Components of Personal Income." Regional Economic Information Service. Mimeo.

———. 1984b. *Local Area Personal Income.* Washington, D.C.: Department of Commerce.

———. 1985. *Survey of Current Business.* Washington, D.C.: GPO.

U.S. Bureau of the Census. 1982a. *Classified Index of Industries and Occupations, 1980.* Washington, D.C.: GPO.

———. 1982b. *General Social and Economic Characteristics.* Washington, D.C.: GPO.

———. 1982c. *Number of Inhabitants, Characteristics of the Population.* Washington, D.C.: GPO.

———. 1982d. "Income Survey Development Program: 1979." *Current Population Reports.* Washington. D.C.: GPO.

———. 1983. *Detailed Population Characteristics.* Washington, D.C.: GPO.

———. 1984a. *Money Income of Households, Families, and Persons in the United States: 1982.* Washington, D.C.: GPO.

———. 1984b. *Summary Tape File 4.* Washington, D.C.: Bureau of the Census. [*STF4*]

———. 1984c. *Census of Service Industries.* Washington, D.C.: GPO.

————. 1984d. *Census of Mineral Industries.* Washington, D.C.: GPO.

————. 1984e. *Census of Wholesale Trade.* Washington, D.C.: GPO.

————. 1984f. *Census of Manufactures.* Washington, D.C.: GPO.

————. 1984g. *Census of Agriculture.* Vol. 1. Washington, D.C.: GPO.

U.S. Bureau of Labor Statistics. 1976–77. *Consumer Expenditure Survey Series: Interview Survey, 1972–73.* Report 455-3, 1976; Report 455-4, 1977. Washington, D.C.: GPO.

————. 1979. "Family Expenditure Data to be Available on a Continuing Basis." *Monthly Labor Review* 102(April): 53–54.

————. 1982a. *Employment and Earnings.* Washington, D.C.: GPO.

————. 1982b. "National Industry/Occupation Matrix." Washington, D.C.: Department of Labor. Computer tape.

————. 1985. *Time-Series Data for Input-Output Industries-Output, Price, and Employment.* Preliminary Report. Washington, D.C.: GPO.

U.S. Department of Interior. 1981. *Energy Resources on Federally Administered Lands.* Washington, D.C.: GPO.

————. 1982. *Managing the Nation's Public Lands.* Washington, D.C.: GPO.

U.S. Department of Treasury. 1984. *Tax Reform for Fairness, Simplicity and Economic Growth.* Washington. D.C.: GPO.

U.S. Environmental Protection Agency. 1973. *Compilation of Air Pollution Emission Factors.* 2d ed. Research Triangle Park, N.C.: U.S. EPA.

————. 1975. *Environmental Assessment Guidelines for Selected New Source Industries.* Washington, D.C.: U.S. EPA.

U.S. Forest Service. 1980. *Land Areas of the National Forest System.* Washington, D.C.: GPO.

————. 1981. *An Assessment of the Forest and Range Land Situation in the United States.* Report No. 22. Washington, D.C.: U.S. Forest Service.

————. 1983a. *Report of the Forest Service, Fiscal Year 1982.* Washington, D.C.: GPO.

————. 1983b. *IMPLAN.* Ft. Collins, Colo.: Rocky Mountain Experiment Station.

————. 1985a. *Draft Environmental Impact Statement, Land and Resource Management Plan, Monongahela National Forest.* Washington, D.C.: GPO.

————. 1985b. *Proposed Land and Resource Management Plan, Monongahela National Forest.* Washington, D.C.: GPO.

————. 1985c. "Monongahela National Forest." Elkins, W. Va. Mimeo.

————. 1986. "U.S. Input-Output Table, 1982." Ft. Collins, Colo.: Rocky Mountain Experiment Station. Computer tape.

U.S. Geological Survey. 1968. *Mineral Resources of the Appalachian Region.* Geological Survey Professional Paper 580. Washington, D.C.: U.S. Department of Interior.

Value Line, Inc. 1984. *The Value Line Investment Survey.* New York.

Verba, S., and N. Nie. 1972. *Participation in America: Political Democracy and Social Equality.* New York: Harper & Row.

Warkov, S. 1978. *Energy Policy in the U.S.* Cambridge, Mass.: Ballinger.

Weber, R. E. 1979. "A Synthesis of Methods Proposed for Estimating Gross State Product." *Journal of Regional Science* 19(May): 217–30.

Weiskoff, R. 1976. "Income Distribution and Export Promotion in Puerto Rico." In *Advances in Input-Output Analysis,* edited by K. Polenske and J. Skolka. Cambridge, Mass.: Ballinger.

West Virginia Chamber of Commerce. 1983. *West Virginia Statistical Profile.* Charleston, W. Va.

West Virginia Department of Employment Security. 1977. *Employment and Wages.* Charleston, W. Va.

————. 1982. *Employment and Wages.* Charleston, W. Va.

Whaley, R. S. 1970. "Multiple Use Decision-Making—Where Do We Go from Here?" *Natural Resources Journal* 10:171–82.

Wilson, W. 1976. "Capital for Coal Mine Development." *Coal Mining and Processing* 13(January): 68–78.

Zeckhauser, R. 1974. "Risk Spreading and Distribution." In *Redistribution through Public Choice,* edited by H. Hochman and G. Peterson. New York: Columbia University Press.

Index

About the Authors

Adam Rose is professor of Mineral Resource Economics and an associate of the Regional Research Institute at West Virginia University. He is the author of *Forecasting Natural Gas Demand in a Changing World, Frontiers of Input-Output Analysis,* and *Geothermal Energy and Regional Development.* He has also published numerous articles in the fields of energy and natural resource economics, regional science, and input-output analysis. He is a recipient of the American Planning Association Outstanding Program Planning Honor Award.

Brandt Stevens is assistant professor of economics at Illinois State University.

Gregg Davis is assistant professor of economics at Northeast Louisiana University.

Natural Resource Policy and Income Distribution

Designed by Ann Walston.

Composed by the Composing Room of Michigan, Inc., in Times Roman.

Printed by Thomson-Shore, Inc., on 60-lb. Glatfelter Offset,
and bound by John H. Dekker and Sons, Inc., in Holliston Roxite.

DATE DUE

JAN 2 3			
GAYLORD			PRINTED IN U.S.A.